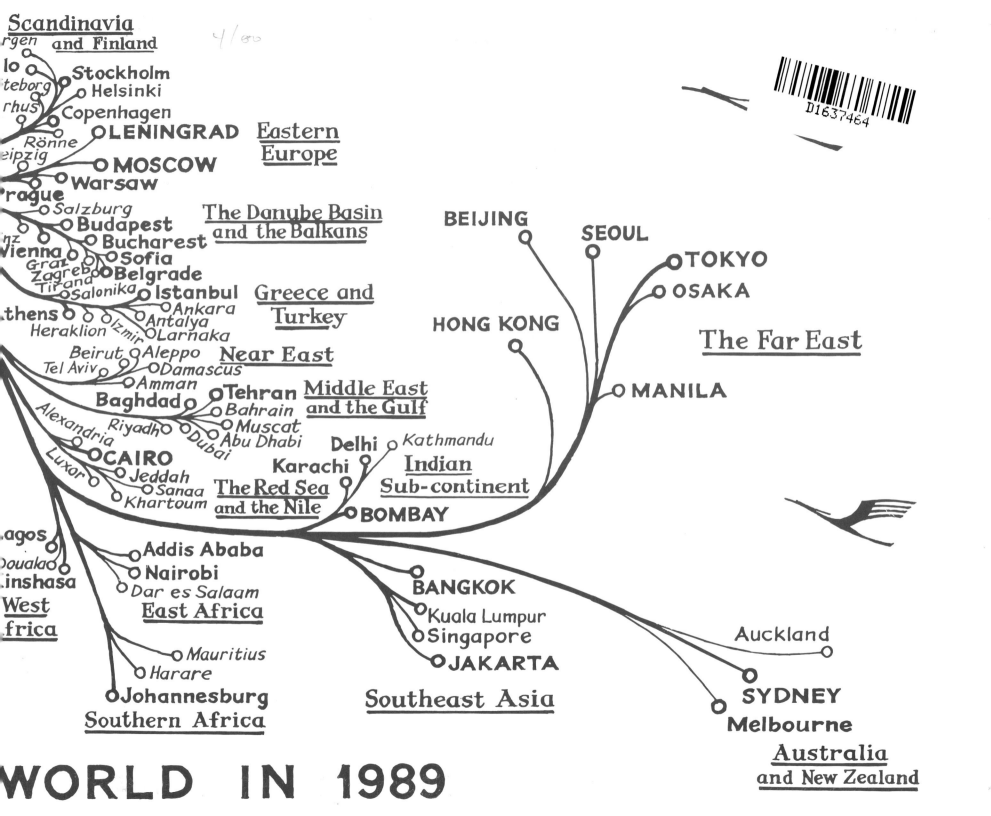

Scandinavia
and Finland

rgen
lo
teborg
rhus
Rönne
eipzig
Prague
nz
Vienna
Graz
Zagreb
Tirana
Athens
Heraklion
West
frica
Lagos
Douala
Kinshasa

Stockholm
Helsinki
Copenhagen
**LENINGRAD**   Eastern
Europe
**MOSCOW**
**Warsaw**
Salzburg
**Budapest**   The Danube Basin
**Bucharest**   and the Balkans
**Sofia**
**Belgrade**
Salonika   **Istanbul**   Greece and
Ankara   Turkey
Antalya
Izmir   Larnaka
Beirut   Aleppo   Near East
Tel Aviv   Damascus
Amman
**Baghdad**   **Tehran**   Middle East
Bahrain   and the Gulf
Alexandria   Riyadh   Muscat
**CAIRO**   Dubai   Abu Dhabi
Luxor   **Karachi**   **Delhi**   Kathmandu
Jeddah   Indian
Sanaa   The Red Sea   Sub-continent
Khartoum   and the Nile
**BOMBAY**

BEIJING   SEOUL
**TOKYO**
**OSAKA**

HONG KONG   The Far East

MANILA

**Addis Ababa**
**Nairobi**
Dar es Salaam
East Africa

Mauritius
Harare
**Johannesburg**
Southern Africa

**BANGKOK**
Kuala Lumpur
Singapore
**JAKARTA**

Southeast Asia

Auckland

**SYDNEY**
Melbourne

Australia
and New Zealand

# WORLD IN 1989

# Lufthansa

## AN AIRLINE AND ITS AIRCRAFT

OTHER BOOKS BY R. E. G. DAVIES

A History of the World's Airlines
Airlines of the United States Since 1914
Airlines of Latin America Since 1919
Continental Airlines: The First Fifty Years
Rebels and Reformers of the Airways
Pan Am: An Airline and Its Aircraft

# Lufthansa

## AN AIRLINE AND ITS AIRCRAFT

By R. E. G. Davies

Illustrated by Mike Machat

ORION BOOKS/NEW YORK

This book is dedicated to Werner Bittner, Lufthansa's archivist, whose approach to his vocation is perfectionistic but not pedantic. His meticulous record-keeping has provided a resource which is as inexhaustible as his patience with those, including this author, who constantly seek his help.

Also, to Günther Ott, whose generosity in sharing with me the results of a lifetime of laborious research into the "old" Luft Hansa has been more valuable than a roomful of reference books. His meticulous review of the prewar fleet lists has contributed substantially to the historical accuracy of this book.

Text and maps copyright © 1991 by R. E. G. Davies

Illustrations copyright © 1991 by Mike Machat

Published by Orion Books, a division of Crown Publishers, Inc., 201 East 50th Street, New York, New York 10022

ORION and colophon are trademarks of Crown Publishers, Inc.

Manufactured in Japan

Designed by R. E. G. Davies

Library of Congress Cataloging-in-Publication Data
Davies, R. E. G. (Ronald Edward George)
     Lufthansa: an airline and its aircraft by R. E. G. Davies;
  illustrated by Mike Machat.
        p. cm.
     Includes index.
     1. Deutsche Lufthansa (1953–     )—History. 2. Deutsche Lufthansa
  (1926–     )—History. 3. Airlines—History. 4. Airlines—
  Germany (West)—History. I. Title.
HE9849.D4D38 1991
387.7′065′43—dc19                                                    88-22463
                                                                          CIP

ISBN 0-517-57022-X

10 9 8 7 6 5 4 3 2 1

First Edition

# Contents

## Another 1000 Airplanes

Pan American Airways had operated an estimated 982 commercial aircraft by the time the first book in this series appeared. The German national airline, including the "old" Deutsche Luft Hansa and the new Lufthansa German Airlines, has comfortably exceeded that number, even if the fleets of its predecessor airlines are excluded. The total listed individually in this book is more than 1100

A word about the registration numbers: In the early months following World War I, as the airlines struggled to their feet, no national system existed, and Deutsche Luft Reederei, for example, had its own numbering system until regulations were introduced. This system was again changed in 1934 when a group of four letters replaced the numbers that had previously been prefixed by the international letter code, D, for Deutschland. Until about 1938 the lettering group consisted of a vowel, consonant, vowel, and consonant, in that order, and each aircraft could therefore be familiarly known by its acronym. Eventually, however, the permutation was exhausted.

The first letter of the four-letter group was -A for multi-engined types, -U for single-engined types, and -O or -I for single-engined *Reiseflugzeuge*, or "travel" aircraft. The Junkers-F 13s were all in the -U category. Incidentally, -E and -Y were allocated for sport aircraft.

During the early years, Junkers aircraft had a letter prefix to the type number. No official or authoritative ruling can be traced to define the system, if there was one. The -F types appear to have been single-engined, but all single-engined types were not -Fs. The -G may have indicated *Grossflugzeug*, or large aircraft; the -W *Wettbewerb* (competition), because it is believed they were built for such a purpose; and the -A *Arbeitsflugzeug*, or "working aircraft." But none of these explanations can be regarded as more than speculative, pending the discovery of an official Junkers rulebook on the practice, which was discontinued in the early 1930s.

## Acknowledgments

In compiling this account of Lufthansa and its ancestors, I inevitably made use of the work of other aviation historians who have toiled for many years, as I have, in trying to record accurately the details of long-forgotten episodes, and to trace the complexities of the ever-changing fleet composition. Certain of these veteran researchers must be recognized for their outstanding contributions in providing the foundations on which this book was prepared and on which systematic further research can still be pursued.

The sleuthlike investigations of **Günther Ott** into the prehistory of the "old" Luft Hansa, its aircraft during the interwar years, and its exploits during World War II, have been of incalculable importance. And I feel especially privileged to have had Günther review the text of my work, make corrections, and offer advice.

The works of **John Stroud**, doyen of commercial aircraft historians, particularly his classic *European Transport Aircraft Since 1910*, and his "Wings of Peace" series of articles for *Aeroplane Monthly*, have been invaluable. I have consulted the published works and other research carried out by **Wolfgang Wagner** and **Heinz Nowarra**, while for a balanced analysis of transport airships, I am indebted to **Peter Brooks** and **John Provan**, both of whom have generously allowed me to select material from their own publications.

The detailed listings of aircraft were assembled from Lufthansa's own archives, presided over by the industrious and ever-helpful **Werner Bittner**, and these were supplemented by material supplied by John Stroud, Günther Ott, and Wolfgang Wagner.

Unless otherwise indicated, all the photographs in this book have been provided by Lufthansa's immaculately referenced archives. Others have been supplied from the collections of John Provan, Peter Bowers, Günther Ott, and Sam Parker.

I am also grateful for much help from Peter Grosz, Kurt Weil, Matthew Muller, and Peter Moeller. Frau M. Hünerbach helped to select the fine photographs from Lufthansa's impressive collection; Bob van der Linden acted once again as my technical conscience and as meticulous proofreader, while Donna Corbett coped with the index.

I can truthfully state that without the help of these good people, this book could not have been produced.

## Special Notes

German law forbids the prominent display of symbols of unconstitutional organizations. Respecting this law, and understanding the reasons for it, the artist has omitted the National Socialist Party emblem from the precision drawings of those aircraft that were introduced between 1933 and 1945.

To avoid excessive duplication of aircraft descriptive material already included in the first book of this series, *Pan Am: An Airline and Its Aircraft*, cross-reference is sometimes made (for example, for the Boeing jets) to the relevant pages of that book. However, all information essential to the Lufthansa story is included here.

The discerning reader may detect what appears to be a discrepancy in the spelling of Lufthansa. Until 30 June 1933 the official name of the airline was Deutsche Luft Hansa A.G. It was then changed to Deutsche Lufthansa by decision of the General Assembly. The "new" postwar airline is generally known worldwide as Lufthansa German Airlines.

For the purists among the aircraft connoisseurs: note that the nomenclature of all Junkers aircraft types takes the form Junkers-F, Junkers-Ju, etc.—the hyphen and letter code following immediately after the manufacturer's name.

## Further Reading

I cannot recommend much further reading in English except *The Lufthansa Story*, a much-better-than-average account published by Lufthansa itself. But for those interested in the detailed development of the "old" Lufthansa's aircraft, John Stroud's masterly *European Transport Aircraft Since 1910* is indispensable, representing as it does a fair slice of his lifetime's dedicated work. For the Zeppelin airships, Peter Brooks's *Historic Airships* is a classic work on lighter-than-air craft but is unfortunately out of print and difficult to obtain. John Provan's meticulous work has, as yet, been published only privately.

For those conversant with the German language, however, far more books and magazine articles are available, notably *Die Flugzeuge der Deutschen Lufthansa* by Erich H. Heimann, and *Der Deutsche Luftverkehr—Die Pionierjahre 1919–1925* by Wolfgang Wagner. The many monographs published in *Luftfahrt International* and *Modell Magazin* by Günther Ott are representative of historical aviation research at its best, as are John Stroud's "Wings of Peace" series in *Aeroplane Monthly*.

## Author

Last year, in choosing the launching subject for this series of books on the world's great airlines, Pan American's long record of technical leadership as the "World's Most Experienced Airline" was a vital criterion for selection.

There have been five main eras of development in the 70 years of international air transport history: (1) Infancy (1919–1929); (2) Great Flying Boats (1930–1945); (3) Great Piston-Engined Airliners (1946–1958); (4) First Jet Age (1958–1970); and (5) Wide-Bodied or "Jumbo" Jet Age (1970–    ). Of the five eras, Pan Am launched three, a record that no other airline can match.

Choice of the second airline for the series was difficult. But given that the selected candidate should be (a) foreign, to preserve an impartial perspective of world, as opposed to U.S. airline progress, and (b) an innovator, to remind us that U.S. airlines have not always been the frontrunners, Lufthansa German Airlines was an ideal choice.

With a large fleet of Junkers-F 13s and their offspring, the "old" Luft Hansa dominated Europe's airways during the 1920s and 1930s, and can thus lay claim to having led the way during the Infancy period; and had not World War II intervened, it may well have stolen a march on the aviation world with the Focke-Wulf Fw 200 Condor, and launched the third era.

The history of the German national airline includes, moreover, the spice of adventure, the badge of courage during the pioneering years, and a powerful element of drama during its precarious survival and final demise in World War II. These episodes give the lie to the fashionable myth that only military men have good tales to tell.

Lufthansa's story reaches deep into aviation's almost distant past. Germany was the first country to recognize the possibilities of air transport. The enterprising airship activities before World War I serve as a fascinating introductory prelude to the events which led to the creation of the national airline in 1926. D.L.H.—as it was known throughout the aviation world during the interwar years—inherited the now familiar crane insignia as the hallmark of airline quality. As long ago as 1919, one of its ancestors led the way not only in devising this insignia, but, far more important, in developing the methods of how to operate an airline. Though less visible than the aircraft on the routes, Martin Wronsky's shrewd analyses in the offices of Deutsche Luft-Reederei were to lay the foundations for Lufthansa's later success. Mighty airships may have attracted public attention, fame, and eventual notoriety; but D.L.H. kept a steady course of disciplined service to the public, at the same time constantly experimenting in every branch of aeronautical technology and operational practice, in an effort to improve the state of the airline art.

The tradition continues today. Now that progress in airliner technology is measured by desperately engineered fractional improvements, Lufthansa has concentrated on penetratingly accurate decision-making in a fiercely competitive environment. With a built-in handicap of a ten-year late start since World War II, because of political restraints, it has hardly put a foot wrong. It was the launching customer for an American-built airliner, a farsighted decision, bearing in mind that the Boeing 737 has become the world's biggest-selling single aircraft type in the commercial airline world.

When Lufthansa makes a move, other airlines take notice. It has joined the ranks of a privileged few at the pinnacle of power of one of the world's most influential industries. As a member of a dedicated production team, I too feel privileged to be able to write its history.

R. E. G. Davies

## Artist

Once more into the fray! If Pan American and its subtle changes in color schemes were a challenge, Lufthansa has been no less a stimulant to the eternal search for accuracy and precision. Lufthansa's long history having started long before color photography was invented, authentic source data have often been difficult to track down. The stark simplicity of the Junkers era was offset by the sheer antiquity of the reference material. For Lufthansa's ancestors, a blue was either light or dark or medium, with no documented PMS color scale to set the exact shade. And records of the sand-colored tones of the undoped early airship fabric varied according to the individual imaginations of the contemporary artists.

These tribulations were happily offset by the pleasure in being able to portray the handsome colors of Lufthansa's postwar modern aircraft, especially the glorious yellow that van Gogh himself would have enjoyed.

The German national airline offers further proof of the constancy of Machat's Law—that aircraft allegedly painted in the same color scheme are seldom actually so painted. There was a case of a seasoned Lufthansa passenger who carefully noted the names of all the aircraft he traveled in, and was surprised to pull in to the gate alongside another aircraft with the same name as his own. This, I hasten to add, is not typical of Lufthansa's characteristically meticulous custom and procedure; but nevertheless I have inserted explanatory notes, where appropriate, which may be of general interest to the reader as well as of assistance to the model makers.

Mike Machat

## Publisher

We would like to echo Ron Davies's and Mike Machat's pleasure in being able to produce this, the second in our series about the world's great airlines. Lufthansa's exciting story, from its prehistory to its current era of pace-setting challenge to its rivals, is published here for the first time in English and distributed to the English-speaking world.

As a great airline with proud traditions, Lufthansa has already documented its own history, and English versions have been distributed among the aviation fraternity. But this book will reach a much wider audience than that of the cognoscenti. It was written with the airline's encouragement and support but not, we should stress, with its censorship. Ron Davies's insistence upon literary autonomy was respected, and Lufthansa recognized that the author's objective was to extract the true drama, adventure, even romance from a story that was exciting enough without resort to sensationalism.

Few airlines have endured such fundamental problems as Lufthansa. Its ancestors survived the worst monetary inflation in world history, when a mountain of marks would not purchase a spark plug; it lived through the political trauma of National Socialism, and it had to rebuild itself against airlines ten years ahead of it in technology and organization when it reemerged only 33 years ago.

Mike Machat has supported the author with the same level of superb professional artistry evident in the Pan American book which launched the series and set the standards, and we have retained the same format and style. We feel that here is another reference book that also gives joy to the eye—a visually pleasing production that can be used as a reliable reference.

And underscoring this consideration is the thought that Lufthansa's history makes a fascinating and, at times, exciting story.

The Publisher

# The Dawn of Air Transport

## The Very First

The credit for recognizing that the transport of people and goods by air was a practical possibility must go to the airship promoters in Germany before World War I. On 8 September 1908, Ferdinand, Count von Zeppelin, founded the **Luftschiffbau Zeppelin GmbH** at Friedrichshafen, on the shore of the Bodensee (Lake Constance). Little more than a year later, on 16 November 1909, to put theory and construction into operational practice, and making use of Zeppelin's products, the **Deutsche Luftschiffahrts A.G. (DELAG)** was formed in Frankfurt-am-Main. The capital was subscribed partly by German cities and partly by the **Hamburg-Amerikanische Packetfahrt A.G. (HAPAG)**, trading as the **Hamburg-Amerika Linie**. The first general manager, Alfred Colsman, also held that position at the Zeppelin works.

DELAG moved into action with a speed that even today would be considered to be courageous. The city fathers, possibly thinking of the prestige attached to the possession of an airship station, provided installations to receive the new and exciting machines; and DELAG ordered its first airship, the *Deutschland,* from Friedrichshafen.

## The Service Record

DELAG got off to a bad start. On 28 June 1910, only a week after its first flight, the *Deutschland* crashed into some trees after an engine failure. Happily the only casualty, apart from pride and wrecked metal, was one broken leg. Another airship, the LZ 6, built a year previously and modified early in 1910 as the LZ 6A, was pressed into service. Hugo Eckener replaced Captain Kahlenburg as DELAG's chief commander, but he too was unlucky, as LZ 6A was destroyed by a hangar fire after three weeks' service.

In 1911, a replacement ship, the *Ersatz-Deutschland,* went into service, but it lasted only a month, as it was wrecked in a crosswind while emerging from its hangar, despite the efforts of at least 250 ground handling staff.

Most organizations would probably have quietly wound up their affairs. But the old Count (he was 73) prevailed upon the DELAG board to give the airship project one more chance, showing great faith in his chief designer, L. Dürr, who was to retain his position until the last of the great dirigibles, the LZ 130 *Graf Zeppelin II.*

The material outcome of this decision was the *Schwaben,* and it was a success. It flew throughout the 1911 summer and for three more months in the summer of 1912, before a storm caused it to burn to destruction. But the *Schwaben's* design improvements over those of previous types encouraged both Zeppelin and DELAG to press on with their program. Thereafter three more fine airships went into service, the *Viktoria Luise* and the *Hansa* in 1912 and the *Sachsen* in 1913. All three flew reliably and well until the outbreak of World War I, when they were transferred to the army.

The formidable record of DELAG's operations is shown in the table on page 4.

## DELAG's Claim to Fame

The seven airships of the pre–World War I DELAG fleet did not carry passengers or goods according to a regular timetable or on fixed routes. They carried people mainly on sightseeing flights, not only from their home bases but from other German cities. Their arrival, usually at weekends, was invariably met with great excitement and enthusiasm. As the airships moved from city to city, the opportunity was offered—and eagerly taken—for citizens to ride in this new and unusual form of transport. But as yet the airships were not competitive with surface modes. Average speeds were barely 40 mph, less than that of an express train.

Pride of place for the world's first *scheduled* air service goes to the **St. Petersburg–Tampa Airboat Line**, in Florida, which, for three months in 1914, operated a diminutive **Benoist XIV** flying boat, carrying two people at a time. This airline carried about 1200 passengers over the 18 miles between St. Petersburg and Tampa. In contrast, DELAG carried 34,000 people, mostly over longer distances, during the 1910–1914 period, and more than 10,000 of them paid for the privilege. The *Schwaben* carried up to 20 people per flight and was the first airborne vehicle to provide onboard service. Heinrich Kubis was the world's first air steward and later became chief steward of the *Hindenburg.*

In one respect, DELAG shared a great honor with the 1914 Florida airline. It never killed a passenger, and the only injury was that broken leg in 1910.

The *Schwaben,* one of **DELAG**'s most successful airships.

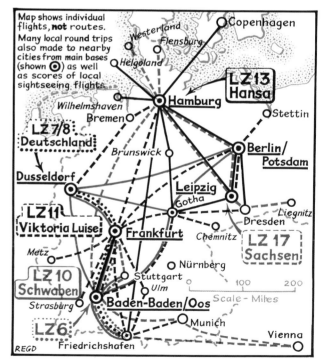

Map shows individual flights, **not** routes. Many local round trips also made to nearby cities from main bases (shown ◉) as well as scores of local sightseeing flights.

LZ 13 Hansa
LZ 7/8 Deutschland
LZ 11 Viktoria Luise
LZ 17 Sachsen
LZ 10 Schwaben
LZ 6

Copenhagen
Westerland
Flensburg
Helgoland
Wilhelmshaven
Bremen
Stettin
Hamburg
Brunswick
Berlin/Potsdam
Dusseldorf
Leipzig
Gotha
Liegnitz
Dresden
Frankfurt
Chemnitz
Metz
Nürnberg
Stuttgart
Ulm
Baden-Baden/Oos
Strasburg
Munich
Vienna
Friedrichshafen

Scale - Miles
0   100   200

REGD

# Zeppelin LZ 10 *Schwaben*

## 20 seats • 44 mph

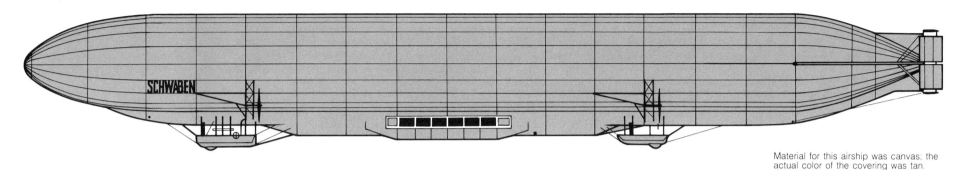

Material for this airship was canvas; the actual color of the covering was tan.

Maybach A-Z (150 hp) × 3 • 45,520 lb max. gross lift • 900 statute miles range

## The Father of the Dirigible Airship

The rigid airship is almost synonymous with the company promoted by **Ferdinand, Count von Zeppelin**, born in 1838. A wealthy former cavalry general, he became interested in ballooning and by the 1880s was convinced that powered rigid airships had a great future. A patent for such a design (by Theodor Kober) was taken out on 28 December 1897. Having

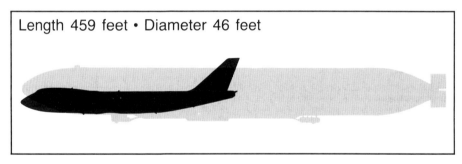

Length 459 feet • Diameter 46 feet

### THE DELAG FLEET
#### 1910–1914

| Airship | | | Date of First Flight | Dimensions (ft) | | Max. Seats | Engines | | | Max. Gross Lift (lb) | Cruise Speed (mph) | Normal Range (st. miles) |
|---|---|---|---|---|---|---|---|---|---|---|---|---|
| Type | No. | Name | | Length | Diam. | | No. | Type | Hp (each) | | | |
| D | LZ 6A | (unnamed) | 21 Aug. 1910 | 473 | 43 | 12 | 2 | Daimler J4L | 115 | 38,360 | 34 | 1250 |
| | | | | | | | 1 | Maybach A-Z | 140 | | | |
| E | LZ 7 | *Deutschland* | 19 June 1910 | 486 | 46 | 20 | 3 | Daimler J4F | 120 | 49,380 | 37 | 1000 |
| | LZ 8 | *Ersatz-Deutschland* | 30 March 1911 | | | | | | | | | |
| F | LZ 10 | *Schwaben* | 26 June 1911 | 459 | 46 | 20 | 3 | Maybach A-Z | 150 | 45,520 | 44 | 900 |
| G | LZ 11 | *Viktoria Luise* | 14 Feb. 1912 | 486 | 46 | 25 | 3 | Maybach B-Y | 170 | 47,840 | 44 | 700 |
| | LZ 13 | *Hansa* | 30 July 1912 | | | | | | | | | |
| H | LZ 17 | *Sachsen* | 3 May 1913 | 519 | 49 | 25 | 3 | Maybach B-Y | 180 | 57,540 | 47 | 1400 |

#### 1919

| Type | No. | Name | Date of First Flight | Length | Diam. | Max. Seats | No. | Type | Hp (each) | Max. Gross Lift (lb) | Cruise Speed (mph) | Normal Range (st. miles) |
|---|---|---|---|---|---|---|---|---|---|---|---|---|
| Y | LZ 120 | *Bodensee* | 20 Aug. 1919 | 397 | 61 | 22 | 4 | Maybach Mb IVa | 245 | 51,150 | 82 | 1050 |

attracted much support from official and other sources, Zeppelin formed a joint stock company "for the promotion of air navigation with dirigibles" in May 1898. A small factory and shed were set up at Manzell, on the shores of the Bodensee, on rent-free land provided by the King of Württemberg. The main construction hangar was built on floating pontoons on the lake.

## First of a Thoroughbred Line

The first Zeppelin, **LZ 1**, made its first flight on 2 July 1900. Its aluminum-zinc-alloy structure was 420 feet long, and the gasbags were filled with hydrogen. It was powered by two 14-hp gasoline engines, and flew, not too successfully, at less than 20 mph. But it was the beginning.

Five years were to pass before **LZ 2** was built, and this was only after the company had folded through lack of funds. But Zeppelin persevered doggedly and gained support after a public appeal. More ships followed from 1905 onward, each successive one an improvement. By the end of the decade the carriage of passengers became practical, and LZ 7 *Deutschland* had the honor of being the first to do so. As shown in the tables on this and the following page, this proudly named airship was the forerunner of a great fleet.

# The First Scheduled Airship Service

## The *Bodensee* Flights

With a speed exceeding that of the fastest train, the *Bodensee's* 80 mph encouraged **DELAG** to venture into competitive scheduled service. Between 24 August and 5 December 1919 a regular service was operated between Friedrichshafen and Berlin, northbound on one day, southbound on the next. Until 4 October a stop was made at Munich, but thereafter the flights were nonstop over the 370 miles.

During the 104 days, 103 flights were made, of which 78 were commercially scheduled. The fare was about $100, although equivalent real values at the time were obliterated by galloping inflation. The *Bodensee* carried 2253 passengers before it was forced into exile—see opposite page.

### DELAG AIRSHIP OPERATIONS
#### 1910–1914

| Airship No. | Airship Name (and base) | Date of First Flight | Period of Service Began | Period of Service Ended | Passengers Carried Total | Passengers Carried Paying | No. of DELAG Flights | Hours Flown | Remarks |
|---|---|---|---|---|---|---|---|---|---|
| LZ 7 | Deutschland (Düsseldorf) | 19 June 1910 | 22 June 1910 | 28 June 1910 | 220 | 142 | 7 | 20 | Crashed at Wallendorf |
| LZ 6A | (unnamed) (Baden-Baden) | 25 Aug. 1909 | 21 Aug. 1910 | 14 Sept. 1910 | 1100 | 726 | 34 | 66 | Destroyed by fire in hangar |
| LZ 8 | Ersatz-Deutschland (Frankfurt) | 30 March 1911 | 11 April 1911 | 16 May 1911 | 458 | 129 | 22 | 47 | Wrecked at base by high winds |
| LZ 10 | Schwaben (Baden-Baden) | 26 June 1911 | 15 July 1911 | 28 June 1912 | 4354 | 1553 | 218 | 480 | Burned out during storm[1] |
| LZ 11 | Viktoria Luise (Frankfurt) | 14 Feb. 1912 | 4 March 1912 | 31 July 1914 | 9738 | 2995 | 489 | 981 | Transferred to army |
| LZ 13 | Hansa (Hamburg) | 30 July 1912 | Aug. 1912 | 31 July 1914 | 8321 | 2187 | 399 | 841 | Transferred to army |
| LZ 17 | Sachsen (Leipzig) | 3 May 1913 | June 1913 | 31 July 1914 | 9837 | 2465 | 419 | 741 | Transferred to army |
| TOTAL | | | 22 June 1910 | 31 July 1914 | 34,028 | 10,179 | 1588 | 3176 | |

[1]The burning was caused by the ignition of leaking gas by static electricity discharged from the rubber gas cells. Thereafter all gas cells were made from expensive "gold beater's skin"—the lining of cows' stomachs; 50,000 stomachs were needed for each cell, with 12–15 cells per airship.

#### 1919

| Airship No. | Airship Name (and base) | Date of First Flight | Period of Service Began | Period of Service Ended | Passengers Carried Total | Passengers Carried Paying | No. of DELAG Flights | Hours Flown | Remarks |
|---|---|---|---|---|---|---|---|---|---|
| LZ 120 | Bodensee (Friedrichshafen) | 20 Aug. 1919 | 24 Aug. 1919 | 5 Dec. 1919 | 4050 | 2253 | 103 | 531 | Surrendered to Allies as war reparations. |

The route taken by the Afrika-Zeppelin **L 59** in 1917 on its remarkable round-trip flight of 4200 miles *(left)*.

The *Bodensee's* scheduled route in 1919 *(below)*.

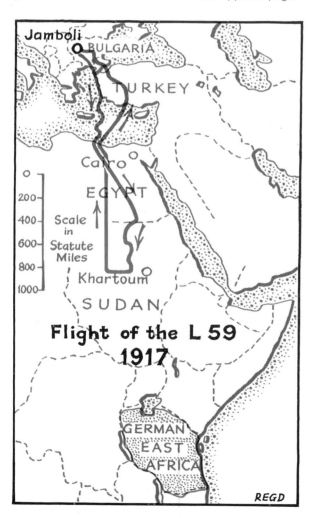

Scale in Statute Miles

**Flight of the L 59 1917**

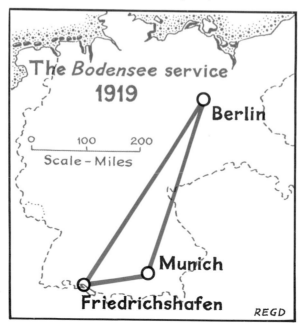

**The Bodensee service 1919**

Scale - Miles

The *Viktoria Luise*, fifth airship of **DELAG**'s fleet of seven.

The *Bodensee*. **DELAG**'s postwar contender for scheduled air service, while under construction.

# Zeppelin LZ 120 *Bodensee*

## 22 seats • 82 mph

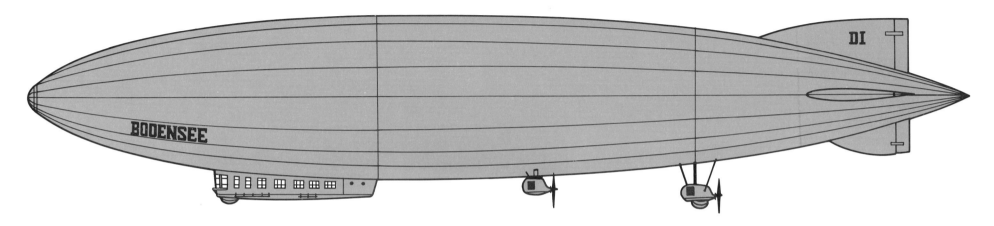

Maybach Mb IVa (245 hp) × 4 • 51,150 lb max. gross lift • 1050 statute miles range

## Wartime Progress

During World War I the **Zeppelin** works improved its technology to a remarkable degree. Under the design leadership of Dr. Ludwig Dürr, the work force grew to almost 23,000 workers, of whom 13,600 were at Friedrichshafen. Among the staff of engineers were Claude Dornier and Adolf Rohrbach, both of whom were to make their own personal marks in the science of aeronautics.

The military airships gradually became bigger and faster. The most important single advance was in the **L 30**, completed on 28 May 1916. For this superb airship, the technical knowledge of the Zeppelin company was pooled with that of its rival, **Schütte-Lanz**. The aluminum-zinc alloy was replaced by duralumin, a new and stronger alloy patented by the Düren Metallwerke A.G. The use of duralumin and other structural improvements, combined with six Maybach engines, permitted an airship with 2½ times the gas capacity of the largest prewar DELAG ship, the *Sachsen*.

To escape the predatory Allied warplanes, more than a match for the Zeppelins, variations of the L 30 produced the L 48 and L 53 "Height-Climbers," while another version led to the L 57 and L 59 Afrika-Zeppelins, with extended range. On 21–25 November 1917, in an attempt to carry supplies to beleaguered German forces in East Africa, **L 59** carried a load of no less than 15 tons from Jamboli, Bulgaria, to a point near Khartoum, Sudan, where she was ordered to return. The round-trip distance was 4200 miles, a world's long-distance record for aircraft that was to hold for many years.

Half of the Zeppelins built during World War I were of the L 30 class or its derivatives. Count von Zeppelin lived just long enough to witness their first production. He died on 8 March 1917.

### Length 397 feet • Diameter 61 feet

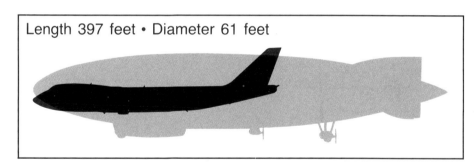

## Back to the Drawing Board

Formidable though these new airships were, the Zeppelin works quickly adapted to **DELAG** requirements when the war ended. Incorporating all the design and structural improvements learned from 1914 to 1918, a new airship, LZ 120, the *Bodensee*, was actually shorter than the prewar ships; but with almost twice the power and aerodynamically cleaner, it was twice as fast.

The *Bodensee* went into scheduled service for a few months in 1919 (see opposite page), but its fate was sealed by the bitterness raging between the ex-combatants. It had to be handed over to Italy in July 1921 as war reparations and was renamed *Esperia*. A sister ship, LZ 121, *Nordstern,* had met a similar fate, having been handed over to France a month previously and renamed *Mediterranée*.

# The World's First Sustained Airline

## A Brave Start

**Deutsche Luft-Reederei (D.L.R.)** came into being in Berlin on 13 December 1917. It was a reorganization of the Gummiwerke Oberspree GmbH, an affiliated company of the **Allgemeine Elektrizitäts-Gesellschaft (A.E.G.),** and had a capital of 2,500,000 marks. D.L.R. was initiated by Walter Mackenthun, a prewar military pilot, and was strongly supported by Walter Rathenau, the far-sighted chief executive of A.E.G. It was registered as a company on 28 May 1918 and was ready to start when the German Air Ministry authorized civil airline operations on 8 January 1919. Four weeks later, on 5 February, D.L.R. opened an air service from the Johannistal airfield in Berlin to the seat of the new government at Weimar. An intermediate stop at Leipzig was added later.

The first flight carried newspapers, mail was carried the next day, and the first passenger was carried on 10 February. During the ensuing weeks, in spite of foul weather and thick snow, D.L.R. maintained the service, using two-seat **A.E.G. J II** and two-seat **L.V.G. C V** biplanes. It was the first sustained daily air service in the world to open to all categories of air traffic.

## A Difficult First Season

Other routes were opened from Berlin during 1919, radiating from Berlin to Hamburg (on 1 March), Gelsenkirchen (on 15 April), and Warnemünde, gateway to Scandinavia. Special air service was offered to the Leipziger Messe (Leipzig Fair) and from Hamburg to Westerland for summer holidays on the beaches. When regular services had to be suspended for a while on 1 August 1919 because of a fuel shortage, D.L.R. had carried 1574 passengers in its first half year of operation.

On 28 August D.L.R. became a founding member of the **International Air Traffic Association (IATA)**—see panel—but fortunes were mixed during the first testing years. The route network changed bewilderingly (see maps), partly because of the restrictions placed on commercial flying into the Ruhr and the Rhineland by the Allied occupying powers after the Treaty of Versailles.

A.E.G. J II of **Deutsche Luft-Reederei**, with cabin modification.

ORIGINAL MEMBERS OF THE INTERNATIONAL AIR TRAFFIC ASSOCIATION (IATA), FOUNDED 28 AUGUST 1919

| Country | Company | Abbreviation |
|---|---|---|
| Great Britain | Air Transport & Travel | A.T.&T. |
| Netherlands | Koninklijke Luchtvaart Maatschappij voor Nederland an Kolonien | K.L.M. |
| Sweden | Svenska Luft Trafik A.B. | S.L.A. |
| Denmark | Det Danske Luftfartselskab | D.D.L. |
| Norway | Det Norske Luftfartsrederi | D.N.L. |
| Germany | Deutsche Luft-Reederei | D.L.R. |

ADDITIONAL MEMBERS, 1920

| | | |
|---|---|---|
| Danzig Free State | Danziger Luft-Reederei | — |
| Great Britain | The Daimler Airway | — |

The crane insignia of **Deutsche Luft-Reederei**, inherited by **Deutsche Luft Hansa**, and still the symbol of today's airline.

**Martin Wronsky**, driving force behind German airline development during its formative years.

## Laying the Foundations

In spite of the difficulties that made D.L.R.'s life a series of minor crises, progress was made. On 18 October 1920 a coastal survey flight was made along the Baltic coast from Warnemünde to Riga, via Königsberg, Memel, and Libau. On 15 November the Ruhr route was reinstated, and a fleet of motorcycles linked Gelsenkirchen with the other industrial cities in the area. The world's first airline pool service, the **Europa Nord-West Flug**, opened on 3 August 1920 with D.L.R. coordinating with the Dutch K.L.M. and the Danish D.D.L.

During 1921 a similar disjointed collection of aircraft and routes was maintained. On 27 April, D.L.R. became part of a holding company, **Aero-Union** (page 8), in which the Zeppelin and the Hamburg-Amerika Linie concerns joined A.E.G. with a financial interest.

## The Legacy

Deutsche Luft-Reederei worked under the umbrella of the Aero-Union group until the end of the 1922 summer season. On 6 February 1923 it was absorbed into the new group **Deutscher Aero Lloyd A.G.** On the last day of 1922 it had made a token flight to Lympne, England, with a Dornier Komet (D-223), the first German aircraft to land in England after World War I. On 10 January 1923, not to be outdone, Junkers made a similar flight to Croydon with a Junkers-F 13 (D-220).

D.L.R. did much to lay the foundations of organized air transport. The first critical examination and statistical analysis of the disciplines involved were formulated in the earliest years by Martin Wronsky, a D.L.R. director, who was later to become the commercial director of **Deutsche Luft Hansa**.

**L.V.G. C VI** biplane of **D.L.R.** loading mail.

# A.E.G. J II K  2 seats • 93 mph (max.)

### THE DEUTSCHE LUFT REEDEREI FLEET
Counting and identifying the fleet of Deutsche Luft Reederei, possibly as many as 70 or 80 aircraft, has defied the ingenuity of many meticulous and indefatigable researchers. The problem is complicated by the existence, in the early 1920s, of three numbering systems, and seldom can more than one be positively linked with the constructor's number. From March 1919 to May 1920, aircraft were registered on the Luftfahrzeugrolle referred to below as LFRA. This was cancelled by order of the Allied control commission and replaced by a second register, referred to as LFR B. To these were added D.L.R.'s own fleet number. Fortunately for the numerologists, none of the aircraft survived to adopt yet another (lettered) series in 1934.

D.L.R.'s place in history is so important that this listing, however incomplete, is considered appropriate to mark D.L.R.'s pioneering role in air transport.

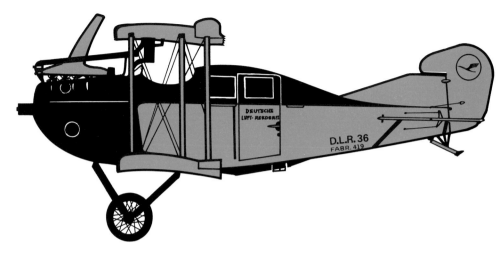

1 Benz Bz IV (200 hp) • 370 statute miles range • 3,570 lb max. gross takeoff weight

## L.V.G. C VI

| Const. No. | Regist. Nos. | Const. No. | Regist. Nos. | Const. No. | Regist. Nos. | Const. No. | Regist. Nos. | Const. No. | Regist. Nos. |
|---|---|---|---|---|---|---|---|---|---|
| 4012 | D-202(A) | 4721 | D-208(A) | 5058 | D-46(A) | 5071 | D-35(B) | 5083 | D-62(A) |
| 4100 | D-203(A) | 4722 | D-209(A) | " | DLR 31 | 5072 | D-54(A) | " | D-17(B) |
| 4587 | D-37(A) | 4830 | DLR 11 | 5059 | D-47(A) | " | D-112(B) | 5086 | D-63(A) |
| " | D-12(B) | 4963 | D-40(A) | 5060 | D-60(B) | 5074 | D-56(A) | 5087 | D-274(A) |
| 4590 | D-38(A) | 4978 | D-41(A) | 5061 | D-265(A) | 5075 | D-57(A) | 5089 | D-275(A) |
| " | D-13(B) | 4991 | D-43(A) | 5062 | D-49(A) | 5076 | D-58(A) | 5091 | D-277(A) |
| " | DLR 6 | " | DLR 10 | 5063 | D-15(B) | 5078 | DLR 43 | " | DLR 44 |
| 4619 | D-205(A) | 4993 | D-44(A) | 5065 | D-51(A) | 5081 | D-61(A) | 5097 | D-18(B) |
| 4621 | D-206(A) | 5050 | D-45(A) | 5067 | D-52(A) | 5082 | D-271(A) | " | DLR 42 |
| 4643 | D-207(A) | 5053 | D-14(B) | 5068 | D-53(A) | " | D-16(B) | 5098 | D-279(A) |
| " | D-123(B) | " | DLR 47 | 5070 | D-276(A) | | | 5099 | D-280 |
| " | DLR 84 | | | | | | | " | DLR 19 |

**Note** (A) indicates Luftfahrzeugrolle A (1919–1920); (B) indicates L.F.R. B (1920–1934). Several known numbers cannot be matched with the constructor's number. These are: (A) D-59, D-71, D-489 (also D-43 in B series); (B) D-34, 36, 37, 62, 64, 65, 76; DLR 21, 45. c/n 5068 was registered as O-BAFC in Belgium in March 1920.

## L.V.G. C V

| Const. No. | Regist. Nos. | Const. No. | Regist. Nos. | Const. No. | Regist. Nos. | Const. No. | Regist. Nos. | Const. No. | Regist. Nos. |
|---|---|---|---|---|---|---|---|---|---|
| 117 | D-189(A) | 591 | D-485(A) | 699 | D-73(B) | 1050 | D-255(A) | 14470 | D-483(A) |
| 150 | D-9(B) | " | D-117(B) | 1044 | D-252(A) | 14549 | D-260(A) | " | D-11(B) |
| 315 | D-10(B) | 695 | DLR 62 | | | | | | |
| " | DLR 59 | | | | | | | | |

**Note** No constructor's numbers for (B) D-58, 59, 147.

## A.E.G. J II

| Const. No. | Regist. Nos. | Const. No. | Regist. Nos. | Const. No. | Regist. Nos. | Const. No. | Regist. Nos. | Const. No. | Regist. Nos. |
|---|---|---|---|---|---|---|---|---|---|
| 310 | D-479(B) | 417 | D-68(B) | 439 | D-74(B) | 6748 | D-38(B) | 6840 | D-5(A) |
| " | DLR 97 | 418 | DLR 39 | 5053 | D-14(B) | " | DLR 74 | 6845 | D-6(A) |
| 415 | DLR 15 | 419 | D-23(B) | 6741 | D-24(B) | 6839 | D-25(B) | 6865 | D-26(B) |
| 416 | DLR 14 | " | DLR 36 | | | | | | |

**Note** No constructor's numbers for (B) 124, 150, 151; DLR 3, 4, 13, 32.

## Friedrichshafen FF45

| Const. No. | Regist. Nos. | Const. No. | Regist. Nos. |
|---|---|---|---|
| 234 | D-27(B) | 1037 | D-121(A) |
| 238 | D-118(A) | " | D-28(B) |
| 239 | D-119(B) | " | DLR 503 |
| | | 505 | D-117(A) |

## Fr. FF49

| Const. No. | Regist. Nos. |
|---|---|
| 1304 | D-146(B) |
| 1365 | D-49(B) |

## A.E.G.N 1

| Const. No. | Regist. Nos. |
|---|---|
| 6748 | D-38(B) |

## Staaken RXIV

| Const. No. | Regist. Nos. |
|---|---|
| R 69 | D-129(A) |
| R 70 | D-130(A) |
| R 71 | D-131(A) |

**Note** No constructor's numbers for FF 45s DLR 504, 505, 506, 508. DLR also had a Fokker DVII and a Hansa-Brandenburg W33 (DLR W 15). No constructor's numbers for FF 49s W3, 5, 6, 7, 8.

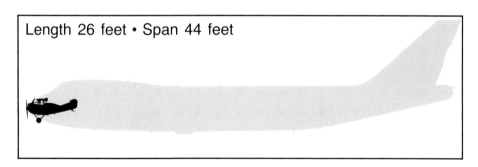

Length 26 feet • Span 44 feet

At first, like the aircraft of the victorious Allies, large, ponderous bombers such as the Friedrichshafen G IIIa were readily available to carry goods and people when Germany turned its aeronautical swords into plowshares. Three Staaken R XIV four-engined giants were even used briefly. But in general the Germans had to improvise with small aircraft because of the strict enforcement of the terms of the Treaty of Versailles after 10 January 1920.

The **A.E.G. J II** was introduced by **Deutsche Luft-Reederei** soon after starting service early in 1919. It was a neat conversion of the 1917-vintage wartime J II general-purpose biplane, built typically of a steel tube framework and wooden ribs, covered with fabric. As the illustrations show, a small cabin roof and sides were added to the fuselage to protect the contents, including some passengers, from the elements. More than 600 of the type were built, some of which were designated K, for Kabine, and quite a few graduated into service with A.E.G.'s pioneering airline, carrying for the first time, in March 1919, the famous crane insignia that was to become the trademark of Germany's national airline, and which Lufthansa proudly carries today.

# Aero-Union

## The First Airline Group

Within a year or two of the start of permanent airline operations in Germany, the need to coordinate the many diverse activities was becoming apparent. Air transport could not yet pay for itself but it clearly had a future, and the industry attracted fresh capital that led to reorganization.

**Aero-Union A.G.** was incorporated on 27 April 1921 by the **Allgemeine Elektrizitäts-Gesellschaft (A.E.G.)** (pages 6–7), the **Hamburg-Amerikanische Packetfahrt A. G. (HAPAG),** and the **Luftschiffbau Zeppelin GmbH,** which at this time also owned the Dornier Flugzeugbau GmbH. It was a nonoperating holding company, which, however, introduced the combined talents of important and influential enterprises of considerable stature. While A.E.G. was no longer producing aircraft, HAPAG and Zeppelin could provide marketing skills as well as aircraft. A.E.G. and HAPAG each held 40% and Zeppelin held 20% of the shares. Some incentive for the merger appears to have come from the growing strength of the Lloyd Luftdienst group, whose parent, the Norddeutscher Lloyd (N.D.L) shipping line, had gained access to precious fuel supplies (see page 12).

The operating members of the group were **Deutsche Luft-Reederei (D.L.R.)** (page 6); **Danziger Luft-Reederei** (this page); and **Deutsch-Russische Luftverkehrsgesellschaft (Deruluft)** (page 10). Together they composed a formidable amalgamation, one which was to have a critical influence on subsequent airline development in Germany. For on 6 February 1923, after less than two years of a "paper" existence, it joined with **Lloyd Luftdienst,** which was backed by N.D.L., to form **Deutscher Aero Lloyd,** one of the two immediate ancestors of **Deutsche Luft Hansa.**

## The Danzig Compromise

Under articles 100–108 of the Treaty of Versailles, the Free City of Danzig (now Gdańsk) was created to reconcile the rights of the 96% German population with the aspirations of the youthful new Polish republic, which desperately needed a good commercial seaport on the Baltic. Under the protection of the League of Nations, Danzig and its adjoining territory were formally proclaimed a Free City on 15 November 1920. Poland's economic interests were protected by a customs union, but the city retained its German character, and much of the commercial activity was linked with Berlin, East Prussia, and the Baltic coast region of Pomerania.

## Airlines of Its Own

Because of this special situation, under which only Danzig-registered aircraft could fly over the "Polish Corridor," the diminutive quasi-state was privileged to have its own airlines. Seeking outlets for eastern expansion, **Deutsche Luft-Reederei (D.L.R.)** established, in October 1919, an affiliated

**A.E.G. N 1** of **Deutsche Luft-Reederei.**

company, the **Danziger Luft-Reederei.** Service opened on 29 July 1921, from Danzig to Riga, via Königsberg and Memel, using original Fokker F. III five-seat single-engined monoplanes.

From the start, Danziger Luft-Reederei had been a member of IATA (page 6) and it became a component of the **Aero-Union** group, merging with **Danziger Lloyd Luftdienst** to become **Danziger Aero Lloyd,** under the umbrella of Deutscher Aero Lloyd, after 6 February 1923.

Meanwhile, **Danziger Luftpost,** representing the Junkers competition, started a route on 26 July 1921 from Danzig to Riga via Kovno, Lithuania, and a month later this service was extended to Reval (Tallinn), Estonia.

"All aboard" (by ladder) on an **L.V.G. C VI** of D.L.R.

**Otto Julius Merkel,** who organized Deutscher Aero Lloyd, and was later a member of Luft Hansa's executive board.

# Sablatnig P III    6 seats • 93 mph

## International Sortie

One early pioneer airline promoter, often forgotten by latter-day aviation historians, was Dr Josef Sablatnig, who had built night bombers at his Berlin factory toward the end of World War I. He converted one of these aircraft (in the manner of the A.E.G. J II K) with a fully enclosed cabin, heated and lighted, big enough for four seats. Designated the **Sablatnig P I**, it had the distinction of making the first overseas international flight by a German airplane when, on 21 April 1919, it flew from Berlin to Copenhagen and Stockholm, to reinforce German interest in airline development to Scandinavia.

## Lloyd-Luftverkehr Sablatnig

On 19 March 1919, the **Sablatnig Flugzeugbau** began a scheduled air service from Berlin to Warnemünde with a Sablatnig N I. On 5 July of that year, in cooperation with Deutsche Luft-Reederei, it added another from Berlin to the Baltic coast at Swinemünde and in September extended this to Copenhagen through its associated company, Dansk Luft Expres. Two P Is were used on this route, somewhat intermittently, during that summer until a fuel shortage toward the end of the year forced a closure.

On 8 October Sablatnig joined with the Bremen-based Norddeutscher Lloyd shipping line to establish **Lloyd-Luftverkehr Sablatnig, GmbH**. It started a permanent route from Berlin to Bremen and linked Bremen with the Ruhr area at Gelsenkirchen. However, this latter route had to be curtailed at Münster because of the Allied occupation of the Rhineland.

Already, in 1920, a new aircraft type, the Sablatnig P III, had been introduced, and in 1921 additional summer holiday routes were opened from Bremen to Wangerooge and along the Baltic coast—the Ostseebäderdienst—from Travemünde to Swinemünde, via Warnemünde and Sassnitz.

The **Sablatnig P I**, typical of the first attempts to adapt aircraft for commercial use.

## 1 Benz Bz IV (200 hp) • 4,815 lb max. gross takeoff weight • 325 statute miles range

**FLEET OF LLOYD-LUFTVERKEHR SABLATNIG** (and other Sablatnig aircraft known to have been in airline use)

### Sablatnig P I

| Const. No. | Regist. No. | Airline |
|---|---|---|
| 252 | D-3 | LLVS |
| 253 | D-4 | LLVS |
| 254 | D-5 | LLVS |
| 255 | D-6 | LLVS |
|  | D-70 | LLVS |
| 128 | D-77 | LLVS |
|  | D-78 | LLVS |
| — | D-93 | LLVS |
| — | D-94 | LLVS |
| — | D-164 | LLVS |
| — | D-106 | LLVS |
| — | D-127 | D.L.E. |

Abbrev. LLVS: Lloyd-Luftverkehr Sablatnig. D.L.E. Dansk Luft Expres, an affiliated company in Denmark.

Lloyd-Luftverkehr Sablatnig also operated four Friedrichshafen floatplanes, listed below:

| Type | Const. No. | Regist. No. |
|---|---|---|
| 49 | 1368 | D-85 |
| 49 | 223 | D-86 |
| 71a | — | D-120 |
| 71a | — | D-121 |

### Sablatnig P III

| Const. No. | Regist. No. | D.L.H. name | Year built | Remarks |
|---|---|---|---|---|
| 386 | D-2 | Hornisse | 1921 | Ex-Aeronaut (E 12), Junkers 1925, scrapped March 1932 |
| 258 | D-50 |  |  | LLVS, D.A.L., Norddeutsche LVG October 1924, written off 17 October 1926 |
| 152 | D143 | Biene | 1923 | LLVS, D.A.L., scrapped March 1932 |
| 273 | D-156 |  |  | Sablatnig, D.L.E. 1921, Aeronaut (E 5) |
| 261 | D-165 |  |  | Sablatnig (fate unknown) |
|  | D-166 |  |  | Sablatnig (fate unknown) |
| 262 | D-171 | Hummel | 1923 | A. Comte (CH 54) April 1921; LLVS July 1921, D.A.L., written off 21 April 1927 |
| 265 | D-395 | Wespe | 1924 | D.A.L., scrapped May 1928 |
|  | D-415 |  |  | D.V.S. written off 23 August 1928 |
| 268 | D-451 | Fliege |  | D.A.L., leased to OLAG 1928 (A-52), scrapped March 1932 |
| 275 | D-453 |  |  | Luftbild GmbH July 1925, written off 31 May 1927 |
|  | D-577 |  |  | Luftreederei Weisser Stern 1926/27 |
|  | D-581 | Libelle | 1921 | Ex-Aeronaut (E 10), Junkers, leased to OLAG (A-54) 1928; in museum 1932–1944 |
| 269 | D-727 | Hornisse | 1924 | D.A.L. July 1925, written off 7 August 1926 |
|  | D-730 |  |  | D.A.L. July 1925, written off 23 July 1925 |
| 270 | D-770 | Mücke | 1924 | D.A.L. July 1925, scrapped March 1932 |
|  | D-962 | Moskito | 1923 | Ex-Aeronaut (E 11), Junkers, written off 23 Sept 1927 |
|  | D-984 | Ameise | 1923 | Ex-Aeronaut (E 8), Junkers, written off 30 July 1927 |

Note   All the named aircraft were inherited by D.L.H. on its formation in 1926. The Aeronaut ones came via Junkers Luftverkehr, which had acquired them in exchange for Junkers-F 13s on a two-for-one basis.

# Deruluft

## Eyes Toward the East

Germany showed remarkable enterprise and vitality in developing air transport after World War I. Restricted though Germany was by the severe terms of the peace treaties, German entrepreneurs found ways and means of legitimate evasion, largely by doing abroad what they were not allowed to do at home.

Rebuffed in the west—relations with France were particularly frigid for several years—they turned to the Soviet Union, which was eagerly seeking commercial and industrial partnerships. On 24 November 1921 a joint Soviet-German airline was founded, with Aero-Union as the German partner, and aptly named **Deutsch-Russische Luftverkehrs GmbH (Deruluft)**.

**Fokker F III** of **Deruluft**.

With a frozen engine, gluelike oil, and no battery, it took three men to swing the propeller at Kovno during the 1920s.

## A Vital Link

On 16 April 1922 the **Treaty of Rapallo** (see panel) normalized relations between Germany and the Soviet Union. Almost immediately deeds followed words. Deruluft began service from Königsberg to Moscow, via Kovno (Kaunas) and Smolensk, on 1 May 1922. At first the **Fokker F.III**s carried the mail and officials only; but on 27 August the service was opened to the public. During the first year 109 trips were completed and almost 300 passengers were carried. The eight-hour flight from Königsberg was a great improvement on the two days by train.

## A Fine Service Record

Because of Deruluft's multinational ownership, it was not absorbed into the mergers that created Deutscher Aero Lloyd in 1923 and Deutsche Luft Hansa in 1926. The new German flag-carrier, however, took over the 50% shareholding from D.A.L. and leased many aircraft and crews to Deruluft. The backbone of the fleet during the late 1920s was the **Dornier Merkur**. Later, on the new route to Leningrad, opened on 6 June 1928, Deruluft used the Junkers-F 13. The journey time from Berlin was 14 hours.

Deruluft survived until 31 March 1937, operating improved equipment such as the **Rohrbach Roland** (page 23), the **Tupolev ANT-9**, and the **Junkers-Ju 52/3m** (pages 44–47). The last-named was fitted with outsize skis during the winter. There is no record as to whether or not the crew was also supplied with skis in case of an emergency landing.

A **Deruluft Dornier Merkur** at Königsberg.

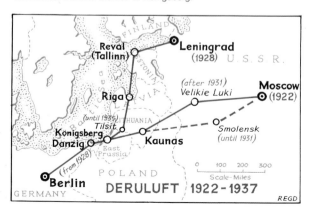

DERULUFT 1922-1937

POLITICAL AND COMMERCIAL DEVELOPMENTS
influencing German airline progress
before creation of Deutsche Luft Hansa

| Date | | Event | Effect |
|---|---|---|---|
| 1918 | 11 Nov. | Token flights by Sablatnig, Berlin-Kiel | Demonstrated German air-mindedness |
| 1919 | 19 Jan. | First postwar general election in Germany | Permitted universal suffrage |
| | 6 Feb. | First meeting of National Assembly at Weimar ("Weimar government") | The **Deutsche Luft-Reederei (D.L.R.)** service between Weimar and Berlin was the first regular postwar air service in Europe |
| | 7 May | Peace treaty imposed on Germany | Among many harsh conditions imposed on Germany, aircraft construction and airline operation were severely restricted |
| | 28 June | **Treaty of Versailles** signed | |
| | 28 Aug. | International Air Traffic Association (IATA) founded | D.L.R. was one of six founding members |
| 1920 | 10 Jan. | Treaty of Versailles effective | Permitted commercial aviation |
| 1921 | April–May | French troops occupied Rhineland | Restricted airline operations in Rhineland-Ruhr area |
| | 21 Nov. | **Deruluft** formed jointly by Aero-Union and Soviet government | |
| 1922 | 16 April | Treaty of Rapallo signed | Germany recognized Soviet Union and opened way for airline development |
| | 1 May | Deruluft started scheduled service | |
| 1923 | 15 Nov. | Height of financial crisis ($1 equal to 2,500,000,000,000 German marks) | Worst example of inflation in history |
| 1924 | 9 April | "Dawes Report" completed | Restructured impossibly harsh reparations payments schedule |
| | 30 Aug. | London Agreement adopted Dawes Report | |
| 1925 | 16 Oct. | Pact of Locarno signed | Guaranteed new frontiers of Germany and permitted more flexibility in aviation |
| | Dec. | British and French troops evacuated northern third of Rhineland area, including Cologne and Ruhr | Airline operations permanently resumed in Rhineland-Ruhr area |
| 1926 | 6 Jan. | Deutsche Luft Hansa AG (D.L.H.) formed as merger of Deutscher Aero Lloyd and Junkers | Created largest airline in Europe |
| | 10 Sept. | Germany joined **League of Nations** | Improved political and commercial climate |

# Fokker-Grulich F. III    5 seats  •  95 mph

## Link with a Legend

During World War I, the Dutch aircraft constructor Anthony Fokker had built some of Germany's best combat aircraft at factories initially in Johannistal, Berlin, and later at Schwerin, Mecklenburg. The Fokker Flugzeugwerke now turned its postwar attentions to civil aircraft and started a new line of commercial transports. Until June 1921 the Schwerin factory, renamed Schwerin Industriewerke after Fokker's return to the Netherlands in 1918, produced the **Fokker F.II** and the **Fokker F.III**, characterized by a wood-covered tubular steel frame and thick wooden wing construction. Both types were used by airlines in the Lloyd group, and the F.III inaugurated Deruluft's service to Moscow, the aircraft having been re-imported from the Netherlands immediately after the Armistice.

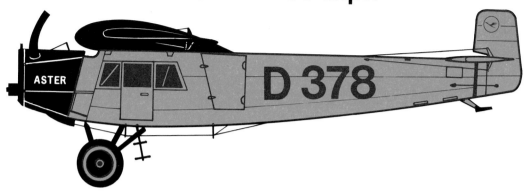

1 BMW Va (320 hp) • 5070 lb max. gross takeoff weight • 350 statute miles range

By the late 1920s the mainline fleets of almost all the airlines of Europe were to include either Dutch-built Fokker trimotors or German-built Junkers metal landplanes, in an early example of manufacturing rivalry for export markets. But the later Fokker transports were not built in Germany.

## Fokker-Grulich

Starting in 1924, the F.IIs and F.IIIs continued to be built in Berlin as **Fokker-Grulich** types, the name taken from Dr. Karl Grulich, who was to become the technical manager of Deutscher Aero Lloyd and who had coordinated disjointed aircraft construction as much of German industry disintegrated during the inevitable postwar decline. Only a thin definition separated aircraft manufacture from operation. Deutscher Aero Lloyd, for example, was involved in Fokker-Grulich F.II and F.III construction, along with Albatros, which built the wings. It refrained from ordering Junkers-F 13s, however, as this action would have supported a competitor. In contrast, the Junkers organization, which had over-produced the F 13, at first supplied aircraft, provided technical support, and even printed comprehensive timetables for innumerable airlines, and only later decided to put its own name to an operating company.

### THE FOKKER-GRULICH F II FLEET

| Const. No. | Regist. No. Original | Regist. No. 1934 | D.L.H. Name | Remarks |
|---|---|---|---|---|
| 1500 | D-57 | | | Prototype V.45, used by D.L.R. 1920 |
| 1503 | D-175 | | Moldau | Ex-Danziger Luft Reederei Dz3, D.A.L., written off 16 June 1931 |
| | D-715 | | | Aero Lloyd, to Balair August 1925 as CH-151 |
| 1570 | D-717 | | Weichsel | Scrapped July 1935 |
| 1581 | D-728 | | Mulde | Scrapped July 1935 |
| 1582 | D-741 | D-OVYF | Pregel | Written off 10 June 1936 |
| 1583 | D-742 | D-OSUP | Swine | Scrapped Oct. 1936 |
| 1584 | D-752 | D-ORAN | Nagold | Scrapped Feb. 1937—the last F 11 |
| 1585 | D-756 | | Dievenow | Scrapped July 1935 |
| 1571 | D-757 | | Spree | Written off 24 August 1929 |
| 1586 | D-758 | | Trave | Written off 26 July 1930 |
| 1587 | D-765 | | Eider | Written off 2 May 1932 |
| 1588 | D-766 | | Lahn | Written off 23 Nov. 1931 |
| 1589 | D-767 | | Ruhr | Scrapped July 1935 |
| 1572 | D-780 | | Havel | Written off 22 July 1929 |
| 1590 | D-782 | | Sieg | Scrapped March 1932 |
| 1591 | D-783 | D-OFAV | Wupper | Scrapped Aug. 1937 |
| 1592 | D-784 | | Iller | Written off 3 Aug. 1927 |
| 1593 | D-785 | D-OJIP | Lech | Written off 24 June 1936 |
| 1594 | D-786 | D-OGOT | Werra | Written off 24 July 1934 |
| 1596 | D-423 | | | Used by Deutsche Verkehrs-fliegerschule 1925–1930 |

Note  All except D-57, D-175, and possibly D-423 were built by Deutscher Aero Lloyd in 1925 and designated Fokker-Grulich F 11, with BMW IV engines. Some were re-engined with BMW Va engines and redesignated F 11b. The earlier ones were built by Fokker at Schwerin. Besides D-175, one or two were used by Danziger Luft Reederei, including Dz 4, but their fate is unknown.

### THE FOKKER-GRULICH F III FLEET

| Const. No. | Regist. No. Original | Regist. No. Other | D.L.H. Name | Date Written Off |
|---|---|---|---|---|
| 1531 | D-180 | Dz 8 | Main | 6 Sept. 1982 |
| 1539 | D-1028 | Dz 5 | Rhein | 17 Aug. 1928 |
| 1551 | D-353 | | Donau | July 1935 |
| 1552 | D-378 | | Alster | July 1935 |
| 1553 | D-447 | | Ems | 3 Oct. 1927 |
| 1554 | D-468 | | Weser | 8 Oct. 1926 |
| 1555 | D-489 | | Etsch | Nov. 1928 |
| 1556 | D-503 | D-ORIP | Leine | Oct. 1936 |
| 1557 | D-516 | | Elbe | 30 June 1926 |
| 1559 | D-533 | | Oder | Sept 1929 |
| 1563 | D-575 | | Isar | July 1935 |
| 1564 | D-594 | D-OTIK | Fulda | July 1935 |
| 1565 | D-701 | | Saale | July 1935 |
| 1566 | D-716 | D-OLYK | Schwarza | Oct. 1936 |
| 1567 | D-729 | | Unstrut | 22 April 1927 |
| 1568 | D-743 | | Inn | 3 June 1933 |

Note  Prototype F III registered as H-NABA (Netherlands), later to Malert, Hungary as H-MABB. D-197 with Deruluft, 1922. Four aircraft were sold to Aero Lloyd in 1925, later transferred to D.D.L., Denmark; and six aircraft were leased from Deruluft in 1927–28.

### THE FOKKER-GRULICH AIRCRAFT

| Type | Dimensions Length | Dimensions Span | Dimensions Height | Pass. Seats | Max Payload (lb) | Engines No. | Engines Type | Engines Hp (each) | Max. Gross TOW (lb) | Cruise Speed (mph) | Normal Range (st. miles) | Approx. No. Built |
|---|---|---|---|---|---|---|---|---|---|---|---|---|
| F II | 38'3" | 52'10" | 10'6" | 4[1] | 880 | 1 | B.M.W. IV | 250 | 4800 | 75 | 300 | 26 |
| F III[3] | 36'4" | 57'9" | 12'0" | 5 | 1000 | 1 | B.M.W. Va[2] | 320 | 5070 | 95 | 350 | 50–60 |

[1]Inside cabin only. One passenger could be carried in the open cockpit alongside the pilot! [2]Some Fokker-Grulich F IIIs had Armstrong-Siddeley Pumas. Deruluft aircraft had Rolls-Royce Eagles. [3]Later, a single Grulich V1 (registered in the Soviet Union as RR2) and a Grulich V2 (RR5) were developments of the F III.

# The Lloyd Group

## Lloyd Luftdienst Bremen

The **Hamburg-Amerikanische Packetfahrt** (**HAPAG**) had been the first transport organization in the world to promote air travel. In 1910 it had participated in the pioneer airship line DELAG (page 2); in 1919 it had backed Deutsche Luft-Reederei as general sales agent (page 6); and in April 1921 it helped to promote the first aviation holding group, **Aero-Union** (page 8). Possibly viewing this as a potentially competitive threat to be nipped in the bud, HAPAG's long-established rival, **Norddeutscher Lloyd** (**N.D.L.**) of Bremen, moved into the airline arena. On 8 March 1921 it established the **Lloyd-Luftdienst GmbH**.

This was essentially a booking and travel agency, representing numerous small airlines as associates, all flying under the Lloyd banner, which coordinated their marketing. One considerable advantage was that, immediately after the end of World War I, N.D.L. became closely associated with Deutsche Petroleum A.G. and had thus gained access to vital fuel supplies during a critical period of fuel shortages.

The initial route under direct control was from Berlin to Bremen, when N.D.L. joined with the Sablatnig Flugzeugbau to start a **Lloyd-Luftverkehr Sablatnig** service on 8 October 1920. This connected the shipping line's home base with the German capital and also provided an air link with Bremen from the industrial Ruhr area.

**Lloyd Ostflug** was then incorporated on 7 November 1920, in association with the aircraft constructor Albatros, which had started a service from Berlin to Königsberg, via

Stettin and Danzig, as early as 11 November 1919. The route was no ordinary one. The Junkers Flugzeugwerke and the Ostdeutsche Landwerkstätten (holder of the traffic license) were also involved. Under the terms of the treaty of Versailles, Poland had been given its "Corridor" to the Baltic Sea, severing East Prussia geographically from the Fatherland. Germans had the Hobson's Choice of either going by the long and circuitous sea route or traveling through Poland if they wished to move from the main part of Germany to the dismembered piece. Flying by Lloyd Ostflug had obvious attractions.

Like D.L.R., which had set up a sister company in Danzig, to use modern Fokker F.II and F.III aircraft, registered in Danzig to meet the legal situation created by the new Free State (page 8), Lloyd Ostflug was linked with Danziger Luftpost as an operator of the new Junkers-F 13s, with Danzig registrations to circumvent the restrictions of the Versailles Treaty, imposed on all aircraft built after January 1920. **Danziger Lloyd Luftdienst** merged with **Danziger Luft-Reederei** (page 8) to become **Danziger Aero Lloyd** after February 1923.

An Austrian affiliate, **Austro-Lloyd Luftdienst**, was incorporated in Vienna in October 1922, with support from the Lombard and Escompte banks, and absorbing the Wiener Flugverkehrsgesellschaft. The objective was to connect the Austrian capital with Berlin and other German cities as well as with Agram (Zagreb), Trieste, and Budapest; but there is no record of Austro-Lloyd's ever having operated, and it was probably set up solely to hold the route licenses.

## Deutscher Aero Lloyd

On 6 February 1923 the HAPAG and Lloyd shipping lines decided to merge their respective aviation activities to form the **Deutscher Aero Lloyd** (**D.A.L.**), which combined HAPAG's **Aero**-Union (essentially Deutsche Luft-Reederei) and the **Lloyd** Luftdienst combination of Lloyd-Luftverkehr Sablatnig, Lloyd-Ostflug, and Deutscher Luft-Lloyd. A.E.G. withdrew and the Deutsche Bank, represented by Dr. Weigelt, became a major shareholder. Mackenthun and A.E.G.'s von Rieben resigned as managers of D.L.R.

The new group resumed service on 23 April 1923 on the international service from Rotterdam to Copenhagen, in cooperation with K.L.M. and D.D.L., using **Dornier Komet IIs**, inherited from the Zeppelin works interest in Aero-Union. On 5 May it opened a joint Berlin-London through service, in partnership with the British Daimler Airway, via Hamburg, Bremen, and Amsterdam. In March 1924, Komet IIs also linked Berlin with Vienna, via Dresden.

But the most important single development of all was when a **Dornier Komet III** made a flight on 15 April 1925 from Berlin to Milan, via Munich. The event had a double significance. Not only did a German airline reach out to a Latin country; it also demonstrated that a commercial aircraft, carrying people and goods, could fly across the Alps, hitherto considered to be an almost insuperable barrier for flying.

This **Fokker-Grulich F II** was built in 1925 and retired in 1936.

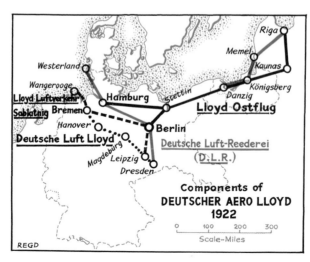

**Lloyd Ostflug**

**Deutsche Luft-Reederei (D.L.R.)**

**Components of DEUTSCHER AERO LLOYD 1922**

Scale-Miles

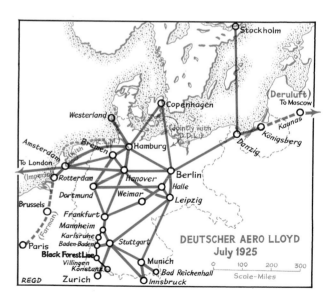

**DEUTSCHER AERO LLOYD July 1925**

Scale-Miles

# Dornier Komet III  6 seats • 96 mph

## An Uncertain Beginning

Claude Dornier had been a leading designer at Luftschiffbau Zeppelin, based at Friedrichshafen, on the Bodensee (Lake Constance). In 1914 he was put in charge of a new plant at Lindau, a short distance along the shore of the lake. He initiated the line of flying boats which was to make him famous. As the war ended, the first commercial type, the Gs I, was under construction. It could carry six passengers, first flew on 31 July 1919, and made some demonstrations. But it fell victim to the Treaty of Versailles and had to be sunk near Kiel on 25 April 1920.

To meet the imposed limitations on aircraft construction, Dornier produced a smaller type, the Delphin, a kind of telescoped Gs I, with improvised modifications. Its broad beam and high engine mounting did little for its aesthetics, but its metal construction gave it an inherent strength.

## An Unusual Switch

Seldom does a basic aircraft design start as a hydroplane and then, as it were, come ashore. Many landplanes have been subsequently fitted with floats, but the reverse procedure has been a rare occurrence. The **Dornier Komet** of October 1920 was one of the exceptions, especially as it was a direct derivative of a flying boat, the Delphin. The small single-engined Komet four-seater had the same wing and bracing struts and almost the same fuselage, but its engine was mounted within the line of the fuselage.

It was not a pretty airplane but was efficient enough to pay its dues. It flew first with **Deutscher Aero Lloyd** in 1923 and then with **Deutsche Luft Hansa** in 1926. It was not an outstanding type but it came at the right time and carried the German commercial airline flag on some of the early international routes. A few were exported, to Spain, Colombia, and the U.S.S.R. D.L.H. used them until 1928 on short routes.

Its development, the Komet III, quickly modified to become the Merkur, was easier on the eye, more efficient, and more successful (see page 21).

1 Rolls-Royce Eagle (360 hp) • 6610 lb max. gross takeoff weight • 650 statute miles range

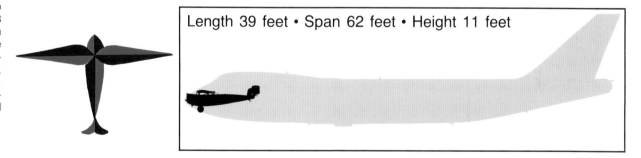

Length 39 feet • Span 62 feet • Height 11 feet

THE DORNIER LANDPLANES

| Type | First Flight Date | Dimensions | | | Pass. Seats | Engines | | | Max. Gross TOW (lb) | Cruise Speed (mph) | Normal Range (st. miles) | Approx. No. Built |
|---|---|---|---|---|---|---|---|---|---|---|---|---|
| | | Length | Span | Height | | No. | Type | Hp (each) | | | | |
| Komet I | 10 Feb. 21 | 31'2" | 55'9" | | 4 | 1 | B.M.W. IIIa | 185 | 4520 | 81 | 370 | 1[1] |
| Komet II | 9 Oct. 22 | 33'9" | 55'9" | | 4 | 1 | B.M.W. IV | 250 | 4850 | 84 | 300 | 19 |
| Komet III | 7 Dec. 24 | 39'4" | 62'4" | 11'4" | 6 | 1 | R-R Eagle | 360 | 6610 | 96 | 650 | 20[2] |
| Merkur | 10 Feb. 25 | 41'0" | 64'3" | 11'4" | 6 | 1 | B.M.W. VI | 450/600 | 7900 | 112 | 460 | 50 |

[1]The Komet I was only the prototype, with the pilot's seat aft of the wing, and predictably unsuitable. [2]Most of the Komet IIIs were converted into Merkurs. (The Komet I and II were designated Do P, and the Komet III and Merkur designated Do B.)

# Junkers Enterprise

## Postwar Airline Dilemma

With the economy shattered and a currency so unstable that it led to unimaginable monetary inflation, the establishment of a German national airline was impracticable in the early 1920s. Airlines were formed in haphazard fashion. No less than 56 companies applied to the German Air Ministry in 1920 for licenses to operate, and all except 14 were granted permission. Many of them probably had only the vaguest idea of how to organize or what was needed in the way of equipment or installations. There was a great deal of "keeping up with Joneses." If Bavaria had an airline then Württemberg had to have one too. And the prospect of gaining access to government subsidies was no doubt tempting, an opportunity too good to pass up.

### THE JUNKERS-F 13 FLEET OF DEUTSCHE LUFTHANSA AND ITS PREDECESSORS

| Const. No. | Regist. No. Original | Regist. No. 1934 | Name | Other Operators | Disposal |
|---|---|---|---|---|---|
| 531 | D-1 | — | Nachtigall | Junkers 1920; Bayer, L.L. (T) 1923 | 1938 H |
|  | D-183 |  | Hertha |  |  |
| 616 | D-192 | D-OTOR | Meise | Junkers 1921 (T) |  |
| 583 | D-193 | D-OHYR | Drossel | Ad Astra (CH 91) |  |
| 581 | D-203 | D-ODEM | Bussard | Junkers 1920 (T) | 1934 D |
| 591 | D-206 | — | Zeisig | Junkers 1920 Rumpler 1923 (T) | 1927* |
| 592 | D-207 | — | Falke |  | 1934* |
| 636 | D-225 | D-ONUZ | Piepmatz | Junkers (R-RECH) | 1935 D |
| 641 | D-230 | — | Wiedehopf | Junkers 1923 | 1933 D |
| 644 | D-232 | — | Truthahn | Rumpler 1923 (T); Condor 1928 | 1933* |
| 757 | D-247 | D-OPAH | Stein-Schmätzer | Deruluft (RR-41); Aeronaut (E 16). |  |
| 650 | D-260 | — | Eisvogel | Deruluft (RR-40); Aeronaut (E 15). |  |
| 660 | D-272 | — | Silbermöve |  | 1926* |
| 665 | D-290 | — | Haubenlerche |  | 1926* |
| 786 | D-298 | — | Schneeammer | (Severa charter, 1928) |  |
| 545 | D-332 | D-OKUF | Elster | Junkers, 1920; Danzig (Dz 36 and 42); TREU 1923; ÖLAG (A-68) | 1938 H 1940 L |
| 724 | D-333 | D-ONOL | Mandelkrähe |  | 1934 D |
| 682 | D-338 | D-OVAS | Nebelkrähe |  | 1934 D |
| 584 | D-347 | — | Schwalbe | Ex-D-162 (Dz 38); Bayer. L.L. 1923 (T) Condor 1929 |  |
| 717 | D-354 | — | Rackelhuhn | (To Severa) | 1928 |
| 718 | D-355 | D-OZEP | Seeschwalbe |  | 1936 R |

### THE JUNKERS-F 13 FLEET OF DEUTSCHE LUFTHANSA AND ITS PREDECESSORS

| Const. No. | Regist. No. Original | Regist. No. 1934 | Name | Other Operators | Disposal |
|---|---|---|---|---|---|
| 720 | D-357 | D-OGUZ | Goldhähnchen |  | 1935 D |
| 723 | D-366 | D-OHIL | Eismöwe | Deruluft 1929–35 | 1935* |
| 750 | D-367 | — | Turmschwalbe | Condor 1928, re-regis. in 1946 | (1947) |
| 725 | D-368 | — | Waldkauz | Condor 1929 | 1945* |
| 726 | D-369 | — | Blaukehichen | (From D.V.L. 1928) |  |
| 730 | D-372 | — | Königsadler | Deruluft 1929 |  |
| 734 | D-373 | D-OPOX | Stösser | Westflug GmbH 1927 | 1939 H 1940 L |
| 738 | D-376 | D-OBAZ | Kronenreiher | Sudwestdeutsche LV 1923 (T); Flugfelag Islands, 1931–32 | 1936* |
| 739 | D-409 | — | Fliegenschnäpper | Sudwestdeutsche LV 1923 (T) | 1925* |
| 740 | D-410 | — | Steppenhuhn | Sudwestdeutsche LV 1923 (T); Flugfelag Islands 1929 | 1931 sunk (Reykjavik) |
| 695 | D-419 | D-OLEF | Weih | DDL (T-DKOV) | 1934 D |
| 697 | D-420 | D-OHAH | Seeadler | (Govt. weather service, 1934–35) | 1935 R |
| 699 | D-422 | — | Eidergans | ÖLAG (A-32, 45, 67) | 1930* |
| 702 | D-424 | D-OXET | Emmerling | LURAG 1923; Europa Union 1925; to Deruluft 1929–36 | 1936 R |
| 703 | D-425 | D-OBON | Milan | LURAG 1923, Europa Union 1925 |  |
| 704 | D-426 | D-OJAL | Sprosser | ÖLAG (A-38) | 1934 D |
| 707 | D-429 | D-OHUN | Haselhuhn |  | 1934 D |
| 743 | D-433 | D-OKAX | Baumläufer | ÖLAG (A-29) | 1934 D |
| 746 | D-436 | — | Schneehuhn | Eurasia (EU IV) |  |
| 547 | D-454 | D-OMIZ | Adler | Ex D-158, Danzig (Dz 31, 37, Junkers Russland (R-RECB) | 1934 D |
| 765 | D-462 | — | Königsfischer | Sudwestdeutsche L.V. 1928; Deruluft (URSS-320, D 301) 1930 |  |
| 764 | D-463 | D-OMUH | Tauchente |  | 1938 H 1940 L |
| 763 | D-464 | D-ONIL | Laubsänger | Flugfelag Islands 1928–29 | 1939 H 1940 L |
| 761 | D-466 | D-OSAF | Prachtfasan |  | 1934 D |
| 694 | D-534 | — | Auerhahn | DDL (T-DBOT) | 1933* |

### THE JUNKERS-F 13 FLEET OF DEUTSCHE LUFTHANSA AND ITS PREDECESSORS

| Const. No. | Regist. No. Original | Regist. No. 1934 | Name | Other Operators | Disposal |
|---|---|---|---|---|---|
| 688 | D-550 | — | Brachvogel | ÖLAG (A-95) | * |
| 768 | D-556 | D-OVAX | Präriehuhn | (From Bad-Pfälzische Lufthansa, 1930–33) |  |
| 748 | D-557 | D-OGEX | Leiervogel | Schlesische LV (T) 1924 | 1934 D |
| 752 | D-558 | D-OKES | Mauersegler | Schlesische L.V. 1924 (T); Deruluft, 1929 |  |
| 756 | D-560 | — | Himmelsziege |  | 1927* |
| 681 | D-561 | D-OZYR | Fischreiher | Oberschlesische L.V. (T) | 1934 D |
| 685 | D-564 | D-OFEN | Goldammer |  | 1936 R |
| 687 | D-565 | D-OGIT | Kleiber | ÖLAG (A-53) |  |
| 705 | D-571 | — | Blaurake | (From Bad-Pfälzische Lufthansa 1929) |  |
| 719 | D-579 | — | Schneegans | (To D.L.H. 1928) | 1932 D |
| 706 | D-582 | D-OLAS | Dommel | Sachsische L.V. 1924 (T) | 1934 D |
| 742 | D-583 | — | Wildente | ÖLAG (A-39) | 1928 |
| 747 | D-600 | — | Ringeltaube | (From D.V.L. 1929); Eurasia (EU III 1930) |  |
| 696 | D-724 | — | Kolkrabe |  | 1932* |
| 790 | D-838 | D-ONIQ | Plattmönch | (From D.V.S. 1927) | 1927* |
| 791 | D-869 | D-OHYK | Lori | (From D.V.S. 1927) |  |
| 532 | D-1036 | — | Kasuar | Ex-Danzig (Dz34); D.A. Lloyd Annelise |  |
| 569 | D-1183 | D-OLOF | Albatros | Ex-Danzig (Dz 30); Junkers Russland |  |
| 690 | D-1391 | — | Steinadler | (To D.L.H. 1928) | 1928 (Sweden) |
| 2032 | D-1579 | D-OVUM | Karmingimpel | (From Bad-Pfälzische Lufthansa 1934) | 1934 D |
| 823 | — | D-OTAL | Blaumeise | From Ala Littoria, 1934 | 1935 R |
| 2008 | D-1182 | D-OMAS | Rotkehlchen | From Ala Littoria, 1934 | 1935 D |
| 2022 | D-1374 | D-ODEN | Kohlmeise | From Ala Littoria, 1934 | 1935 D |
| 2071 | — | D-ONOR | Hänfling | From Ala Littoria, 1934 | 1936 R |
| 2026 | — | D-OLAP | Sonnenvogel | ÖLAG (A-48, OE-LAH) | 1939 H |

**Abbrev.** T: Trans-Europa-Union (TREU), D: Deutsche Verkehrsschule (DVL), R: Reichsluftfahrtministerium, L: Luftwaffe, H: Hansa Flugdienst.
**Note** Aircraft that crashed or were damaged beyond repair shown by *

# Junkers-F 13

## 4 seats • 105 mph

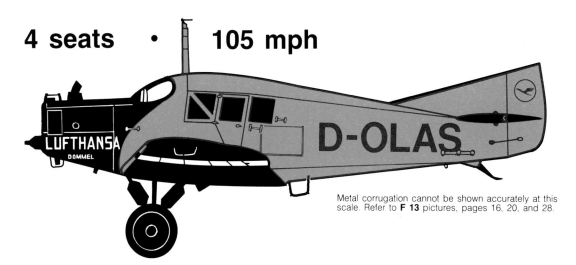

Metal corrugation cannot be shown accurately at this scale. Refer to **F 13** pictures, pages 16, 20, and 28.

1 Junkers-L 5 (280 hp) • 5500 lb max. gross takeoff weight • 400 statute miles range

## The Tail Wags the Dog

The best commercial aircraft by far to emerge in Germany during the immediate postwar years was the **Junkers-F 13** (see opposite page). It was to go down in history as one of the most significant transport aircraft of all time. Yet Junkers could find no German customer for its product because the Lloyd groups had their own manufacturing associates, such as Fokker and Dornier.

It therefore created a precedent. All over the world, during air transport's formative years, airlines were founded first and then they shopped around for aircraft to operate. **Junkers Flugzeugwerke** of Dessau turned this orthodox procedure upside down. It produced a superb aircraft first and then shopped around for airlines to operate it.

The result was that half the airlines of central and northern Europe were created by the Junkers-F 13, as shown on pages 16–17.

## The First Metal Airliner

Even before World War I, in 1909, Professor Hugo Junkers had prepared the first outlines of a metal-built airplane, a cantilever monoplane with a thick wing and a fuselage that derived much of its strength from sheet-metal skin rather than from wire bracing. This was considered to be almost revolutionary at the time and was never expected to succeed. Nevertheless, the first of the series, the J 1, flew on 12 December 1915, and during the war further monoplanes and even a biplane were produced. At first the fuselage and wing were covered with smooth metal, but later types used corrugated duralumin—rather in the style of the familiar iron sheets used for roofing—for strength. By the time the last military aircraft came off the line in 1918, the series numbering had reached J 11.

It is said that on Armistice Day, 11 November 1918, in one of the best-known incidents in the chronicle of airplane technology development, Professor Junkers instructed designer Otto Reuter and his team to switch from military to commercial aircraft construction. The result was a modified J 10, at first called the J 12, but this was never built, as it was superseded by the improved J 13 project, later produced as the F 13. Its wing was formed of strongly braced tubular spars—effectively a lightweight girder—and the entire structure was clad in corrugated duralumin, combining unidirectional strength with light weight. The tubular steel/wooden and fabric aircraft of the same period were fragile compared with the sturdy F 13.

## Cometh the Hour . . .

The pilot Monz flew the first prototype on 25 June 1919, and the F 13 went into service on 18 July. It was one of the most important transport airplanes ever built. Unlike the ponderous bomber conversions such as the Handley Pages and Farmans, the modified A.E.G.s, or the awkward cousins of the first Dornier flying boats, the F 13 *looked* like an airplane designed from the start to carry passengers. The enclosed cabin carried four in cushioned seats, with seatbelts, lighting, and picture windows.

Construction continued into the early 1930s—not without problems (see page 17)—and 322 were built altogether. **Deutsche Luft Hansa** had 55, and in the early and middle 1920s they became a familiar sight all over Europe as airlines brought them into service, working in partnership with Junkers (pages 16–17). They were exported all over the world, even to the United States, where, however, they were not a complete success, because of some accidents (see panel on page 17). They started historic services in Colombia (page 28), Persia (page 30), Bolivia (page 31), the U.S.S.R. (page 30), and Brazil (page 32).

Deutsche Lufthansa was still operating F 13s in 1937, and two, built in 1924, were still on the 1938 register, valued in the books at 1 mark each. The Brazilian airline VARIG retired the last F 13 in 1948, so that the absolute lifespan of this truly early bird was 29 years, far longer than that of many a famous airliner built decades later. Several F 13s are preserved, in museums in Munich, Stockholm, Paris, Porto Alegre, and—a particularly fine example—Budapest.

| Const. No. | Regist. No. | Name |
|---|---|---|
| 534 | D-219 | Stieglitz |
| 565 | D-201 | Uhu |
| 570 | D-251 | Eule |
| 572 | D-252 | Lerche |
| 590 | D-194 | Kuckkuck |
| 614 | R-RECE | (USSR, Persien) |
| 630 | R-RECF | (USSR) |
| 643 | D-231 | Wachtel (USSR, Persien) |

| Const. No. | Regist. No. | Name |
|---|---|---|
| 651 | R-RECI | (USSR) |
| 663 | D-288 | Würger |
| 683 | D-339 | Distelfink |
| 686 | D-549 | Sittich |
| 698 | D-421 | Hahn |
| 708 | D-319 | Turteltaube |
| 709 | D-320 | Kormoran |
| 710 | D-321 | Edelfalke |
| 711 | D-322 | Alk |

| Const. No. | Regist. No. | Name |
|---|---|---|
| 712 | D-340 | Krickente |
| 713 | D-341 | Spottvogel |
| 714 | D-342 | Kreuzschnabel |
| 715 | D-343 | Schleiereule |
| 716 | D-337 | Lachmöwe |
| 721 | D-358 | Schwarzspecht |
| 722 | D-359 | Rauchschwalbe |
| 727 | D-336 | Sturmöwe |
| 729 | D-371 | Singdrossel |

| Const. No. | Regist. No. | Name |
|---|---|---|
| 741 | D-431 | Steissvogel |
| 745 | D-435 | Rohrsänger |
| 755 | D-559 | Ziegenmelker |
| 762 | D-465 | Grünspecht |
| 774 | D-812 | Fischadler |
| 775 | D-82 | Wasseramsel |
| 776 | D-63 | Gimpelhäher |
| 2001 | D-1126 | (Persien) |

Note   Many Junkers-F 13s of **Junkers Luftverkehr** did not pass to Deutsche Luft Hansa. Some served in the U.S.S.R. or Persia, as indicated. Some F 13s (c/n 799/D-833 *Spiegelhahn*; 2015/D-1378/D-OLOF; 2016/D-1382/D-ONUS) were owned by Seeflugzeug-Versuchsabteilung GmbH (Severa), a military support agency, which in 1929 changed its name to Lufthansa Abt Küstenflug, leading to some confusion, and later to Flugdienst GmbH.

# The Europa-Union

## Spreading the Junkers Net

With the Lloyd group of companies gaining stature and influence, Junkers realized that strength came not from diversity but from cooperation and ostensible unity.

Accordingly it formed two important international groups, the **Trans-Europa-Union**, on 14 May 1923, and the **Ost-Europa-Union**, on 22 October of the same year. After a year, the name of the latter was changed to the **Nord-Europa-Union**.

Serving a greater population and a commercially more advanced region, Trans-Europa was the stronger group, and had the advantage that all the component companies shared a common language. Junkers also had a shareholding in the pilots' training school, the **Deutsche Verkehrsflieger-Schule (D.V.S.)**, founded at Berlin's Staaken airfield in 1925.

On 7 May 1925, two years after the birth of the two Unions, a move was made to unite both into one all-embracing organization, the **Europa-Union**, together with other related Junkers affiliates. But this idea was never put into practice, and an even greater unification was only a few months ahead.

## The One That Got Away

One of the foreign affiliates of the Junkers group was **Aerolloyd Warschau**, formed by Dr. Wygard on 1 September 1922 with subsidy support from the Polish government. It began service four days later on routes from Warsaw to Danzig (Gdansk) and Lemberg (Lvov) with the ever-present **Junkers-F 13**s.

Sturdily independent at last after more than a century of foreign rule, Aerolloyd Warschau broke free of German control and the name was changed to **Aerolot** on 9 May 1925. Nevertheless, the ubiquitous Junkers-F 13 remained as the service aircraft until the arrival of trimotored Fokkers at the end of 1929.

The "cleaning brigade" working on a **Junkers-F 13** in the 1920s.

Hugo Junkers.

### TRANS-EUROPA-UNION (TREU)—Founded 14 May 1923—Based at Munich

| Company and Location | Date Founded | Date of First Service | Remarks |
|---|---|---|---|
| Ad Astra Aero Zurich | 20 Sept. 1919 | 1 June 1922 | Created as a merger of several Swiss companies, all founded in 1919. |
| Rumpler Luftverkehr Munich | 30 Sept. 1922 | 30 Sept. 1922 | Earlier services, March 1919, Augsburg-Berlin, operated by an affiliate of the Rumpler Flugzeugwerke. |
| Aero-Express R.T. Budapest | 1 Jan. 1923 | 15 July 1923 | Flew pleasure flights to Lake Balaton in June 1923; service ended in 1924 when Hungarian govt. granted exclusive rights to MALERT. |
| Österreichische Luftverkehrs, A.G. (ÖLAG) Vienna | May 1923 | 14 May 1923 | Founded by Austrian banking and railroad interests, in association with Junkers. |
| Bayerischer Luft Lloyd Munich | 16 June 1919 | 11 April 1921 | Originally associated with Rumpler in 1919; fleet demolished, under provisions of Versailles Treaty, 1920. |
| Junkers Luftverkehr A.G. Berlin | 13 Aug. 1924 | 13 Aug. 1924 | Airline operations originally by affiliate of Junkers formed 1 Jan. 1922 as Junkers-Werke Abteilung Luftverkehr. |
| Südwestdeutsche Luftverkehrs A.G. Frankfurt | May 1924 | — | These were primarily agencies for travel and ground services, operating as **Junkers Luftverkehr**. |
| Sächsische Luftverkehrs A.G. Dresden | 12 March 1924 | 11 Aug. 1924 | |
| Schlesische Luftverkehrs A.G. Breslau | Jan. 1925 / Feb. 1925 | 13 March 1925 / 13 March 1925 | |
| Oberschlesische Luftverkehrs A.G. Gleiwitz | 24 Feb. 1925 | 20 April 1925 | |
| Luftverkehrsgesellschaft Ruhrgebiet A.G. (LURAG) Essen | May 1925 | — | |
| Bayerische Luftverkehrs A.G. Munich | | | |

### OST-EUROPA-UNION—Founded 22 October 1923—Based at Riga name changed in 1924 to NORD–EUROPA-UNION—Based at Reval

| Company and Location | Date Founded | Date of First Service | Remarks |
|---|---|---|---|
| Latvijas Gaisa Satikmes A/S Riga | 1921 | July 1923 | Established in association with Junkers and absorbed in 1925. |
| A-S Aeronaut Reval | (end) 1921 | (Summer) 1922 | Founded by Lloyd-Luftverkehr Sablatnig, with participation from Denmark and Sweden. |
| Aero O/Y Helsinki | 9 Oct. 1923 | 20 March 1924 | Founded by Bruno Lucander, Junkers representative in Finland. |
| Junkers Luftverkehr A.G. Berlin | 13 Aug. 1924 | 13 Aug. 1924 | (See Trans-Europa-Union) |
| Danziger Luftpost GmbH Danzig | 26 Feb. 1921 | 1922 | Initially operated Königsberg-Memel-Riga-Reval route of Lloyd Ostflug. |
| Lloyd Ostflug Danzig | 7 Nov. 1920 | 27 Dec. 1920 | Founded jointly by Norddeutscher Lloyd, Albatros, Junkers, and Ostdeutsche Landwerkstätten; Junkers disassociated in 1923 and Berlin-Danzig-Konigsberg route operated alternately by Junkers and Lloyd groups. |

# Triumph Over Adversity

## Jack of All Trades

By the mid-1920s, even before the formation of Deutsche Luft Hansa, the Junkers group was deploying other types such as the small Junkers-A 20 mail carrier in 1923. A year later came the Junkers-G 24, a three-engined nine-seat aircraft that was the harbinger of bigger and better airliners in the years to come. But during these rather turbulent years the little **Junkers-F 13** resisted the inroads of these challengers, having earned itself great respect, even affection, among its operators, because of its strength, resilience, reliability, and adaptability.

Curiously it was able to demonstrate its special qualities at the geographical extremities of the Nord-Europa-Union and Trans-Europa-Union groups. To cross the Gulf of Finland, the Estonian **Aeronaut** and the Finnish **Aero O/Y** both converted the F 13 to use floats in the summer and skis in the winter. In that severe northern climate, where to start the engine was a formidable test of stamina, it could theoretically have taxied across the gulf. Down south, the Hungarian Aero-Express and initially the Austrian **ÖLAG** both had F 13 floatplanes to follow the River Danube between Vienna and the riverfront moorings of the Hotel Gellert in Budapest.

As the accompanying panel shows, the adolescence of the Junkers-F 13 did not go smoothly. Given an orderly development period, free of restrictions, the innovative design would have ensured its complete and universal dominance. Its technical superiority was backed by efficient organization and a corporate strength derived from a fine *esprit de corps* at all levels of the staff. Its numerical designation gave the lie to superstition. It was one of the greatest airplanes in aeronautical history, and to call it an airliner, even before the term came into use, would not be misrepresenting its true destiny.

### THE D.L.H. JUNKERS-A 20 FLEET

| Const. No. | Regist. No. Original | Regist. No. 1934 | Name | Remarks |
|---|---|---|---|---|
| 353 | D-392 | D-IBUX | Erde | Written off 1937 |
| 457 | D-394 | — | Mars | To D.V.S. July 1928 |
| 459 | D-404 | — | Saturn | Destroyed 1934 |
| 461 | D-440 | — | Orion | Bulgarian Traffic Management 1932 |
| 464 | D.443 | — | Merkur | Destroyed 1928 |
| 862 | D-574 | D-IBUP | Aldebaran | Sold (or to R.L.M.) 1936 |
| 822 | D-592 | D-ISYN | Kassiopeia | To R.V.M. 1929 |
| 863 | D-599 | D-IBIT | Betelgeüze | Sold (or to R.L.M.) 1936 |
| 865 | D-704 | — | Castor | To R.V.M. 1929 |
| 866 | D-712 | — | Pollux | Sold 1927 |

### JUNKERS-F 13 AIRCRAFT IN THE TRANS-EUROPA-UNION FLEET

| Airline | Base | Const. No. | Regist. | Name |
|---|---|---|---|---|
| Ad Astra Aero A G | Zurich, Switzerland | 583 | CH 91 | Drossel |
| | | 587 | CH 92 | Specht |
| | | 593 | CH 93 | Dohle |
| | | 617 | CH 94 | Star |
| Bayerische Luft Lloyd GmbH | Munich, Germany | 531 | "D1" | Nachtigall |
| | | 584 | 347 | Schwalbe |
| Österreichische Luftverkehrs A G | Vienna, Austria | 575 | A3 | Taube |
| | | 534 | A2 | Stieglitz |
| Rumpler Luftverkehr A G | Munich, Germany | 644 | D-232 | Truthahn |
| | | 591 | D-206 | Zeisig |
| Sächsische Luftverkehrs A G | Dresden, Germany | 687 | D-565 | Kleiber |
| | | 706 | D-582 | Dommel |
| Südwestdeutsche Luftverkehrs A G | Frankfurt, Germany | 739 | D-409 | Fliegenschnäpper |
| | | 738 | D-376 | Kronenreiher |
| | | 740 | D-410 | Steppenhuhn |
| Aero Express R.T. | Budapest, Hungary | 635 | H-MACB | Ente |
| | | 640 | H-MACF | Strauss |
| Junkers-Luftverkehr A G | Dessau, Germany | 545 | D-332 | Elster |
| | | 581 | D-203 | Bussard |
| | | 616 | D-192 | Meise |
| | | 641 | D-230 | Wiedehopf |

**Note** The Austrian (briefly) and the Hungarian aircraft were floatplanes, for use on the River Danube. Ad Astra also had some Junkers-G 24s.

### JUNKERS-F 13 AIRCRAFT IN THE NORD-EUROPA-UNION FLEET

| Airline | Base | Const. No. | Regist. German | Regist. National | Name |
|---|---|---|---|---|---|
| Aero O/Y | Helsinki, Finland | 700 | D-335 | K-SALA | Regenpfeifer |
| | | 760 | D-506 | K-SALB | Bergfink |
| A-S Aeronaut | Tallinn, Estonia | 646 | D-255 | E 13 | Schwan |
| | | 650 | D-260 | E 15 | Biene |
| | | 757 | D-247 | E 16 | Steinschmätzer |
| Latvijas Gaisa Satikmes A/S | Riga, Latvia | 579 | D-202 | B-LATA / B-LATB | Condor |

**Note** Aero O/Y and Aeronaut aircraft were fitted with floats in the summer and skis in the winter.
**Special Note** When Deutsche Luft Hansa was formed on 6 January 1926, all Junkers airline activities were under the name of Europa Union, even though the traffic license had been revoked by the German Aviation Board. Furthermore, most of the foreign airlines had declined to join Europa Union, as the main purpose of its formation was perceived to be a device to raise funds for the financially ailing Junkers Flugzeugwerke.

### POST–WORLD WAR I RESTRICTIONS ON AIRCRAFT CONSTRUCTION

| Date | | Situation or Development |
|---|---|---|
| 1919 | March (1919)– April (1920) | About 600 aircraft registered. Most of these were former military types, converted to civilian use. Others were mainly Junkers-F 13s. |
| 1920 | 10 January | Effective date of the Treaty of Versailles. Germany prohibited from building any aircraft for six months, while Allied Commission set up to consider problem. |
| | April–May | Every German aircraft confiscated by Allies. |
| | 22 May | Some aircraft released, but had to be repurchased by the previous owners and used only for commercial purposes. A new register of commercial aircraft was initiated. |
| 1921 | 5 May–July | Under the "London Ultimatum" all aircraft were again confiscated, under a new German law, enforced by the Allies. The old register was cancelled. Eleven F 13s, awaiting shipment at Hamburg, ostensibly for the U.S., were impounded. 25 F 13s were seized by the Allies as reparation. |
| | 10 August | The cost of all aircraft had to be validated only after approval by the Allied Commission. |
| 1922 | 14 April (effective 5 May) | The ban on aircraft construction was lifted, but there were severe restrictions on aircraft size, engine power, and other features to ensure that aircraft could not carry bombs. |
| | 16 April | (The Treaty of Rapallo normalized relations between Germany and the Soviet Union—see page 10.) Dornier and Junkers set up production in Moscow, Sweden, Switzerland, and Italy. |
| 1926 | 6 January | (Deutsche Luft Hansa A.G. formed.) |
| | 21 May | A conference in Paris lifted the ban on aircraft manufacture. |
| | 8 July | A German law ratified the Paris agreement. |

The **Junkers-A 20**, even smaller than the F 13, and used primarily for training and carrying mail.

# Formation of Deutsche Luft Hansa

## Too Many Cooks . . .

By 1925, the two big airline groups, **Deutscher Aero Lloyd** and the **Junkers Luftverkehr**, were competing intensely. The former operated routes mainly to the countries of northwest Europe. The latter, through its Trans-Europa-Union and Nord-Europa-Union affiliates, commanded the airways of central and northern Europe. Aero Lloyd and Junkers overlapped on certain routes, competing on some, cooperating on others, as in the case of the link with East Prussia. The Lloyd group used aircraft from every manufacturer except Junkers (not counting the ones in Danzig). The Junkers group flew only aircraft of its own manufacture.

The two shared, however, a common denominator. They both depended upon some form of subsidy for financial survival, drawing support from parent shipping lines or manufacturers, or from benevolent states or municipalities. There seemed to be no immediate prospect for improvement, and at the end of 1925 a decision was made to put an end to the mildly chaotic situation.

## The Merger

The guiding hand behind the merger of D.A.L. and Junkers was Ernst Brandenburg, head of the aviation department of the German Ministry of Transport. He refused to bail out Junkers by denying traffic rights to Europa-Union but struck a bargain by taking over the shareholding of Junkers Luftverkehr, thereby enabling the Junkers manufacturing activity to continue.

Dr. Kurt Weigelt, representing the Deutsche Bank and Deutsche Petroleum—key sources of finance and fuel—cooperated with Brandenburg. Weigelt had helped to form Lloyd Luftverkehr Sablatnig in 1919, Deutscher Luft Lloyd in 1920, Deruluft in 1921, and Deutscher Aero Lloyd in 1923. He now produced a brochure, *Fusion in the Field of Air Traffic*, recommending the amalgamation of the Aero Lloyd and the Junkers groups. The latter, short of bargaining power, was obliged to accede to the plan. The International Air Traffic Association (IATA), strongly influenced by Martin Wronsky, promoting Aero Lloyd's interests, frowned on the covert control of the air transport affairs of sovereign nations, and thus Junkers was forced out.

Thus, at a meeting at the Kaiserhof Hotel in Berlin, on 6 January 1926, **Deutsche Luft Hansa (D.L.H.)** was born. It took over all the airlines and affiliates of the Aero Lloyd and Junkers groups. The new company's name was suggested by the Junkers chief of public relations, Fischer von Poturzyn, who invoked a historic association with the aspirations of the former Hanseatic League, the great German trading guild that included the ports of Hamburg, Bremen, and Lübeck.

Of the stock of D.L.H., 26% (the "Junkers" share) was held by the German government, 19% by other German provinces and cities, 27.5% by regional companies, and 27.5% by private organizations. The initial capital of 50,000 marks was raised to 25,000,000 marks on 15 June 1926, subscribed mainly by the individual shareholders listed on this page. Junkers kept its shares in all foreign airlines, except ÖLAG (Austria), as the German government had no wish to subsidize, directly or indirectly, foreign countries.

The first chairman was Emil Georg von Stauss, of the Deutsche Bank. From Aero Lloyd came Martin Wronsky and Otto Julius Merkel, as directors, and Walter Luz. From Junkers came Erhard Milch as a director and Carl August Freiherr von Gablenz. Dr. Konrad Adenauer, Mayor of Cologne, was a board member. They were a formidable talent, as well they might be—for they were conducting the fortunes of an airline which, in 1925, had through its ancestors provided two-fifths of the total traffic of the world's air transport industry.

**Dr. Kurt Weigelt** devised the framework of the first Luft Hansa, became vice-chairman in 1936, and was chairman of the postwar Lufthansa.

### DEUTSCHE LUFT HANSA AFFILIATES, 1926

| Deutscher Aero Lloyd | | | | Junkers Luftverkehr | | | |
|---|---|---|---|---|---|---|---|
| Company | Location | D.A.L. % | Remarks | Company | Location | Junkers % | Remarks |
| Deruluft | Berlin | 50.0 | 50% by Soviet Union | Badischer L.V.G. | Karlsruhe | 11.0 | Jointly with Baden |
| Danziger Aero Lloyd | Danzig | 100.0 | Danzig affiliate | Bayrischer Luftlloyd | Munich | 50.0 | Jointly with Bavaria |
| Mitteldeutscher Aero Lloyd | Leipzig | 42.9 | Jointly with Saxon interests | Bayrischer L.V.G. | Munich | 13.3 | Jointly with Bavaria |
| L.V. Württemberg | Stuttgart | 5.7 | Jointly with Württemberg | Luftverkehrsgesellschaft Ruhrgebiet (LURAG) | Essen | 11.0 | Jointly with the Ruhrgebiet |
| Adria Aero Lloyd | Tirana | 55.0 | Albanian affiliate | Norddeutscher L.V.G. | Bremen | 25.0 | Link with Aero Lloyd Group |
| Aero Lloyd | Berlin | 100.0 | Insurance | | | | |
| Condor Syndikat | Berlin | 36.6 | Aircraft trading | Oberschlesischer L.V.G. | Gleiwitz | 3.6 | Jointly with Upper Silesia |
| Austro Lloyd Luftbild | Vienna | 100.0 | Austrian affiliate | | | | |
| Luftfahrtverlag | Berlin | 100.0 | Publisher | Rumpler Luftverkehr | Berlin | 50.0 | Aircraft constructor |
| Süddeutscher Aero Lloyd | Munich | 13.7 | Jointly with Bavarian interests | Sächsischer L.V.G. | Dresden | 26.0 | Jointly with Saxony |
| | | | | Schlesischer L.V.G. | Breslau | 12.5 | Jointly with Silesia |
| Badisch-Pfälzische L.V.G. | Mannheim | 20.0 | Jointly with Baden-Pfalz (Palatinate) | Sudwestdeutscher L.V.G. | Frankfurt | 16.7 | Jointly with Hesse |
| Hessische Flugbetriebs GmbH | Darmstadt | 15.4 | Airport handling | Westflug | Bielefeld | 41.4 | |
| Udet Flugzeugbau | Munich | 7.7 | Aircraft constructor | "Etag" Erdöl und Teerprodukte | Berlin | 75.0 | Airport materials |
| "Welu" (L.V.G. Westfalen) | Dortmund | 20.0 | Jointly with Westfalen interests | SCADTA | Barranquilla | 5.7 | Colombian affiliate |
| Basler Luftverkehr | Basel | 75.0 | Swiss affiliate | | | | |
| Aero Hansa | Berlin | 100.0 | Original investment on 6 Jan. 1926 | | | | |
| Deutsche Verkehrs-fliegerschule (D.V.S.) | Berlin (Staaken) | 14.3 | Flying school | Deutsche Verkehrsflieger-schule (D.V.S.) | Berlin (Staaken) | 14.3 | Flying school |
| Lloyd Junkers L.V.G.[1] | Berlin | 50.0 | Formerly Lloyd Ostflug | Lloyd Junkers L.V.G.[1] | Berlin | 50.0 | Formerly Lloyd Ostflug |

[1]This company was referred to as "the engagement ring."

# Ancestry of Deutsche Luft Hansa

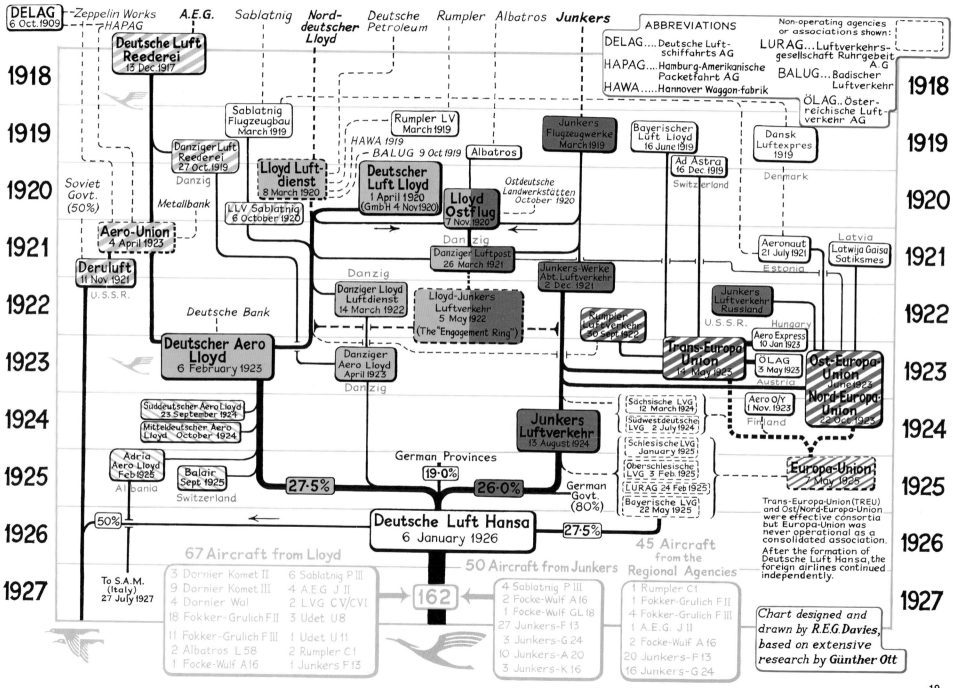

# An Airline of Many Parts

## First Priorities

When **Deutsche Luft Hansa** began service in earnest on 6 April 1926, it inherited 162 individual aircraft of 19 different types. The first priority was to sift out the old types that were either too small, toilworn, or inadequate. Twenty-seven machines in this category, of ten types (listed on this page), were accordingly pensioned off by 1930.

Next came the ten **Sablatnig III**s, sound enough to be honorably retired individually, rather than as a type. The last one, *Hornisse,* was on the fleet inventory until 1932.

The three **Dornier Komet II**s were gone by 1931, but the ten **Komet III**s, far better—and better-looking—machines, were all converted to **Merkur**s, and the type was popular enough to be augmented to a total fleet of 26 by 1928 (page 21, opposite). Four rugged and reliable **Dornier Wal** flying boats were retained and more added to perform pioneering duties on the transoceanic routes, conducting innovative experiments and survey flights (pages 34–39).

## Backbone of the Fleet

Of the 162 aircraft, 80 were Junkers types, of which 48 were the remarkable six-seat **Junkers-F 13**s (page 19). Of the remainder, from the Aero Lloyd group, 34 were **Fokker-Grulich F.II**s and **F.III**s (page 11).

To round off the total, there were 19 **Junkers-G 24**s, the nine-seat three-engined craft developed from the same design and structural principles as the other Junkers metal-built types. First produced in 1924, it was the world's first all-metal trimotored airliner (page 25).

During this initiation period, D.L.H. had one interesting aircraft, the **Arado V-1** (const. no. 47), registered as D-1594. Between 25 and 29 October 1929, it made survey flights to Istanbul and to Seville. Then, appropriately christened *Teneriffa,* it made another survey flight to Tenerife, Canary Islands, on 16 November. Unfortunately, it crashed on its return flight, on 19 December, to end a brief but eventful career.

### DEUTSCHE LUFT HANSA
### AIRCRAFT TYPES RETIRED DURING FIRST FOUR YEARS

| Aircraft | Const. No. | Regist. No. | Name | Year built | Year Ret. |
|---|---|---|---|---|---|
| L.V.G. CV (ex-D.L.R., D.A.L.) | 699 | D.73 | *Maus* | 1919 | 1928 |
| Rumpler C I (ex-Bayerische Rumpler L.V.) | | D-100 | | 1919 | 1927 |
| | | D-103 | | 1919 | 1928 |
| | | D-108 | | 1919 | 1928 |
| Albatros L 58 (ex-D.A.L.) | 10002 | D-246 | *Wolkensegler* | 1923 | 1927 |
| | 10006 | D-576 | | 1923 | 1928 |
| Udet U 8 (ex-D.A.L.) | 227 | D-417 | *Linde* | 1924 | 1926 |
| | 236 | D-483 | *Blindschleiche* | 1924 | 1928 |
| | 237 | D-502 | | 1924 | 1928 |
| Udet U 11 | 828 | D-243 | *Kondor* | 1925 | 1929 |
| Focke-Wulf G.L.18 | 28 | D-967 | *Helgoland* | 1926 | 1929 |
| A.E.G. J II K (ex-D.L.R., D.A.L.) | 5053 | D-14 | | 1919 | 1928 |
| | 6748 | D-38 | | 1919 | 1928 |
| | 417 | D-68 | *Kreuzotter* | 1918 | 1930 |
| | 439 | D-74 | *Viper* | 1919 | 1928 |
| | 6741 | D-24 | | 1919 | 1926 |
| Focke-Wulf A-16 (ex-Bremer Luftverkehr) | 3 | D-467 | *Westerland* | 1924 | 1929 |
| | 5 | D-548 | *Baden* | 1925 | 1930 |
| | 8 | D-659 | *Borkum* | 1925 | 1930 |
| | 7 | D-814 | *Wangerooge* | 1925 | 1928 |
| | 4 | D-647 | *Hansa* | 1925 | 1929 |
| Junkers-K 16 (ex-Junkers Luftverkehr) | 474 | D-500 | *Karlshorst* | 1925 | 1929 |
| | 475 | D-654 | *Kreuznach* | 1925 | 1930 |
| | 470 | D-983 | *Kissingen* | 1925 | 1930 |
| Dornier Komet II (ex-D.L.R., D.A.L.) | 24 | D-223 | *Tiger* | 1920 | 1929 |
| | 30 | D-248 | *Jaguar* | 1922 | 1930 |
| | 45 | D-943 | *Wolf* | 1920 | 1929 |

**Abbrev.** R.V.M.: Reichsverkehrsministerium (Traffic Ministry)
**Note** Many aircraft were withdrawn from service several years before official retirement, most of them scrapped.

This **Fokker-Grulich F II** is believed to have inaugurated D.L.H.'s first service on 6 January 1926.

Passengers boarding a **Junkers-F 13** in the early years of Luft Hansa.

**Erhard Milch**, leading member of the Luft Hansa executive board, welcomes the press from a **Udet Kondor** at the formation of the airline in 1926.

This **Arado V 1**, pictured at La Laguna, Tenerife, made the first cautious step toward South America in 1929.

# Dornier Merkur
## 6 seats • 112 mph

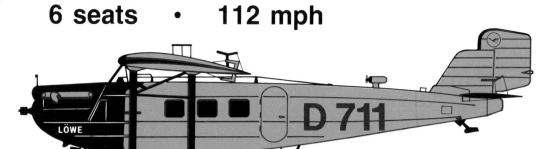

### THE D.L.H. DORNIER MERKURS

| Const. No. | Regist. No. Original | Regist. No. 1934 | Name | Year Built | D.L.H. Deliv. | Disposal and/or Year of Last Service |
|---|---|---|---|---|---|---|
| 63 | D-528 | D-UHUQ | Luchs | 1925 | 1926 | 1934 |
| 64 | D-529 | — | Schakal | 1925 | 1926 | Scrapped 1933 |
| 65 | D-546 | — | Hyäne | 1925 | 1926 | Aug. 1933 |
| 66 | D-552 | — | Gepard | 1925 | 1926 | Scrapped 1927 |
| 71 | D-562 | — | Marder | 1925 | 1926 | To D.V.S. 1934 |
| 74 | D-580 | — | Panther | 1925 | 1926 | To D.V.S. 1934 |
| 75 | D-585 | — | Puma | 1925 | 1926 | Written off 1927 |
| 76 | D-597 | — | Wildkatze | 1925 | 1926 | Scrapped 1933 |
| 78 | D-711 | D-UZYZ | Löwe | 1926 | 1926 | To R.L.M. 1935 |
| 85 | D-1101 | — | Präriewolf | 1927 | 1927 | Written off 1928 |
| 87 | D-1102 | D-UDYF | Edelmarder | 1927 | 1927 | Retired 1934 |
| 88 | D-1103 | D-USYM | Silberfuchs | 1927 | 1927 | Retired 1934 |
| 89 | D-427 | — | Zobel | 1927 | 1928 | Retired 1933 |
| 92 | D-936 | — | Gaúcho | 1927 | 1930 | Ex-VARIG Condor. Retired 1933 |
| 94 | D-1078 | — | Iltis | 1927 | 1927 | Scrapped 1935 |
| 97 | D-1082 | D-UKON | Leopard | 1927 | 1927 | Retired 1934 |
| 98 | D-972 | D-UQET | Königstiger | 1926 | 1926 | To R.L.M. 1935 |
| 121 | D-1076 | — | Silberlöwe | 1927 | 1927 | To Deruluft 1929 |
| 122 | D-1077 | — | Wiesel• | 1927 | 1927 | To Deruluft 1932 |
| 123 | D-1686 | — | Mungo | 1927 | 1929 | |
| 126 | D-1465 | — | Hermelin• | 1927 | 1928 | To Deruluft 1932 |
| 127 | D-1079 | — | Blaufuchs• | 1927 | 1928 | To Deruluft 1929; written off 1932 |
| 128 | D-1080 | — | Weissfuchs• | 1927 | 1928 | To Deruluft 1929 |
| 129 | D-1081 | — | Kreuzfuchs• | 1927 | 1928 | To Deruluft 1929 |
| 130 | D-1451 | — | Nerz• | 1927 | 1928 | To Deruluft 1932 |
| 157 | D-1083 | D-UHAS | Polarfuchs | 1927 | 1927 | |
| 158 | D-1084 | D-UVIZ | Eisbär | 1927 | 1927 | |
| 159 | D-1085 | — | Seelöwe | 1927 | 1927 | July 1931 |
| 160 | D-1086 | — | Bär | 1927 | 1927 | Oct. 1929 |
| 161 | D-1087 | — | Steinmarder | 1927 | 1927 | July 1933 |
| 176 | D-1445 | — | Nerz• | 1928 | 1929 | June 1934 |
| 177 | D-1455 | — | Weissfuchs• | 1928 | 1929 | June 1931 |
| 178 | D-1458 | D-UNEQ | Hermelin• | 1928 | 1929 | To R.L.M. 1935 |
| 174 | D-1595 | — | Wiesel• | 1928 | 1929 | March 1932 |
| 173 | D-1605 | D-ULAV | Kreuzfuchs• | 1928 | 1929 | To R.L.M. 1935 |
| 175 | D-1629 | D-UPEN | Blaufuchs• | 1928 | 1929 | To R.L.M. 1935 |

**Abbrev.** D.V.S.: Deutsche Verkehrsfliegerschule R.L.M.: Reichsluftfahrtministerium
**Notes** 1. The first nine aircraft listed and D-972 *Königstiger* were conversions from **Komet IIIs**. 2. The aircraft indicated with • were the subject of an exchange with **Deruluft**. The last six were designated **Do B Bal** and had more powerful B.M.W. engines.

## 1 BMW VI (450 mph) • 7900 lb max. gross takeoff weight • 460 statute miles range

## The Komet III

On 7 December 1924, a new Komet took to the air. Claude Dornier had cleaned up his design (page 13), installed more powerful engines, and increased the accommodation by 50% to seat six passengers. It was used by **Deutscher Aero Lloyd** and made the first flight by an airliner across the Alps (page 12). The Danish D.D.L. chartered one from Aero Lloyd, and a fleet of seven constituted the main equipment of the Ukrainian airline Ukrvozdukhput, already operating six Dornier Komet IIs.

The Japanese Kawasaki company produced the **Komet III** under license in 1926 and these were used by one of Japan's first airlines, Tozai Teiki Kokukai (T.T.K.), and for carrying newspapers for the leading Japanese daily *Asahi Shimbun*.

*Lineup of D.A.L.'s fleet in 1925: from the left, a **Dornier Komet III, Komet II,** and **Fokker F. III.***

## The Merkur

Dornier seems to have put the finishing touches to the Komet III when the Allies allowed it to use the more powerful B.M.W. VI engine. The resultant minor modifications gave the variant its own name, **Merkur**. It was widely accepted. **Deutsche Luft Hansa** alone had a total of 36, while they composed the flagship fleet of **Deruluft**, which operated perhaps a dozen.

The type was exported to German-affiliated airlines in South America, Syndicato Condor, VARIG, and SCADTA; and the Chilean Air Force had a military variant. A total of about 70 Dornier Merkurs were built, including about 20 Komet IIIs, most of which were converted to Merkurs. The only non-German customer in Europe was Swissair, but one of its two aircraft achieved a certain fame when the Swiss pilot Walter Mittelholzer flew it to Cape Town, South Africa, during the winter of 1926–27. For this special flight, and returning to its ancestral element, the Merkur *Switzerland* was fitted with floats, as was the one supplied to Brazil for Condor and VARIG.

# D.L.H. Gets Under Way

## Into the Night

Simultaneously with its efforts to tidy up its multi-origin fleet, **Deutsche Luft Hansa** began to improve the operational and technical elements of its business. During the early years of air transport, aviators had understandably feared to fly at night. Their instruments were few and unreliable. Even to fly in the clouds or through fog was hazardous in the extreme.

In 1924, **Aero Lloyd** had flown Dornier Delphins at night on the Warnemünde-Karlshamn-Stockholm trans-Baltic route, and—not to be outdone—**Junkers Luftverkehr** had flown across the Baltic with Junkers-A 20 floatplanes. The pilots found their way by what can best be described as lighthouse-spotting. But they were still vulnerable in poor visibility conditions. But even though the lighthouse-keepers helped by reporting the passage of aircraft by telephoning to onward points. These flights were experimental.

On 1 May 1926, following the principles developed by the United States Postal Service as the Lighted Airway, a **Junkers-G 24** opened a regular night service from Berlin to Königsberg, under the direction of Hermann Köhl. Specially installed beacons guided the pilots with a trail of lights. This was an important development, as the aircraft's working time could now be increased. The Berlin-Moscow journey time was reduced by the elimination of a long overnight stop and the night train journey from Berlin to Königsberg.

## Instruments and Radio

At the same time, great improvements were made to the instruments in the aircraft cockpit, so that the pilot did not have to rely almost entirely on his own eyes to find the way. Voluntary instrument-flying was introduced in the **Junkers-G-24** in 1927 by Willi Polte, under von Gablenz's direction, and in 1929, instrument rating became compulsory.

In 1926, radio was fitted to the larger aircraft. Although as yet relatively primitive, it was nevertheless adequate for communication to the ground controllers, who could, during low ceiling visibility, guide the pilots down to the airport by listening for the engine noise on approach and relaying directions.

The **Albatros L 73**, used on Deutsche Luft Hansa's international routes during the early years.

### THE D.L.H. ROHRBACHS

| Const. No. | Registration No. Original | Registration No. 1934 | Name | Year Delivered | Remarks |
|---|---|---|---|---|---|
| **Ro VIII Roland I** | | | | | |
| 18 | D-991 | — | Zugspitze | 1926 | Prototype. Sold to D.V.L. 1928 |
| 19 | D-999 | D-AHIM | Watzmann | 1927 | Transferred to D.V.S., Sept. 1934 |
| 27 | D-1124 | — | Schnee-koppe | 1927 | Scrapped March 1933 |
| 35 | D-1280 | D-AGUN | Feldberg | 1927 | To Iberia 1934 as M-CBBB |
| 36 | D-1292 | — | Brocken | 1927 | To Iberia 1927 as M-CAAC |
| 37 | D-1297 | D-AKIL | Wasser-kuppe | 1927 | Transferred to D.V.S. Oct. 1934 |
| **Ro VIII Roland Ia** | | | | | |
| 38 | D-1314 | D-AMAR | Inselberg | 1928 | To R.L.M. 1935 |
| 39 | D-1327 | D-APIN | Hohentwiel | 1928 | To D.V.S. 1934 |
| 40 | D-1338 | — | Zugspitze | 1928 | Destroyed by fire, March 1931 |
| **Ro VIII Roland II** | | | | | |
| 42 | D-1692 | D-ARAF | Stolzenfels | 1929 | To D.V.S. 1935 |
| 44 | D-1710 | D-ASOL | Rheinstein | 1929 | To R.L.M. 1935 |
| 45 | D-1712 | — | Schönburg | 1929 | To Deruluft 1932; crashed March 1935 |
| 46 | D-1720 | D-AHOL | Niederwald | 1929 | To R.L.M. 1935 |
| 47 | D-1727 | D-AXEV | Freienfels | 1929 | To R.L.M. 1935 |
| 43 | D-1729 | D-ANUZ | Drachenfels | 1929 | To Deruluft, 1933 |
| 48 | D-1735 | D-AVOK | Marksburg | 1929 | To Deruluft 1932 |
| 49 | D-1745 | D-ARUT | Siegburg | 1929 | To R.L.M. 1935 |
| 50 | D-1756 | D-ANAX | Rolandseck | 1929 | Transferred to D.V.S. Oct. 1934 |
| **Ro V Rocco** | | | | | |
| 26 | D-1261 | — | — | 1928 | Owned by Severa and leased to D.L.H. for 2 months in summer |
| **Ro Romar** | | | | | |
| 29 | D-1693 | — | Hamburg | 1929 | Damaged Nov. 1929 |
| 30 | D-1734 | — | Bremen | 1929 | Damaged Sept. 1929 |
| 31 | D-1747 | — | Lübeck | 1929 | Scrapped 1933 |

**Note** All the Rolands except the first two were allocated to D.L.H. by the R.V.M. (Reichsverkehrsministerium). The last six in service were delivered to the R.L.M. (Reichsluftfahrtministerium).

## Three-Engined Comfort and Safety

Further reliability and safety were attained by the introduction of multiengined equipment. First had come the **Junkers-G 24** in 1924 and then the revolutionary **Rohrbach Roland** (see opposite page) in 1926. It was first ordered by Aero Lloyd in 1925 and introduced by D.L.H. as its first successful new type. The Roland could reach an altitude of 16,000 feet—higher than Mont Blanc. Although a Dornier Komet III had flown across the Alps (*through* them would have been more apt) in 1925 (page 12), to do so regularly would have been impossible with an aircraft whose normal ceiling was about 5000 feet. On 13 April 1927, Willi Polte first flew a Roland to Milan. Regular mail and freight service began in 1928, and passengers were carried directly from Munich to Milan in 1931.

Whereas in 1926 the average aircraft utilization was barely more than a year-round average of an hour per day, this improved by the mid-1930s to about three hours. In 1928, passengers in one of the **Junkers-G 31**s were offered snacks and drinks, served by a steward, while in the **Albatros L 73**s the seats could be folded down to ease the strain of night flying.

There were occasional criticisms. Some of the clientele, benefiting from the improved technology, requested compensation for lost flying time if an aircraft arrived early.

The Albatros's cabin had ample room for eight passengers in sleeper seats.

# Rohrbach Roland

**10 seats • 109 mph**

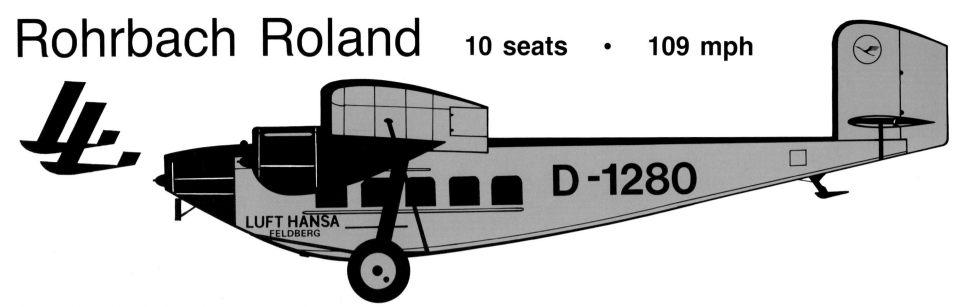

BMW Va (320 hp) × 3 • 800 statute miles range
• 16,315 lb max. gross takeoff weight

### THE ROHRBACHS

| Type | First Flight Date | Dimensions | | | Pass. Seats | Engines | | | | Max. Gross TOW (lb) | Cruise Speed (mph) | Normal Range (st. miles) | No. Built |
| | | Length | Span | Height | | No. | Type | Hp (each) | | | | | |
|---|---|---|---|---|---|---|---|---|---|---|---|---|---|
| Ro VIII Roland I | 1926 | 52'10" | 86'3" | 14'9" | 10 | 3 | B.M.W. IV | 230 | | 15,760 | 109 | 700 | 6 |
| Ro VIII Roland Ia | 1928 | 53'9" | 86'3" | 14'9" | 10 | 3 | B.M.W. Va | 320 | | 16,315 | 110 | 550 | 3 |
| Ro VIII Roland II | 1929 | 53'9" | 86'3" | 14'9" | 10 | 3 | B.M.W. Va | 320 | | 16,315 | 110 | 800 | 9 |
| Ro V Rocco | 1927 | 63'0" | 85'3" | | 10 | 2 | R-R Condor III | 650 | | 21,400 | 104 | 900 | 1 |
| Ro Romar | 1928 | 72'2" | 121'1" | 27'10" | 12 | 3 | B.M.W. VI | 500 | | 40,800 | 110 | 1200 | 3 |

In 1919 the Zeppelin-Werke factory at Staaken, Berlin, had built the E.4/20 four-engined aircraft. Had not the Allied Control Commission prevented its development, it could easily have changed the course of commercial air transport. This would not have been simply because of its size, although its 9-ton loaded weight, its 102-foot wingspan, and its four Maybach engines generating almost 1000 hp clearly put it in a new class. Its significant innovation was the huge single wing which was completely unsupported because of its revolutionary box-spar construction. The E.4/20's construction was not only stronger. It was lighter.

The genius behind this design innovation was a frustrated Dr. Adolf Rohrbach, who founded his own company in 1922, with a production branch in Copenhagen, to circumvent the Versailles Treaty restrictions. But by 1926 these had eased sufficiently to permit **Deutsche Luft Hansa** to take delivery of the prototype of the three-engined, ten-seat **Rohrbach Roland** at Staaken. Built on the same principles as the E.4/20, the name was contracted from Rohrbach Land.

## FOKKER WOODEN WING

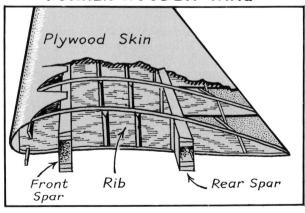

Plywood Skin

Front Spar — Rib — Rear Spar

## JUNKERS ALL-METAL WING

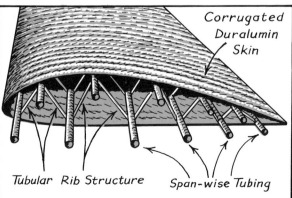

Corrugated Duralumin Skin

Tubular Rib Structure — Span-wise Tubing

## ROHRBACH BOX SPAR WING

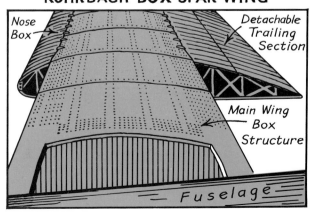

Nose Box — Detachable Trailing Section

Main Wing Box Structure

Fuselage

# First Steps Toward the East

## THE D.L.H. JUNKERS-G 24s
### (including F 24 conversions)

| Const. No. | Regist. No. Original | Regist. No. 1934 | Name | Disposal |
|---|---|---|---|---|
| 840* | D-876 | D-USAH | Diana | Written off 1935 |
| 842* | D-877 | D-UPIT | Amsterdam | Scrapped 1939 |
| 844 | D-878 | — | Haarlem | To D.V.L. Dec. 1929 |
| 902 | D-879 | D-ABIP | Pluto | To R.L.M. 1934 |
| 908 | D-880 | D-ADIL | Hermes | Freighter version; to R.L.M. Nov. 1934 |
| 850* | D-896 | — | Düsseldorf | Written off 1938 |
| 904 | D-899 | — | Juno | Damaged beyond repair Feb. 1929 |
| 909 | D-901 | — | Tyr/Ostmark | To R.L.M. Nov. 1933 |
| 911 | D-903 | — | Hera/Oberschlesien | Damaged beyond repair 1928 |
| 841 | D-915 | — | Wotan | To D.V.S. 1928 |
| 907 | D-944 | — | Artemis | Written off 1926 |
| 916 | D-946 | — | Prometheus | Damaged beyond repair Sept. 1928 |
| 917 | D-949 | D-ANIK | Dyonysos | To R.L.M. 1933 |
| 921 | D-950 | — | Persephone/Potyguar | To Syndicato Condor (P-BAHA) 1928 |
| 839* | D-1016 | D-UMUR | Thor/Österreich | Scrapped 1939 |
| 848* | D-1017 | D-UPOP | Hera/Bayern | Scrapped 1939 |
| 834* | D-1018 | D-ULET | Odin/Helvetia | Written off 1935 |
| 843* | D-1019 | — | Rotterdam | Destroyed April 1934 |
| 849* | D-1020 | D-URIS | Essen | Scrapped 1939 |
| 949 | D-1059 | — | Flora | To Iberia (M-CFFA) March 1932 |
| 933 | D-1062 | D-AJIF | Silvanus | To R.L.M. Jan. 1935 |
| 845* | D-1069 | D-UQAN | Baldur | Written off 1935 |
| 941 | D-1088 | — | Cupido | To R.L.M. March 1934 |
| 927 | D-1089 | D-ADOX | Hestia | To R.L.M. Nov. 1934 |
| 915 | D-1090 | — | Aurora | To Iberia (M-CAFF) March 1932 |
| 912 | D-1092 | — | Loki | To R.L.M. March 1934 |
| 944 | D-1287 | — | Ypiranga | To VARIG (P-BABA) 1928, then Syndicato Condor (PP-CAB); written off 1938 |
| 961 | | | Riachuelo | To Syndicato Condor (P-BAQA, PP-CAS) |
| | — | D-ALAB | Faunus | Ex-ÖLAG 1939; written off 1939 |

Abbrev. R.L.M.: Reichsluftfahrtministerium  D.V.S.: Deutsche Verkehrsfliegerschule
**Note** The first 19 aircraft, delivered to Junkers Luftverkehr in 1925, were part of Deutsche Luft Hansa's original fleet on formation in 1926. D-1059–D-1092 were acquired in 1927; D-1287 in 1928, and *Riachuelo* in 1931. A few names were changed in 1928. Those marked with an asterisk were converted to single-engined F 24 in 1928–1929.

## Destination: China

By the time Deutsche Luft Hansa was founded in 1926, German aircraft had demonstrated their quality everywhere, especially in South America and Asia. They were somewhat at a disadvantage, however. British and other European airmen and airline visionaries could concentrate on the southern route to the Orient, where the British, Dutch, and French still ruled. But the Germans were still restricted in many ways as an aftermath of the bitterness prevailing after World War I.

The products of the **Junkers Flugzeugwerke** were therefore to be seen in what, in the 1920s, were considered to be remote and dangerous corners of the world. Some flights were remarkable in that they were completed at all. All seemed to have a common goal: to explore the potential for commercial air routes to the Middle and Far East without having to fly through colonial territories.

By October 1924, the Soviet airline **Dobrolot** was flying Junkers aircraft from Tashkent, in Central Asia, to Kabul, Afghanistan. The famous Swiss pilot Mittelholzer flew a **Junkers-F 13** from Zurich to Teheran in six weeks during the winter of 1924–25; and a **Junkers-A 20** of the Persian Air Force flew from Teheran to Bushire, on the Persian Gulf, early in March 1925. In July of that year, Dobrolot promoted an experimental expedition from Moscow to Peking, which included a Junkers-F 13.

## First from Berlin to Peking

Transcending these achievements, and relying on Junkers Luftverkehr's preparations in 1925, was the expedition led by Dr. Robert Knauss in 1926, using two new three-engined **Junkers-G 24**s, D-901 and D-903. They left Berlin on 23 July 1926 and arrived in Peking on 30 August. They had flown the 6000-mile route in 17 stages, with inaccurate maps, no weather reporting service, no source of en route spare parts, and—rather riskily—no Chinese permits.

Neither aircraft could take off from Kurgan until Russian workers built a new airstrip. They were again delayed at Tsitsihar, Manchuria, for nine days while diplomats cleared the way. With civil wars raging between Chinese warlords at the time, they were perhaps lucky to reach their destination.

Even in the 1920s Deutsche Luft Hansa's passengers were provided with a special bus service.

REGD

**Route of the G24s** (D-901 – D-903) July–August 1924

Berlin — Königsberg — Smolensk — Moscow — Kazan — Kungur — Krasnoufimsk — Kurgan — Omsk — Novosibirsk — Nijni Udinsk — Irkutsk — Krasnoyarsk — Chita — Manchuli — Harbin — Mukden — Peking

U. S. S. R.
CHINA

Scale—Miles 1000 2000

These two aircraft were originally named *Tyr* and *Hera* respectively. They were later renamed *Ostmark* and *Oberschlesien*

# Junkers-G 24

**9 seats • 113 mph**

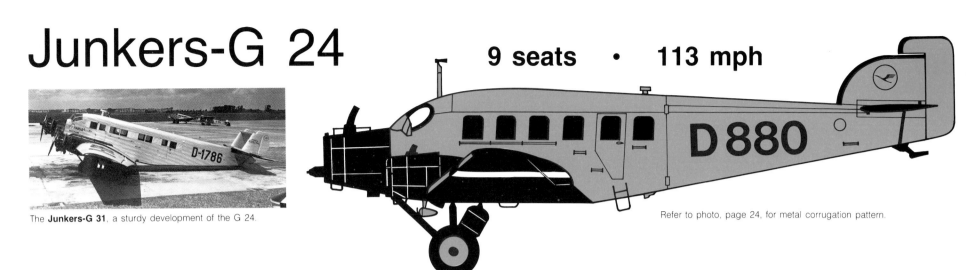

The **Junkers-G 31**, a sturdy development of the G 24.

Refer to photo, page 24, for metal corrugation pattern.

## Junkers-L 5 (280 hp) × 3 • 14,330 lb max. gross takeoff weight • 800 statute miles range

### The World's First All-Metal Trimotor

Many aircraft have been widely ignored by aviation writers despite their contributions to aeronautical progress. One of these was the three-engined series started by Junkers as early as 1923. Drawing on the all-metal formula so convincingly successful with the F 13, the Junkers Flugzeugwerke developed a larger version in 1924, adding the wing-mounted engines for safety and reliability as well as to increase size. Because of the Versailles Treaty restrictions that overshadowed German industry during the early 1920s, the G 24 could not be registered in Germany and flew under Swiss and Swedish flags until 1926. It was sometimes referred to as the "G 23."

Cities and provinces in Germany were official shareholders in local airlines or the Europa-Union, with the objective of directing air traffic in their direction. During these difficult reconstruction years in Germany, there were more ways than one to skin a cat—or to finance an aircraft; and the "G 23" benefited from this procedure.

### The G 24

As the restrictions eased with the signing of the Locarno Pact on 16 October 1925 and the Paris agreements that followed, more powerful engines could be fitted, and this resulted in the **G 24**, of which about 50 were built, including 18 or 19 for the **Junkers Luftverkehr**, and which passed to **Deutsche Luft Hansa** on its formation in 1926. This version was quite successful, working D.L.H.'s main routes and considered to be, with the new Rohrbach Rolands, the flagships of the fleet.

The G 24 was selected in 1926 for a pioneering flight to the Far East (see opposite page), and in March 1927 it set world records for duration and distance for aircraft in its class. Many were exported to European countries and to Latin America.

### The F 24 Conversion

When more powerful engines were available, about half of the G 24 fleet was converted during 1928 and 1929 into single-engined aircraft, the F 24s. One Junkers Jumo diesel or one B.M.W. VIIau engine could provide as much power as the three smaller engines on the G 24. They were the last of the series to be retired by D.L.H., and used as engine test beds just before the outbreak of World War II. Some of them had served for 14 years, alongside their more illustrious progeny, the Junkers-Ju 52/3m.

### The Junkers-G 31

This sturdy development of the G-24 was an excellent aircraft that served D.L.H. well until 1936, when the Junkers-JU 52/3m took over. Three of the G-31s, specially modified for extraordinary assignments, were supplied to the airlines operating to the goldfields in the mountains of New Guinea. During the early 1930s the three Junkers "specials" were estimated to have carried a greater tonnage of air freight than all the other air fleets of the world put together.

#### THE D.L.H. JUNKERS-G 31 FLEET

| Constr. No. | Regist. No. Original | Regist. No. 1934 | Name | Disposal |
|---|---|---|---|---|
| 3002 | D-1310 | D-ADIN | *Hermann Köhl* | To R.L.M. 1935 |
| 3004 | D-1427 | — | *Deutschland* | Destroyed by fire Sept. 1928 |
| 3005 | D-1473 | — | *Rheinland* | Destroyed by fire Dec. 1928 |
| 3006 | D-1523 | D-ADAR | *Nordmark* | To R.L.M. 1935 |
| 3008 | D-1722 | D-ABIL | *Brandenburg* | To R.L.M. 1936 |
| 3007 | D-1770 | D-ABAR | *Preussen* | To R.L.M. 1936 |
| 3009 | D-1786 | D-ADUR | *Westmark* | To R.L.M. 1935 |

**Abbrev.** R.L.M.: Reichsluftfahrtministerium
**Note** All aircraft delivered 1928–1930.

#### THE JUNKERS-G TRIMOTOR SERIES

| Type | First Flight Date | Length | Span | Height | Pass. Seats | Engines No. | Engines Type | Hp (each) | Max. Gross TOW (lb) | Cruise Speed (mph) | Normal Range (st. miles) | No. Built |
|---|---|---|---|---|---|---|---|---|---|---|---|---|
| G 24 | 1925 | 51'6" | 98'1" | 11'5" | 9 | 3 | Junkers-L 5 | 310 | 14,330 | 113 | 800 | 60 |
| F 24 | 1928 | 51'3" | 85'3" | 11'5" | 9 | 1[1] | BMW VIIu[2] | 750 | 10,360 | 115 | 600 | 11 |
| G 31 | 1926 | 56'8" | 99'5" | 19'8" | 15 | 3 | BMW Hornet[3] | 525 | 18,740 | 106 | 800 | 13 |

[1]The F 24 was a single-engined version of the G 24. [2]Other B.M.W. engines were used, also the Junkers Jumo diesel engine. [3]Some G 31s had Gnome-Rhône Jupiters or Siemens Jupiters.

# Foothold in the Orient

## Formation of Eurasia

After earlier negotiations were delayed by civil wars until 1928, when discussions were initiated with the new Kuomintang government in Nanking, Wilhelm Schmidt, representing **Deutsche Luft Hansa**, reached agreement with the Chinese on 21 February 1930 to form a European-Asian airmail company, later named the **Eurasia Aviation Corporation**. The Chinese held two-thirds of the shares, while D.L.H. exercised technical direction and route policy. Unlike other foreign airline associations in China, Eurasia was a true joint venture.

## An Eventful History

Scheduled operations began on 31 May 1931, with two **Junkers-W 33**s. Eurasia's main raison d'être was to provide a secure Far Eastern anchor for a joint German-Soviet service to the Orient. **Deruluft** (page 10) flew from Berlin to Moscow and **Dobrolot** carried the mail as far as Irkutsk. The next stage, to the Manchurian border at Manchuli, was by the **Trans-Siberian Railway**. Finally, Eurasia provided the air link with a Junkers-W 33 to Peiping (Peking; more recently, Beijing) and Shanghai on 31 May 1931.

Unfortunately this venture soon came to an abrupt halt. On 2 July, Johannes Rathje and copilot Otto Kölber were within 100 miles of Manchuli, flying over a remote corner of Mongolia, when a group of soldiers fired at the W 33 Eu II and seriously wounded Kölber. They were taken prisoner, interrogated, and threatened with death by firing squad for alleged espionage. Only intense diplomatic activity enabled them to return to Peiping ten weeks later.

The next idea was to take a more direct route across northwestern China to connect with Dobrolot. A W 33 made a trial flight from 20 December 1931 until 10 January 1932 and further flights were made the following year; but Sino-Soviet relationships deteriorated in 1933, and the promising trans-Asian route was stillborn.

Painstakingly, an internal Chinese network was fashioned (see map). Several W 33s and W 34s were delivered from 1933 to 1935 and three **Junkers-Ju 52/3m**'s were flown out in 1934 and 1935. (See page 58.)

These were adventurous and dangerous times for all the airlines in China. Japanese armed forces began to occupy the eastern Chinese provinces after the "Marco Polo Bridge Incident" at Peiping in 1937. After the German invasion of Poland in 1939, and consequent close relations with the Soviet Union, the idea of operating an air route from Germany to China, with the cooperation of Aeroflot, was revived. Eurasia actually ordered four **Focke-Wulf Fw 200B Condor** long-range airliners for the purpose. Germany's Chinese airline partner survived, however, only until 2 July 1941, when the Kuomintang severed diplomatic relations with Hitler's Reich.

A **Eurasia Junkers-W 33** at Lanchow, China.

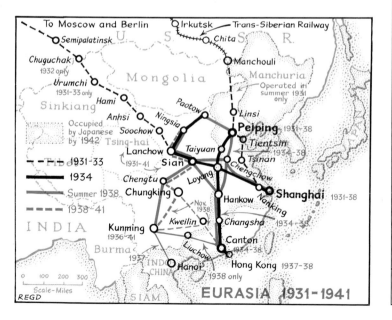

| Eurasia Fleet No. | Service Life From | To | Disposal |
|---|---|---|---|
| **Junkers-F 13** | | | |
| EU-III | March 1931 | 15 Dec. 1932 | Crashed near Shanghai |
| EU-IV | March 1931 | Aug. 1937 | Bombed by Japanese at Shanghai |
| **Junkers-W-33** | | | |
| EU-I | 4 Feb. 1931 | 26 Aug. 1932 | Crashed near Lanchow |
| EU-II | 4 Feb. 1931 | 2 July 1931 | Lost when overflying Mongolia |
| EU-V | 19 June 1932 | 1 Feb. 1933 | Crashed at Sian |
| EU-VI | 16 July 1932 | 1 Sept. 1932 | Crashed at Lanchow |
| EU-VII | 23 Feb. 1933 | | Remained in Hong Kong after repair |
| EU-VIII | 17 March 1933 | Aug. 1937 | Bombed by Japanese at Shanghai |
| **Junkers-W 34** | | | |
| EU-I | 31 May 1933 | 4 July 1935 | Crashed at Lanchow |
| EU-II | 31 May 1933 | | |
| EU-III | 4 Sept. 1933 | 22 Feb. 1935 | Crashed near Changsha |
| EU-V | 11 March 1935 | 27 Sept. 1935 | Crashed near Sian |
| EU-III | 25 March 1935 | 11 May 1935 | Crashed near Canton |
| EU-VI | 25 June 1935 | | Remained in Hong Kong after repair |
| **Junkers-Ju 52/3m** | | | |
| EU-XV | 11 Sept. 1934 | | |
| EU-XVII | 24 Oct. 1935 | 6 May 1939 | Destroyed in Japanese attack at Hanchung |
| EU-XVIII | 29 Dec. 1935 | 1 Aug. 1937 | Crashed at Kunming |
| EU-XIX | 19 July 1936 | | Crashed near Kunming |
| EU-XX | 11 March 1937 | | |
| EU-XXI | 27 May 1937 | 16 July 1938 | Crashed at Hankow |
| EU-XXII | 14 March 1938 | | |
| EU-XXIII | 6 Sept. 1938 | 12 March 1939 | Crashed near Weining |
| EU-XXIV | 26 Aug. 1937 | | Participated in Pamir |
| **Junkers-Ju 160** | | | |
| EU-XVI | 3 Oct. 1935 | 25 Dec. 1935 | Crashed near Shanghai |

# Junkers-W 33　6 seats • 93 mph

## THE DEUTSCHE LUFT HANSA JUNKERS-33/34 FLEET

| Const. No. | Regist. No. Original | Regist. No. 1934 | Name | Year Deliv. | Disposal |
|---|---|---|---|---|---|
| **W 33** | | | | | |
| 2514 | D-1472 | — | *Ural* | 1928 | Scrapped 1932 |
| 2544 | D-1649 | — | *Baikal* | 1929 | Scrapped 1930 |
| 2543 | D-1695 | — | *Balkan* | 1929 | To Eurasia 1933 |
| 2545 | D-1696 | — | *Taurus* | 1929 | To Eurasia 1930 |
| 2557 | D-1826 | — | *Karpathen* | 1930 | Destroyed 1930 |
| 2560 | D-1827 | — | *Sieben-bürgen* | 1930 | To Eurasia 1930 |
| 2561 | D-1839 | D-OFEZ | *Plattensee* | 1930 | With Eurasia 1932–1935 |
| 2563 | D-1855 | — | *Hohe Tatra* | 1930 | To Eurasia 1932 |
| 2564 | D-1894 | — | — | 1930 | To Flugfélag Islands (Island I) 1930–31; Eurasia 1932 |
| 2579 | D-2008 | — | *Beskiden* | 1931 | To D.V.S. 1933 |
| 2580 | D-2009 | D-OTAQ | *Bosporus* | 1931 | To Hansa Flug-dienst 1938 |
| 2582 | D-2016 | D-OVOL | *Sakaria* | 1931 | Scrapped 1942 |
| 2583 | D-2017 | — | *Marmara* | 1931 | Crashed 1932 |
| 2584 | D-2018 | — | *Bukowina* | 1931 | Scrapped 1933 |
| **W 34** | | | | | |
| 2733 | D-2394 | D-OJOH | *Castor* | 1933 | Sold to Hansa Flugdienst 1938 |
| 2734 | D-2395 | D-OMET | *Pollux* | 1933 | Sold to Hansa Flugdienst 1939 |
| 2746 | D-2478 | D-UPOL | *Merkur* | 1933 | To Eurasia 1935 |
| 2743 | D-2535 | — | *Orion* | 1933 | To Eurasia 1933 |
| 2763 | D-3118 | D-UKAM | *Orion* | 1934 | To Eurasia 1935 |
| 2764 | D-3119 | D-UGES | *Wega* | 1934 | Sold to Hansa Flugdienst 1938 |
| 2766 | D-3342 | D-UBAJ | — | 1934 | To D.V.S. 1934 |

**Abbrev.** D.V.S.: Deutsche Verkehrsfliegerschule

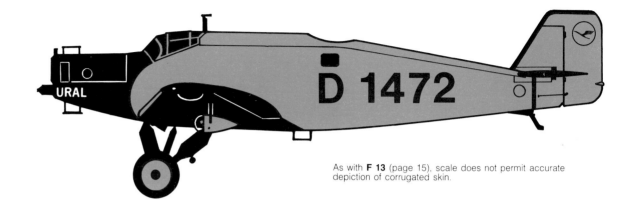

As with **F 13** (page 15), scale does not permit accurate depiction of corrugated skin.

## 1 Junkers-L5 • 5510 lb max. gross takeoff weight • 620 statute miles range

## The Junkers-W 34

A further improvement in performance was possible when radial engines—Gnome-Rhône Jupiters—replaced the water-cooled in-line engines. In this **W 34** the radials were an identifiable feature, distinguishing it from the W 33. Many of them, like the F 13s and W 33s, stayed in service for years, and one was still flying in Canada in 1962. More than 100 W 34s were built, so that the total of the basic type, F 13s, W 33s, and W 34s, exceeded 600, a truly remarkable record for the era and a tribute to the soundness of the design.

Easily the most famous of the series was the W 33 *Bremen*, which made the first nonstop east-west crossing of the North Atlantic (page 34). But the adventures of the little Junkers metal airplanes, from Peking to Peru, would fill a book.

## Freighter Version of a Famous Type

In 1926 the first freighter version of the Junkers-F 13 appeared off the production line at Dessau. Designated the **W 33**, it was possibly the first commercial aircraft designed specifically for this purpose. It was the same size as its predecessor, but its lines were cleaner, with the cockpit faired into the fuselage upper surface. The earlier freighters had no windows at all, but later passenger versions, with six seats, were fitted with them.

Coming into production as it did when Allied restrictions were lifted, it had an engine twice as powerful as the F 13s, thus permitting increased take-off weight and consequent payload and range. This straightforward development, landplanes and floatplanes, supplemented the F 13 fleets of most of the Junkers airline customers overseas as well as with **Deutsche Luft Hansa**. More than 200 were built.

### THE JUNKERS SINGLE-ENGINED TRANSPORT AIRCRAFT

| Type | First Flight Date | Dimensions Length | Span | Height | Pass. seats | Engines No. | Type | Hp (each) | Max Gross TOW (lb) | Cruise Speed (mph) | Normal Range (st. miles) | (Approx.) No. Built |
|---|---|---|---|---|---|---|---|---|---|---|---|---|
| F 13 | 1919 | 34'6" | 58'3" | 11'10" | 4 | 1 | Junkers-L5[1] | 280 | 5510 | 106 | 400 | 322 |
| A 20 | 1923 | 27'5" | 50'4" | 9'10" | 1 | 1 | Mercedes DIIIa | 160 | 3300 | 93 | 300 | (30) |
| W 33 | 1926 | 34'6" | 58'3" | 11'7" | 0[3] | 1 | Junkers-L5 | 310 | 5510 | 93 | 600 | 199 |
| W 34 | 1926 | 33'8" | 58'3" | 11'7" | 4[3] | 1 | Gnome-Rhône Jupiter VI[2] | 420 | 5950 | 109 | 525 | (100) |

[1]The earlier F 13s had 185-hp B.M.W. IIIa, or Mercedes D IIIa, with lower performance. Later versions also had B.M.W. IV and Pratt & Whitney engines. [2]Some W 34s had Pratt & Whitney Hornet, Armstrong Siddeley, or Bristol engines. [3]All W 33s and most of the W 34s were freighter aircraft.

# SCADTA—Oldest Airline in the Americas

## Seizing a Great Opportunity

The first airlines in Latin America were two small and short-lived French-sponsored companies, founded in 1919 in Guiana and Colombia. But German initiative—again in Colombia—established the first American airline of permanence and stability. The present-day Colombian national airline, AVIANCA, can trace its ancestry directly to the **Sociedad Colombo-Alemana de Transportes Aéreos (SCADTA)**, founded by a group of Colombian businessmen and German residents on 5 December 1919, in Barranquilla.

The Colombian government supported the enterprise, recognizing the value of air transport to connect the Caribbean with the capital, Bogotá. High on a plateau at 8400 feet altitude, Bogotá was reached by an arduous two-week riverboat journey up the Magdalena River, then by pack mule or horseback. SCADTA undertook to provide an air service within a single day, using sturdy **Junkers-F 13** floatplanes.

These were imported by an experienced airline manager and pilot, Fritz Hammer. Sent to Colombia to represent Junkers' interest in the airline, he was aided by an inventive engineer, Wilhelm Schnurbusch, and a fine pilot, Hellmuth von Krohn. Though plagued by various mishaps and by illness, the team nevertheless managed to conduct the necessary survey flights during the next two years, while the F 13's metal structure displayed a resilience that no other aircraft of its time could match.

## The von Bauer Years

In 1921, Peter Paul von Bauer, an Austrian industrialist, became so enthused with the SCADTA venture that he emigrated to Colombia, acquired the Gieseking shareholding in 1922, and developed the airline with tremendous flair. He quickly established its name throughout the commercial world, and negotiated an important agreement with the Colombian government whereby SCADTA could actually issue its own airmail stamps. On 19 September 1921, one of air transport history's great occasions, SCADTA opened full passenger and mail service from Barranquilla to Girardot, the Magdalena River port connected by rail to Bogotá.

SCADTA claimed to be the first airline to carry a head of state, President Pedro nel Ospina, in 1922. It rescued the state bank by flying 1½ tons of currency to Bogotá in 1923. It made the audacious Trans-Caribbean Survey (see page 29) in 1925. It introduced improved aircraft, **Junkers-W 33**s, **W 34**s, and **Dornier Wal**s, and expanded the network to serve all the main cities of Colombia. Gaining confidence and accumulating experience, it had by 1929 ventured into Panama, Ecuador, and even Peru, creating the Servicio Bolivariano. But SCADTA sustained accidents too; and far more ominous, was sold to U.S. interests in 1930 by none other than von Bauer himself.

THE GERMAN FLEET OF SCADTA

| Regist. No. | Const. No. | Name | Year Deliv. | Remarks |
|---|---|---|---|---|
| **Junkers-F 13** | | | | |
| A2 | 557 | Colombia | 1920 | There were probably two Colombias: J1 believed to have crashed 1923; A2 transferred to Colombian army for war against Peru, crashed 1933 |
| A4 | 554 | Bogotá | 1920 | Ex-D-29; crashed 1927 |
| A6 | 543 | Huila | 1921 | Ex-D-152 of Lloyd Ostflug (and Dz 152 of Danziger Luftpost) Kasuar; flew 3100 hr |
| A8 | 602 | Magdalena | 1921 | Returned to Junkers in 1929 for study after 3200 hr and almost 400,000 miles |
| A9 | 618 | Cauca | 1921 | Crashed at Barranquilla 1927 |
| A10 | 615 | Caldas | 1921 | Crashed at La Victoria 1926 |
| A12 | 573 | Santander | 1923 | Burned out at El Banco 1930 |
| A16 | | Tolima | 1924 | Crashed at Barranquilla 1924 |
| A18 | | Cúcuta | 1925 | Allocated to COSADA |
| A21 | | Bucaramanga | 1925 | Allocated to COSADA; reregistered C-21 |
| A22 | | Huila (2) | 1927 | Reregistered C-22 |
| A24 | | Antioquia | | |
| A25 | | Boyacá | 1927 | Reregistered C-25; survey flights to Ecuador and Peru; to Colombian army 1932 |
| A26 | | Naraiño | 1928 | Reregistered C-26; retired 1925 |
| C29 | | Atlántico | 1928 | |
| C30 | | Chocó | 1928 | Crashed 1929 |
| C31 | | Valle | 1928 | Crashed 1929 |
| A32 | | Pacífico | 1928 | Rereg. C-32; crashed 1934 |
| C35 | | Darien | 1929 | Crashed 1938 |
| A36 | | Garcia Rovira | 1929 | Rereg. C-36; crashed 1933 |
| C40 | | Córdoba | 1929 | Crashed at Chocó 1936 |
| C41 | | Santa Fé | 1929 | Crashed at Girardot |
| **Dornier Wal** | | | | |
| A19 | 34 | Atlántico | 1925 | Leased from Condor Syndikat (D-1012); transferred to Brazil |
| A20 | | Pacífico | 1925 | Leased from Condor (ex I-DOOR); crashed, Venezuela 1926 |
| C28 | | Colombia | 1928 | Probably third use of name; started service to Panama 1929; to Colombian govt. 1932 |
| **Dornier Merkur (1927)** | | | | |
| A23 | 124 | Simon Bolivar | | Reregistered C-23; retired 1931 |
| C27 | 167 | Pedro nel Ospina | | |
| **Junkers-W 33/34 (1928–1929)** | | | | |
| C33 | | Cundinamarca | | W 33; to Colombian govt. 1932 |
| | | Cundinamarca (2) | | W 34 |
| C53 | | Boyacá | | W 34 |
| C71 | | Huila (3) | | W 34 |
| | | Magdalena (2) | | W 34 |

Several other W 34s were operated but cannot be precisely identified

*Bogotá*, one of **SCADTA**'s wheeled **Junkers-F 13**s, introduced only after several years of waterway operations during the 1920s.

*Cauca*, one of **SCADTA's Junkers-F13s,** on the ramp at Girardot, on the Magdalena River in Colombia.

# Caribbean Reconnaissance

The **Dornier Wal** *Pacífico* at Lake Amatitlán, Guatemala, during its historic survey flight in 1925.

*Cundinamarca*, one of **SCADTA**'s **Junkers-W 34**s, whose radial engine distinguishes it from the W 33.

## A Dramatic Venture

During the 1920s the development of commercial aviation and the establishment of well-structured airlines were far more advanced in Europe than in the United States and most other parts of the world. Airline interests in Germany and France had also obtained overseas bridgeheads for airline partnerships, taking financial and operational risks just as they had taken the initiatives in Europe. SCADTA was Germany's most impressive representative in the New World. Its Junkers-F 13 floatplane service up the Magdalena River was almost a textbook model for its time.

In 1925, SCADTA joined with its new sponsor, the Condor Syndikat (backed by Aero Lloyd), in an undertaking even more daring. Bearing in mind the inadequacies of en-route ground installations, the total lack of navigational aids, and the absence of weather reporting, the Trans-Caribbean Survey flight was a triumph of planning and organization. It was also a shrewd and calculated demonstration to the governments of the Americas (including that of the United States) that German technology was in the vanguard of aviation progress.

Two **Dornier Wal**s, the *Pacífico* and the *Atlántico,* were shipped specially to Colombia and prepared for this remarkable journey. A top-level SCADTA-Condor team left Barranquilla on 18 August and arrived in Havana on 19 September 1925. The intention was clear: to show not only that an airline linking North and South America was feasible, but that a German partnership was ready to begin sevice.

## U.S. Intransigence

The United States was alarmed. Only the *Pacífico* was allowed to proceed, and then only as far as West Palm Beach. Peter Paul von Bauer, head of SCADTA, went to see President Coolidge in Washington, but Silent Cal gave little encouragement. Fritz Hammer, head of the Condor Syndikat, went to New York, seeking financial support, but faced apathy on Wall Street. The delegation had to return to Colombia, empty-handed and frustrated.

Had the negotiations succeeded, SCADTA would undoubtedly have started a trans-Caribbean service and the whole course of airline development in the New World would have been vastly different.

The supreme irony was that the Trans-Caribbean Survey served notice on the United States that it should start to take commercial aviation seriously. Within a few short months of von Bauer and Hammer's departure, several interested groups vied for the privilege of carrying U.S. airmail to the Caribbean and to South America. The Air Mail and Air Commerce Acts were passed in 1926 by a now alerted—and somewhat alarmed—Coolidge administration. One result was that Pan American Airways was founded on 14 March 1927, starting scheduled service from Key West to Havana on 28 October 1928.

Unwittingly, German enterprise may have sown the seeds of its future competition, waged ruthlessly and successfully by the U.S. flag carrier which might never have existed but for the threat of SCADTA in 1925.

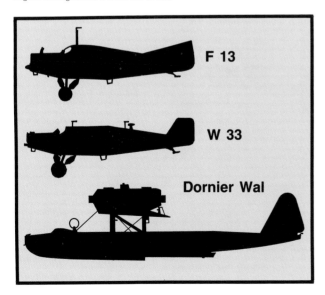

F 13

W 33

Dornier Wal

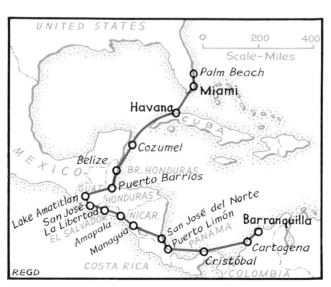

# The Middle East Connection

## Junkers Luftverkehr Persien

In 1927, Kurt Weil, a former World War I pilot who had joined Junkers and had been intimately involved with negotiations to conduct air services in the Soviet Union during the early 1920s, was sent to Persia (now called Iran) to put to the test his theories on how to run an airline profitably. He realized that even a good aircraft was only as reliable as its maintenance, that the fleet must be well utilized, and that with good marketing to generate traffic, an airline need not necessarily depend completely on subsidy to stay viable.

Arriving in Teheran, he found two **Junkers-F 13**s, probably assembled in Moscow from Dessau components. Owned by the Persian air force, they were left in the open air. Backed by a 1924 concession from the Persian government, and after overhauling the aircraft and engines, Weil launched the **Junkers Luftverkehr Persien** in February 1927, with two weekly services: to Pahlevi, on the Caspian Sea; and to Qasr-i-Shirin, on the Iraqi frontier, via Hamadan and Kermanshah.

Having lost its airline system based in Germany, Junkers was keen to demonstrate the efficiency of its products in airline operations. It supported Weil by delivering new aircraft, crews, and ground staff. For his part, Weil set up an agency for bath stoves, one of Junkers's former products that was in demand in Persia.

## A Link with the Gulf

The system grew steadily, with an extension to Baku in February 1928 and to Bushire two months later, via Isfahan and Shiraz. Another extension linked Teheran with Baghdad. Thus, on the map at least—although it must have been an arduous journey—there was an air connection from Berlin to the Persian Gulf. Luftverkehr Persien also opened routes to

**Kurt Weil,** founder of **Junkers Luftverkehr Persien**.

### THE FLEET OF JUNKERS LUFTVERKEHR PERSIEN

| Const. No. | Previous Regist. No. | Previous Owner |
|---|---|---|
| **Junkers-F 13** | | |
| 569 | R-RECK (ex-R-RECG) | Junkers Luftverkehr, U.S.S.R. |
| 614 | R-RECE | "        " |
| 630 | R-RECF | "        " |
| 643 | — | — |
| 651 | R-RECI | Junkers Luftverkehr, U.S.S.R. |
| 2001 | D-1126 Zweigspecht | Junkers Luftverkehrs |

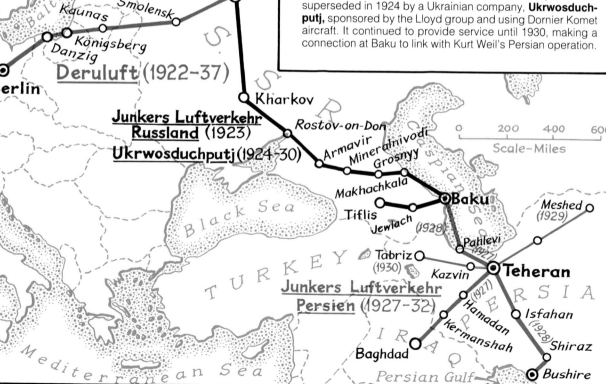

Persia's second largest city, Tabriz, and to the holy city of Meshed. The fleet grew to six Junkers-F 13s and one W 33.

The Persian airline lasted five years, until 1932, when it ceased operations. Most aircraft were returned to Germany and Kurt Weil went back to Berlin. He had operated an airline without complete dependence upon subsidy, built a new airfield at Teheran, and maintained a German commercial presence in a predominantly British sphere of influence. He had proved his point.

## The Moscow-Caspian Connection

When the Junkers company sought to establish assembly lines in foreign countries in order to evade the restrictions imposed by the Allies after World War I, the Moscow suburb of Fili was the site of one of the satellite factories, originally built in 1916 for production of the Sikorsky *Il'ya Muromets*. In connection with the cooperative agreement, Junkers also began an airline connection from Moscow to the Caucasus region via the Ukraine.

This service seems to have operated only intermittently, from 1923, as **Junkers Luftverkehr Russland,** and was superseded in 1924 by a Ukrainian company, **Ukrwosduchputj,** sponsored by the Lloyd group and using Dornier Komet aircraft. It continued to provide service until 1930, making a connection at Baku to link with Kurt Weil's Persian operation.

# Lloyd Aéreo Boliviano

## Pioneer Work by Junkers

The first Junkers mission to Latin America, equipped with two F 13s, was based in Havana in November 1922. It tried to establish airlines in the Caribbean and in South America but came to a tragic end when Hugo Junkers's son, Werner, was killed in an F 13 crash in Brazil in June 1923.

Having made some successful demonstrations in Argentina in 1924–1925, another South American Junkers mission sent a team to Cochabamba, Bolivia. Headed by Dipl-Ing Walter Jastram, the mission included two pilots and a mechanic, who assembled a **Junkers-F 13** which had arrived in three pieces by train. It made its first flight on 27 July 1925 and a few days later carried the first Bolivian fare-paying air passenger, to Sucre, guided by a Bolivian copilot who knew the way.

On 15 September a group of German residents formed **Lloyd Aéreo Boliviano (L.A.B.)**, naming Guillermo Kyllman as the first president. Scheduled service began with the F 13 *El Oriente* on 24 December 1925, from Cochabamba, at almost 8,000 feet altitude, to Santa Cruz, down on the plain closer to sea level. The 2 hr 20 min flight over the 200-mile distance compared favorably with surface modes, which varied from four days to two weeks. L.A.B. may thus have helped to launch Santa Cruz in its rise to prominence as Bolivia's chief commercial city.

During the next few years, L.A.B. steadily expanded its network, adding more Junkers-F 13s and W 34s. Two F 13s were fitted with floats for work on the many Amazon tributaries in northern Bolivia, while in 1928 a landplane opened service to the capital, La Paz, notable for its 12,000-foot altitude, with its airport 1500 feet higher still.

## First Overseas Junkers 52 Trimotor

In 1932, war broke out between Bolivia and Paraguay over the disputed Gran Chaco territory. L.A.B. provided logistics support for the Bolivian armed forces and deployed a Ford Tri-Motor and the first of several **Junkers-Ju 52/3m** trimotors, each able to carry 16 or more troops. L.A.B. was the first operator outside Europe of the famous *Tante Ju*, which also provided normal commercial service.

L.A.B. also put into service, in the spring of 1937, some fast (190 mph) **Junkers-Ju 86**s. These combined civil duties with missions for the Fuerza Aérea Boliviana, in which latter role they were fitted with armament.

The Bolivian airline was dependent on Junkers and later on Deutsche Luft Hansa, which provided technical support throughout the 1930s. It participated in an important airline development when on 24 May 1938 the all-German South American coast-to-coast route opened from Rio de Janeiro to Lima, with Syndicato Condor of Brazil and Lufthansa Sucursal Perú sharing the responsibility with L.A.B.

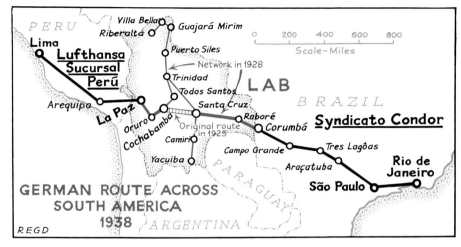

But as war clouds threatened and the United States became alarmed at German influence in South America, the U.S. airline PANAGRA took over D.L.H.'s godfather role in the Bolivian airline scene on 3 June 1941. L.A.B. survives today as the second-oldest airline in the Americas.

*Mamoré*, one of **L.A.B.**'s **Junkers-F 13** floatplanes.

*Illampu*, one of **L.A.B.**'s **Junkers-Ju 52/3m**s, at the Cochabamba base.

### THE FLEET OF LLOYD AÉREO BOLIVIANO (L.A.B.)
during the period of German influence
(before PANAGRA took control, 1941)

| Regist. No. | Const. No. | Name | Remarks |
|---|---|---|---|
| **Junkers-F 13** (First delivery 1925) | | | |
| (L.A.B. is believed to have had nine F 13s, and few can be identified with complete certainty. Their names and constructor's numbers, where known, were *El Oriente* (769), *Beni* (711), *Beni* (788), *Chaco*, *Charcas*, *Illimani*, *Mamoré* (634). There were two *Orientes* and three *Benis*.) | | | |
| **Junkers-W 34** (1929) | | | |
| | 2607 | *Vanguardia* | New; crashed 12 April 1939 |
| | 2608 | *Tunari* | New |
| **Junkers-Ju 52/3m** (1932) | | | |
| CB-17 | 4008 | *Juan del Valle* | First production Ju 52/3m; crashed 3 Nov. 1940 |
| CB-18 | 4009 | *Huanuni* | Second production Ju 52/3m; crashed 15 Dec. 1937 |
| CB-21 | 4061 | *Bolívar* | Sold to Aeroposta (Argentina) |
| CB-22 | 5623 | *Illampu* | Sold to VASP |
| | 4018 | *Chorolque* | Crashed 17 Jan. 1936 |
| **Junkers-W 33** (1933) | | | |
| CB-19 | 2756 | *Mururata* | New; crashed 3 April 1939 |
| CB-20 | — | *Sajama* | New; crashed 13 March 1937 |
| **Junkers-Ju 86** (1937) | | | |
| CB-23 | 13 | *Illimani* | New; from 1932 to 1935, Bolivia at war with Paraguay in dispute over Gran Chaco; L.A.B. provided logistics support |
| | 234 | *Mariscal Sta Cruz* | |
| | 237 | *General Perez* | |
| | 240 | *Mariscal Sucre* | |

**Note** During this period, L.A.B. also had a Ford 5-AT Tri-Motor, three Junkers-A 50 Juniors, a Sikorsky S-38B, and a Grumman Goose.

# The Condor Syndikat and Iberia

## Foundation of a Legendary Enterprise

On 5 May 1924, the **Condor Syndikat** was formed in Berlin to promote the sale of German commercial aircraft overseas. It was backed by Deutscher Aero Lloyd, the Hamburg trading company Schlubach Thiemer, and SCADTA's Peter Paul von Bauer, who had 10% of the shares, to protect his Colombian interests. The driving force behind Condor's marketing initiatives was the director-general, Fritz Hammer.

The first efforts were with SCADTA (see pages 28–29), one of whose two Italian-built **Dornier Wal**s, the *Atlantico*, was transferred to Brazil late in 1926. Deutscher Aero Lloyd had dispatched one of its best pilots, Capt. Rudolf Cramer von Clausbruch, who spearheaded a team of demonstrator pilots. The Condor contingent made a considerable impression on the Brazilian authorities.

## The Linha da Lagôa

Condor duly received an operating certificate and began, on 22 February 1927, the first scheduled air service in Brazil, after an official inaugural on 3 February. This was called the **Linha da Lagôa**, as it operated the Wal flying boat along the shores of the Lagôa dos Patos, from Rio Grande to Porto Alegre, in Brazil's southernmost state, which was populated largely by German immigrants. On 15 June, this Condor Syndikat operation was transferred to a new Brazilian airline, **Viação Aérea Rio Grandense** (**VARIG**), founded in Porto Alegre by businessmen from the German colony and using German equipment, with Condor's assistance. VARIG was to remain a small regional airline for 15 years.

## A Great Brazilian Airline

A newly formed **Syndicato Condor Ltda.** started a coastal route from Rio de Janeiro to Porto Alegre on 9 November 1927 and quickly expanded to become a great Brazilian airline. The new Condor, registered on 1 December, was an echo of the Syndikat, with the same directors, and Fritz Hammer remained as director-general until 1930. The airline consolidated its position in 1928, opening a network of local routes from Salvador. Then on 5 February 1930 it filled in the gaps to complete a Brazilian coastal route from Rio Grande, in the far south, to Natal, on the northeastern corner of Brazil, strategically positioned for possible expansion across the South Atlantic.

On 18 September of that year, von Clausbruch, always in the vanguard of Condor's bent for exploration, started an inland route, from the rail terminus at Corumbá to Cuiabá. Both cities were in the then remote state of Mato Grosso, and the line was extended later to São Paulo, whence a special bus service connected the metropolis with Condor's coastal line at the nearby port city of Santos.

For the *Bandeirante* route to the Mato Grosso and for some segments of the main coastal route, Condor operated the ubiquitous **Junkers-F 13** as well as the Dornier Wals and some **Junkers-W 34**s. Later, Condor built up a sizable fleet of **Junkers-Ju 52/3m**'s for its main network, and also opened, with the smaller types, routes into the heart of Brazil and in the northeastern regions, much to the consternation of U.S. observers, who suspected ulterior motives.

One of Condor's most dramatic achievements was to import, by sea, in June and July 1939, two **Focke-Wulf Fw 200 Condor** four-engined landplanes. By this time Syndicato Condor had established itself as an important partner for both the German aircraft industry and for Lufthansa (see pages 36–39). Its influence on the development of air routes was of considerable importance to the economic development of Brazil. But with that nation favoring the Allied cause, a progressive transfer from German control began in 1941, and in due course, on 16 January 1943, the name was changed to **Serviços Aéreos Cruzeiro do Sul** (**Cruzeiro**), and henceforward the airline became completely Brazilian. By an irony of fate, it survives today as a subsidiary of VARIG, once its junior cousin.

## Iberian Bridgehead

Having staked a claim for traffic rights at the Brazilian end of the South Atlantic route, **Deutsche Luft Hansa** cleared the way for rights of passage along the route, with a European air presence in the Iberian peninsula. On 28 June 1927 it helped to form the **Sociedad Iberica de Aviación** (**Iberia**), an airline in which a Spanish business consortium held 51% and D.L.H. 49%; 24% of D.L.H.'s shares were through trustees. D.L.H. supplied three **Rohrbach Roland** aircraft and the technical support. Iberia began service from Madrid to Barcelona on 14 December 1927, so that with D.L.H. itself providing service from Marseilles to Barcelona from 5 January 1928, there was now a direct air link between the German and Spanish capitals.

The life of the first Iberia was brief. Service was discontinued after less than a year's operations, as the Spanish government, on which all airlines were dependent for subsidy, favored the idea of granting disbursements only to a unified Spanish airline, which was duly formed in 1929. Iberia survived, however, as a legal entity, and was revived by the Falangist forces during the Spanish Civil War and put back into operation in August 1937, with a fleet of **Junkers-Ju 52/3m**'s supplied by Lufthansa. Iberia bought seven of these aircraft on 1 July 1939, but the Spanish government bought all the Lufthansa shares on 7 June 1940. Iberia was completely nationalized on 14 August 1943.

*Ypiranga*, one of **Syndicato Condor**'s **Junkers-G 24**s, upriver in Brazil during the 1930s, and revolutionizing transport in the outback jungles.

**Fritz Hammer**, the driving force, as its marketing director, of the **Condor Syndikat**.

*Caiçara*, a **Junkers-Ju 52/3m** floatplane of **Syndicato Condor**, seen here at its base in Rio de Janeiro.

## THE FLEET OF SYNDICATO CONDOR

| Regist. No. | Const. No. | Name | Remarks |
|---|---|---|---|
| **Dornier Wal (1927)** | | | |
| P-BAAA | 34 | *Atlântico* | Ex-D-1012 Condor Syndikat; with VARIG June–July 1927; reregistered PP-CAA |
| P-BACA | 83 | *Santos Dumont* | Ex-D-1213; crashed 3 Dec. 1928 |
| P-BADA | 82 | *Bartholomeu de Gusmão* | Ex-D-1196; destroyed by fire 11 Feb. 1928 |
| P-BAIA | 106 | *Guanabara* | Ex-D-1443; reregistered PP-CAI |
| P-BALA | 107 | *Olinda* | Ex-D-1488 *Hamburg*; crashed |
| P-BAMA | 108 | *Jangadeiro* | Ex-D-1626 *Flensburg* |
| **Junkers-G 24 (1928)** | | | |
| P-BABA | 944 | *Ypiranga* | Ex-D-1287; with VARIG July–Sept. 1927; rereg. PP-CAB; crashed |
| P-BAHA | 921 | *Potyguar* | Ex-D-950 *Persephone*; crashed |
| P-BAQA | 961 | *Riachuelo* | Ex-D.L.H.; rereg. PP-CAS; crashed |
| **Junkers-F 13 (1928)** | | (All except P-BAFA crashed) | |
| P-BAFA | 750 | *Bandeirante* | Ex-D-367 *Turmschwalbe*; PP-CAF |
| P-BAGA | 644 | *Blumenau* | Ex-D-232 *Truthahn*; PP-CAG |
| P-BAJA | 584 | *Iguassú* | Ex-D-347 *Schwalbe*; PP-CAJ |
| P-BAKA | 725 | *Pirajá* | Ex-D-368 *Waldkauz*; PP-CAK |
| **Dornier Merkur (1930)** | | | |
| P-BAAB | 92 | *Gaúcho* | Ex-VARIG; reregistered PP-CAC |
| **Junkers-W 34 (1931)** | | | |
| P-BANA | 2593 | *Tiéte* | New; rereg. PP-CAN; crashed |
| P-BAOA | 2594 | *Tibagy* | "　　" PP-CAO |
| P-BAPA | 2595 | *Taquary* | "　　" PP-CAP; crashed |
| PP-CAR | 2711 | *Tapajoz* | New; renamed *Turyassu*; crashed |
| PP-CAW | 2791 | *Tacutu* | |
| PP-CBO | 2608 | *Tarauacá* | Ex-SEDTA (Ecuador) HC-SAA |
| **Junkers-Ju 46 (1934)** | | | |
| PP-CAU | 2720 | *Tocantins* | Ex-D-2271 *Bremen* (catapulted floatplane)/*Hamburg* (landplane); crashed |
| PP-CBK | 2744 | *Tingúa* | Ex-D-2744 *Jupiter*; crashed |

Syndicato Condor's **Junkers-Ju 52/3m** *Tupan* in the floating dock at the Cajú base in Rio de Janeiro.

| Focke-Wulf Fw Condor (1939) | | |
|---|---|---|
| PP-CBI | 2996 | *Abaitará* (crashed) |
| PP-CBJ | 2995 | *Arumani* |

| Focke-Wulf Fw 58 Weihe (1940) | | |
|---|---|---|
| PP-CBM | 3102 | *Aquiri* |
| PP-CBN | 3103 | *Cacuri* |

| Junkers-Ju 52/3m (1933) | | | | | | | | |
|---|---|---|---|---|---|---|---|---|
| PP-CAT | 4024 | *Anhangá* | PP-CBB | 4078 | *Tupan* | PP-CBG | 4075 | *Pagé* |
| PP-CAV | 4038 | *Caiçara* | PP-CBC | 5453 | *Guaracy* | PP-CBH | 5109 | *Moré* |
| PP-CAX | 4043 | *Curupira* | PP-CBD | 5478 | *Jacy* | PP-CBL | 5656 | *Los Andes* |
| PP-CAY | 4042 | *Marimbá* | PP-CBE | 5120 | *Yarassú* | PP-CBP | 6800 | *Ibaté* |
| PP-CAZ | 5261 | *Maipo* | PP-CBF | 4079 | *Aracy* | PP-CBR | 5053 | *Uirapurú* |
| PP-CBA | 5283 | *Aconcagua* | (PP-CAT, CAY, CBC crashed) | | | | | |

**Note** The date following the name of each type indicates the year of first service.

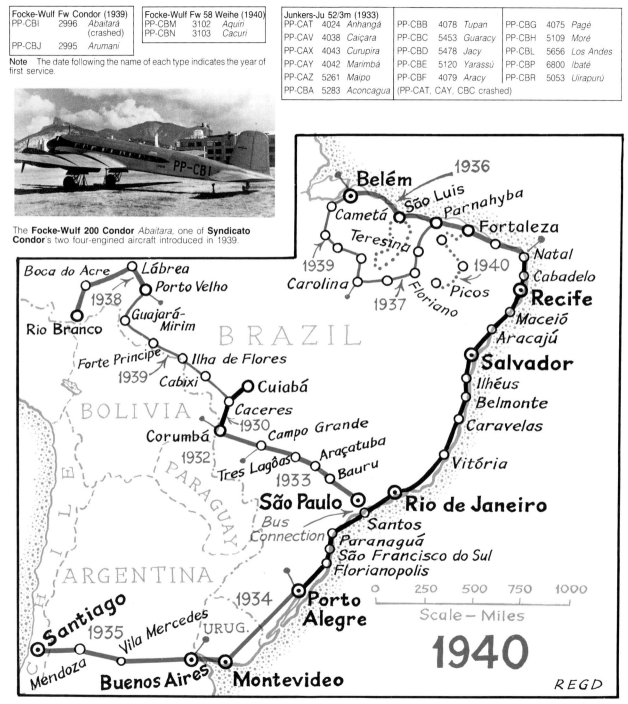

The **Focke-Wulf 200 Condor** *Abaitara*, one of **Syndicato Condor**'s two four-engined aircraft introduced in 1939.

# Early North Atlantic Surveys

## First Steps

As early as April 1927, a Junkers-F 13 floatplane made some flights while accompanying the Nord Deutscher Lloyd pleasure steamer *Lützow.* The aircraft was lowered into the water by the ship's crane. The experiments continued in the following year, using the *Stuttgart,* as sister ship, in this first cautious but innovative exploration of the possibilities of a floatplane partnership.

On 12–13 April 1928, Capt. Hermann Köhl, Baron von Hünefeld, and an Irish air officer, Commandant James Fitzmaurice, flew from Dublin to Greenley Island, Newfoundland, in a Junkers-W 33 landplane, the *Bremen.* This was the first nonstop east-west crossing of the North Atlantic by air and was a sharp reminder to the world that German aviation technology was still a force to be reckoned with.

## Preference for Flying Boats

Impressive as this single sortie was, German aviation opinion shared the contemporary view, also held by British, French, and American airline planners, that the future of transoceanic flight was with seaborne rather than landborne craft, and like the others, D.L.H. pursued various experiments with flying boats and floatplanes. In particular, **Pan American Airways**, working meanwhile from North America, promoted an expedition in 1933 to explore a route to Europe by the northern fringes of the Atlantic. Leading this reconnaissance, named after its depot ship, the *Jelling*, was Charles Lindbergh, flying his famous Lockheed Sirius floatplane, the *Tingmissartoq*, in an aerial circumnavigation of the Atlantic. During the first half of this effort, he was retracing the steps taken by a German aviator who had already covered that part of the ocean three times in successive years.

## Wolfgang von Gronau

Possibly because the world's eyes were focused upon the idea of record-breaking nonstop Atlantic flights, the achievements of one of Germany's finest pioneering aviators, **Wolfgang von Gronau**, are not so well known as those of Lindbergh, Chamberlin, Earhart, Köhl, Mollison, and others. He was the director of the Deutsche Verkehrsflieger-Schule (D.V.S.) seaplane flying schools at Warnemünde and List, on the island of Sylt. His route was by the "stepping-stones" across the northern rim of the Atlantic, flying the relatively shorter stages that were far more practicable for commercial aircraft, which had to carry payloads as well as pilots.

From 18 to 26 August 1930, he flew a **Dornier Wal**, with a crew of three, from List, on the island of Sylt, to New York, 4670 miles, in 47 flying hours, or nine days' elapsed time. From 8 August to 1 September 1931, he flew another Wal from Sylt to Chicago and on to New York again, this time crossing the inhospitable Greenland icecap en route. For the third time, from 22 to 26 July 1932, he followed a similar route from Sylt to Montreal, and then continued across Canada around the world via Alaska and southeastern and southern Asia, to arrive in Friedrichshafen on 10 November and finally to reach List on 23 November.

## Possession Is Nine Points of the Law

For all the German technological leadership, the aspiring flag carrier, **Deutsche Luft Hansa**, was handicapped in its quest for a passage across the Atlantic. Territorial sovereignty was a vital factor during the competitive years of the late 1920s and the 1930s. In the north, **Iceland**, together with

Denmark (by its control over the Faeroe Islands and Greenland), could provide vital staging points and safe haven for transatlantic air services; and the aviation powers, especially Germany and the United States, were anxious to obtain traffic and operational rights. Similarly, **Portugal** ruled over some precious island groups in the Atlantic Ocean farther south, and the Azores, particularly, were to play a key role in the battle for the airline conquest of what was to become the world's most important single air corridor.

## Icelandic Outpost

If an air link across the North Atlantic was to be established by the northern fringe of islands, a base in Iceland was an essential staging point. During the 1920s—and indeed for another two decades—almost all the fishing communities in the fjords around the barren island were accessible only by coastal ships. There were only a few miles of paved roads, and none was passable in the winter. Accordingly, the prospect of air service was very attractive to the Icelandic government.

On 1 May 1928 it formed **Flugfélag Islands**, with Richard Walter as director, to operate seasonal services, using a **Junkers-F 13** floatplane, the *Súlan,* leased from **Deutsche Luft Hansa**, and opened routes around the country during the all-too-brief summer of this northern land. Further services were opened in 1929, and a second F 13, the *Veidibjallan,* was added. By 1931, a third floatplane, the *Alftin,* had reinforced the fleet, but the rigors of the Icelandic climate and sea conditions had taken their toll. With only the *Alftin* left, Flugfélag Islands made its last scheduled flight on 3 August 1931.

The little airline had not been able to operate economically and owed money to D.L.H., which, however, wrote off its losses. One result of this pioneering operation was that a modest floatplane base had been established at Reykjavik. The German airline also reminded the Danish Minister for Iceland (which at that time had not achieved complete independence) that it was entitled to "most favored nation" preference, because of past services rendered. This was long before the International Civil Aviation Organization (ICAO) was formed in 1944, to set up the Five Freedoms of the Air; but there is little doubt that by its initiative in exploring all the options, Deutsche Luft Hansa could have had them for the asking.

No doubt the accumulated experience of the little short-lived Icelandic airline was put to good use by Wolfgang von Gronau when he made his Atlantic flights in 1930, 1931, and 1932.

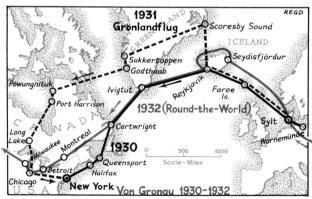

**Wolfgang von Gronau's** pioneering flights across the Atlantic.

Key staging point for transatlantic airline aspirations during the 1920s and 1930s was Iceland. Deutsche Luft Hansa was closely associated with an early airline venture in that country.

# Ocean Liner Interlude

## Trans-Ocean Rivalry

During the latter 1920s, **Norddeutscher Lloyd** had considered trans-ocean commercial flying, regarding the Atlantic as its own preserve. In 1927 its rival, the **Hamburg-Amerika Linie**, supported a plan to fly the Atlantic with a Rohrbach Robbe flying boat, with Ernst Udet as pilot and Kurt Tank as crew member. Both N.D.L. and HAPAG opposed the idea of D.L.H. entering their arena but (as he had done in 1926 with the original Aero Lloyd-Junkers merger) Ernst Brandenburg at the Air Ministry compelled the shipping lines to cooperate with the airline.

## The Experiment

On 22 July 1929 the first German ship-to-land airmail flight took place about 300 miles east of New York. A **Heinkel He 12** floatplane, owned by the shipping company and flown by **Deutsche Luft Hansa** crews, was launched by catapult from the Norddeutscher Lloyd passenger liner *Bremen*, covering the distance in 2½ hours, and saving about half a day. On the ship's return journeys, the He 12 was catapulted from a point near Cherbourg, to fly to Southampton, Amsterdam, Bremerhaven, or sometimes Cologne.

During the following year, eleven such catapulted flights were made. The *Bremen*'s sister ship, the *Europa,* was similarly equipped, the He 12 supplemented initially by the larger **Heinkel He 58** and, in 1932, by the **Junkers-Ju 46**. Until 1935, when an improved system came into use, an average of 17 flights were made each year. These and subsequent developments are described and tabulated on page 52.

Although the total timesaving was not significant, the airmail program had great promotional as well as operational value. The launchings were witnessed by an appreciative and admiring audience of ocean voyagers, many of whom carried a great deal of weight in the corridors of political and industrial power; and the events received much attention from the press. Also, several of the pilots, such as Blankenburg and Graf Schack, gained much experience for the more ambitious catapult flights from the special depot ships over the South and North Atlantic (pages 38–39 and 52–53).

Wolfgang von Gronau made three transatlantic flights by the northern perimeter route in **Dornier Wal**s in 1930, 1931, and 1932.

The first practical experiment in coordinating air and shipping operations was with a **Junkers-F 13** taking off from the sea alongside the Norddeutscher Lloyd *Lützow* in 1927.

Four **Junkers-Ju 46**s were used on both the *Bremen* and the *Europa* from 1932 to 1935.

The **Heinkel He 58** was used with the *Europa* from 1930

The **Heinkel He 12** *New York* was **Nord Deutscher Lloyd**'s first aircraft to be catapulted from an ocean liner, the famous *Bremen,* in 1929.

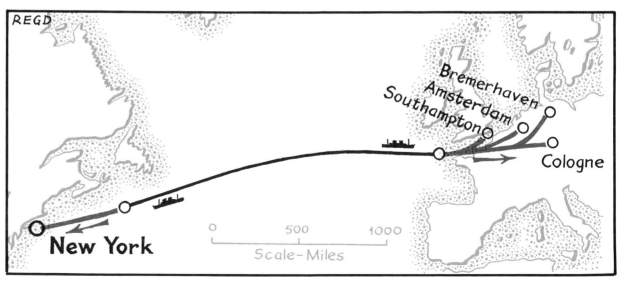

# Preparations for the South Atlantic

## A Formidable Rival

In its ambition to develop an air service across the South Atlantic, **Deutsche Luft Hansa** faced a determined opponent in Marcel Bouilloux-Lafont, a French businessman with substantial interests in Latin America who had purchased the famous French airline Lignes Latécoère, changed its name to **Aéropostale**, and established a legend.

On 1 March 1928, Aéropostale started a mail service from Paris to Buenos Aires, in which the ocean crossing was made by a fleet of submarine-chasers leased from the French navy. Airmail from Paris to Buenos Aires took about eight days, of which 4½ days were by sea. In 1930, the end-to-end time was shortened by about two days when specially built Aéropostale ships replaced the obsolete naval vessels.

Then, on 12–13 May 1930, on one of the most notable flights in commercial airline history, the crew of Jean Mermoz, Jean Dabry, and Léopold Gimié flew an Aéropostale Latécoère 28 floatplane from St. Louis, Senegal, to Natal, Brazil, in 21 hr 15 min. Mail dispatched from France on the morning of Sunday, 11 May, reached the Argentine capital on the next Wednesday evening. Although only an experimental flight, Mermoz's epic achievement was a portent of future French capability.

Fortunately for the German side of this commercial rivalry, the French government condoned a politico-industrial intrigue designed to discredit Bouilloux-Lafont, who was hounded from the leadership of a great airline, which itself fell prey to the jackals who had intrigued against him. On 31 March 1931, Aéropostale was forced into *liquidation judiciaire*, leaving the way clear for German enterprise.

A **Dornier Wal**, **Syndicato Condor**'s *Olinda*, makes the mail transfer to the *Cap Arcona* in 1930, off the island of Fernando de Noronha, Brazil.

## First German South Atlantic Sortie

The German version of the air-ship-air service employed regular ocean liners, which, though not specialized like Aéropostale's fleet, did the job very well. On 22 March 1930 the first link-up was completed off the island of Fernando do Noronha, when mail was transferred from the **Syndicato Condor Dornier Wal** *Jangadeiro* to the flagship of the Hamburg Südamerika Linie, the *Cap Arcona*. Alternating with the sister ship *Cap Polonio,* from Fernando do Noronha to Las Palmas, Canary Islands, where *Deutsche Luft Hansa* took over, this service lasted for three years, until superseded by another bold experiment (page 38).

**Flugkapitän Cramer von Clausbruch**, ace of the D.L.H.-Condor corps of South Atlantic pilots.

Deutsche Luft Hansa · Berlin · Stuttgart · Barcelona · Seville · Las Palmas

The Ocean Liner Connection 1930

Cap Arcona and Cap Polonio

AFRICA

Berlin~Rio in 11 days Air Mail only

Natal · Fernando de Noronha · Recife · Dornier Wal · Salvador · Rio de Janeiro

BRAZIL

Syndicato Condor

Scale-Miles 0 500 1000 1500

REGD

| Const. No. | Registration No. Original | Registration No. 1934 | Name | Year Deliv. | Remarks |
|---|---|---|---|---|---|
| **Do J Wal** | | | | | |
| 41 | D-861 | — | Hai | 1925 | Ex-D.A. Lloyd; to D.V.S. 1929 |
| 42 | D-862 | — | Sägefisch | 1925 | Ex-D.A. Lloyd; cert. withdrawn 1933 |
| 43 | D-863 | — | Thunfisch | 1925 | Ex-D.A. Lloyd; to D.V.S. 1929 |
| 44 | D-864 | — | Hecht | 1925 | Ex-D.A. Lloyd; totally damaged 1930 |
| 82 | D-1196 | — | — | 1927 | To S. Amer., written off 1928 |
| 83 | D-1213 | — | — | 1927 | To S. Amer., written off 1928 |
| 105 | D-1397 | — | Kiel | 1928 | *Lübeck* until 1930 |
| 106 | D-1443 | — | Lübeck | 1928 | To Synd. Condor (P-BALÁ, PP-CAI., *Guanabara*) 1928 |
| 109 | D-1647 | — | Bremer-haven | 1928 | |
| 110 | D-1648 | D-APYL | Helgoland | 1928 | To D.V.S. 1934 |
| 107 | D-1488 | — | Hamburg | 1929 | To Synd. Condor (P-BALÁ, *Olinda*) 1929; written off 1931 |
| 108 | D-1626 | D-ARIP | Flensburg | 1929 | |
| 34 | D-1012 | — | Atlántico | 1930 | Ex-VARIG (ex-Synd. Condor P-BAAA, PP-CAA) |
| **Do J II Wal (8-Ton)** | | | | | |
| 185 | D-2068 | — | Passat | 1931 | To D.V.S. 1934 |
| 210 | D-2069 | D-ABIR | Monsun | 1931 | Sold 1938 |
| **Do J II Wal (10-Ton)** | | | | | |
| 237 | D-2399 | D-AKER | Taifun | 1933 | |
| 299 | — | D-ADYS | Tornado | 1934 | Lost in South Atlantic 1936 |
| 297 | — | D-AFAR | Samum | 1934 | To R.L.M. 1937 |
| 298 | — | D-AGAT | Boreas | 1934 | To R.L.M. 1940 |
| 300 | — | D-ALOX | Passat | 1935 | To R.L.M. 1940 |
| 676 | — | D-AKYM | Mistral | 1936 | Sold 1938 |
| **Do R Super Wal** | | | | | |
| 147 | D-1255 | | Narwal | 1927 | Transferred |
| 143 | D-1337 | | Pottwal | 1928 | |
| 146 | D-1447 | | Graf Zeppelin | 1928 | Transferred |
| 172 | D-1500 | | Blauwal | 1928 | Renamed *Eckener* |
| 190 | D-1761 | | Rügen | 1928 | |
| 192 | D-1774 | | Fehmarn | | |

# Dornier Do J Wal
## 10 seats • 91 mph

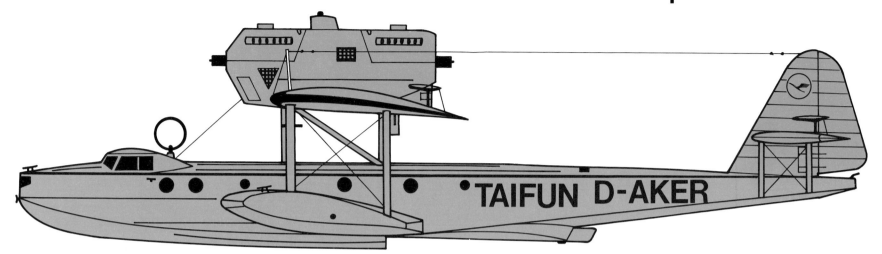

Hispano-Suiza (300 hp) × 2 • 12,570 lb max. gross takeoff weight • 500 statute miles range

## The First Great Flying Boat

No flying boat of the interwar period was produced in such large numbers or was deployed to so many places, from Brindisi to Buenos Aires, from Stockholm to Shanghai, as the **Dornier Do J Wal**. It first flew on 6 November 1922, and when production ceased 14 years later, about 300 had been built, in about 20 different versions, and using almost every engine of acceptable power rating. Boldly defying the restrictions of the Treaty of Versailles, the Wal was first produced in Italy, by Construzione Meccaniche S.A. (C.M.A.S.A.) in Pisa, and later by Piaggio. The Italians produced about half of the Wals built.

Wals from Pisa went into airline service in Italy, Germany, Colombia, and Brazil. **Deutscher Aero Lloyd** had four and put them on the trans-Baltic Danzig-Stockholm route in 1925. The Italian airlines had 26 altogether. Kawasaki built them in Japan, to be used by N.K.K.K., the Japanese airline, on the route to China. Production lines started in 1928 in Spain and the Netherlands, and finally, in 1932, back where it was designed, at Freidrichshafen.

Here the larger and more powerful **Super Wal**, with a cabin accommodating up to 19 passengers instead of ten, had been produced in 1926. Most Super Wals had four engines, mounted in tandem in the two nacelles above the wing.

In 1933, the **"8-Ton" Wal**, with a bigger wing and more powerful B.M.W. engines, used the extra permitted weight to carry enough fuel for experimental flights across the South Atlantic (pages 36, 38, 39), while in 1933 the **"10-Ton" Wal** added even more range and provided—at last—an enclosed cockpit for the pilots of that pioneering enterprise.

The Wal won the respect of all the crews who flew in her. In 1925 two of them gave the United States a shock by demonstrating a feasible air service to link the two Americas (page 29); in 1926 Major Ramon Franco and his crew flew from southern Spain to Buenos Aires, via the Canary Islands, to make only the second South Atlantic crossing. From 1930 to 1932 von Gronau took them on the northern route across the North Atlantic. And Roald Amundsen used Wals in his attempt to fly to the North Pole. The Dornier Wal deserves its place in the aircraft hall of fame.

Length 57 feet • Span 74 feet • Height 18 feet

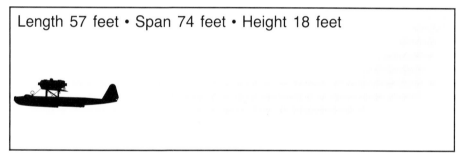

THE DORNIER WALS

| Type | First Flight Date | Dimensions | | Pass. Seats | Engines | | | Max. Gross TOW (lb) | Cruise Speed (mph) | Normal Range (st. miles) | Approx. No. Built |
| | | Length | Span | | No. | Type | Hp (each) | | | | |
|---|---|---|---|---|---|---|---|---|---|---|---|
| Do J Wal | 6 Nov. 1922 | 56'7" | 73'10" | 10 | 2 | Hispano-Suiza[1] | 300 | 12,570 | 91 | 500 | ⎫ |
| Do J II Wal (8-Ton) | 1932 | 59'8" | 76'1" | — | 2 | B.M.W. VI[1] | 600 | 17,640 | 120 | 1000 | ⎬ 300 |
| Do J II Wal (10-Ton) | 3 May 1933 | 59'8" | 89'3" | — | 2 | B.M.W. VI[1] | 690 | 22,050 | 114 | 2000 | ⎭ |
| Do R2 Super Wal | 30 Sept. 1926 | 77'5" | 93'6" | 19 | 2 | R-R Condor[2] | 650 | 27,780 | 109 | 600 | ⎫ ⎬ 20 |
| Do R4 Super Wal | 15 Sept. 1928 | 77'5" | 93'6" | 19 | 4 | Bristol Jupiter[3] | 480 | 28,880 | 116 | 600 | ⎭ |

[1]Other engines used included Rolls-Royce Eagle IX (360 hp), B.M.W. VI (600), Farman 12 We (500), FIAT A24R (750), Hispano-Suiza 12 Lb (600), Lorraine-Dietrich 12 Ed (450), Napier Lion (450), Siemens Sh 20 (560), Bristol Jupiter, and many others. [2]Other engines included Packard 3A-2500 (800 hp) and Napier Lion (450). [3]Also used Pratt & Whitney Hornet (575 hp).

# South Atlantic Mail Service

## The Depot Ship Idea

In 1933 one of air transport's most enterprising pioneer ideas for furthering long-distance airmail services was put to the test at Bathurst, in British Gambia, West Africa. The **Deutsche Luft Hansa (D.L.H.) Dornier Wal** *Monsun* made an experimental catapult-assisted takeoff from the specially equipped depot ship *Westfalen* (page 39) and alighted on the "drag-sail" (see opposite) in the open sea near Bathurst on 2 June. Two days later, Capt. Jobst von Studnitz flew the *Monsun* from Bathurst to the *Westfalen,* now at its rendezvous about 400 miles to the southwest. Hauled on board, refueled, and catapulted off again on 6 June, the *Monsun* arrived at Natal the next day.

## A Daunting Experience

The routine South Atlantic airmail service that developed made severe demands on the pilots, all of whom had qualified to receive their License for High-seas Navigation. The normal cruising altitude was only about 30 feet, as the ground effect (if this term can be applied to the sea) increased the speed by about 10 mph. Capt. Cramer von Clausbruch claimed that the ocean transfer involved a "double-refueling"—a strong drink for the pilot as well as one for the aircraft. Little wonder: the 38,000-hp Heinkel pneumatic catapult launched the aircraft in about two seconds.

## First Transocean Airmail Service

The **Pan American Airways** transpacific *China Clipper* inaugural flight from San Francisco to Manila on 22–29 November 1935 was undoubtedly the outstanding step in the history of airline ocean conquest. But the *Graf Zeppelin* had already started regular airship services across the South Atlantic during the summer seasons (page 40), while on 3 February 1934, a **D.L.H.** Heinkel He 70 took the mail from Berlin to Seville, whence a Junkers 52/3m carried it to Bathurst. On 7 February the Wal *Taifun* took the mail on to Natal, having been catapulted from the *Westfalen,* which had steamed westward from Bathurst. The **Syndicato Condor** Junkers-W 34 *Tieté* then reached Buenos Aires in a further 26 hr 51 min from Natal. On the eastbound flights, the Wal made a rendezvous with the depot ship, which had continued to steam farther westward.

The service was completely successful. On 30 March 1935, after the introduction of night services on the overland segments of the route, the D.L.H.-Condor weekly schedule was speeded up to three days to Rio de Janeiro, with an extra half a day to Buenos Aires. On 7 October of that year, Condor extended its route to Santiago, Chile, and airmail delivery was now possible from the German capital to the Pacific Ocean in four days. Simultaneously, the German schedules were alternated with those of Air France, to eliminate wasteful competition.

## The Dornier Do 26

Described by John Stroud as "probably the cleanest flying boat ever produced," the **Dornier Do 26** was ordered by D.L.H.—by then the name was Deutsche Lufthansa—for nonstop Lisbon–New York service. It was powered by Junkers Jumo diesel engines, which were mounted in tandem pairs, and the rear ones could be elevated on takeoff to avoid water injection from spray. They made 18 mail crossings on the South Atlantic route, and *Seeadler* made a remarkable flight in February 1939 to carry relief supplies to Chile after an earthquake. But the Do 26 never went into regular service, as intended.

The **Dornier Wal** *Taifun* is launched from the *Westfalen/Schwabenland.*

The **Dornier Wal** *Monsun,* the first to make the catapult-assisted South Atlantic crossing, is hauled aboard the *Westfalen.*

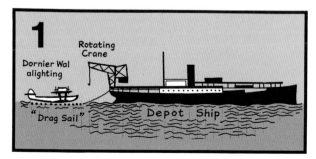

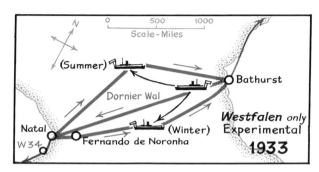

This map shows the close scheduling cooperation necessary to ensure the regularity of the German South Atlantic mail service in the 1930s.

### THE DORNIER DO 26

| Const. No. | Regist. No. | Name | Remarks |
|---|---|---|---|
| 792 | D-AGNT | *Seeadler* | Prototype; first flight 21 May 1938 |
| | D-AWDS | *Seefalke* | Completed 1939 |
| | D-ASRA | *Seemöwe* | Completed after start of World War II; delivered to Luftwaffe with three others and carried supplies to Narvik, Norway; only six built |

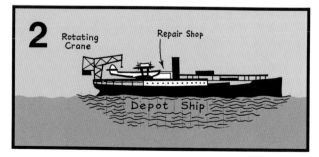

# The Catapult Ships

**The *Westfalen*** Converted merchant ship (ex-N.D.L.); 5243 tons; length 410 feet

Pioneer of the ingenious fleet of Lufthansa catapult-equipped depot ships was the *Westfalen*. Its first trials took place on 29 May 1933, using the Heinkel K-6 pneumatic catapult. In subsequent months the operational system was perfected. The sequence of the transfer, using the "drag-sail" to assist the Dornier Wal's alighting on the high seas, is illustrated in the sequence of drawings below.

**The *Schwabenland*** Diesel motor ship (ex-Schwartzenfels); 8188 tons; length 468 feet

Improvements were made later in the spring of 1934. The *Schwabenland* was stationed off the African coast near Bathurst, while the *Westfalen* was moved to a location near the island of Fernando de Noronha, off the coast of Brazil. This coincided with the introduction of the **"10-Ton" Wal**, an improved version, with longer range. With two depot ships, one at each end of the transatlantic crossing, takeoffs from the ocean were no longer necessary, and greater payloads of fuel and mail were possible.

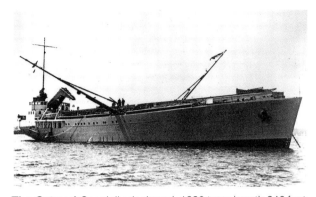

**The *Ostmark*** Specially designed; 1280 tons; length 246 feet

In 1936, energetically pursuing this method of achieving the necessary combination of range and payload to achieve transocean range (equally elusive for aircraft manufacturers all over the world), Deutsche Lufthansa introduced another depot ship, the *Ostmark*. In spite of its smaller size, it was even more efficient in recovering and launching the aircraft. The orthodox centrally positioned foremast was replaced by a pair of masts, one each side. These could be lowered sideways so as to allow free space for the launch. By this device, longer catapult rails could be installed, permitting heavier loads on the Dornier Wals (see page 52).

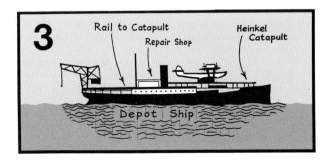

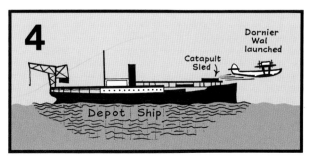

**D.L.H.**

**Syndicato Condor**

**The *Friesenland*** Specially designed; 5434 tons; length 452 feet

This fine ship incorporated all the innovative design characteristics learned by the operating experience of the previous ships. It was deployed on the North Atlantic in 1937 and could handle the larger **Blohm & Voss Ha 139** and **Dornier 26** aircraft, which were too much for the *Ostmark*. At the end of the North Atlantic trials, the *Friesenland* transferred to the South Atlantic.

Incidentally, the aircraft were catapulted from the bows of the *Westfalen* and the *Ostmark* but from the sterns of the *Schwabenland* and the *Friesenland*.

# South Atlantic Airship Service

## Experimental and Proving Flights

In 1930 the *Graf Zeppelin* made a trial flight from Friedrichshafen to Recife (then called Pernambuco) at the northeastern corner of South America. It arrived there on 22 May and three days later was safely moored at the Campo dos Affonsos field at Rio de Janeiro. Much of the mail consignment went to the German communities in southern Brazil. The next year, the *Graf* made three more round trips and the **Luftschiffbau Zeppelin** was confident enough to begin scheduled service on a limited commercial basis.

## Transatlantic Scheduled Passenger Service

Between April and October 1932, the *Graf Zeppelin* flew nine round trips. The giant airship could accommodate 20 passengers in ten two-berth cabins, for which privilege individual one-way tickets cost about $450 at the prevailing rate of exchange—about $5000 in today's money. The southbound flights took almost exactly three days and the northbound ones rather more than 3½ days. Depending on conditions, the flights were made either nonstop from Friedrichshafen to Recife or with a stop at Seville, Spain.

On 22 March 1935 the Zeppelin company joined with the Reichsluftfahrtministerium (R.L.M.), together with **Deutsche Lufthansa**, to become **Deutsche Zeppelin-Reederei**.

As the accompanying table shows, the service frequency was increased during the mid-1930s and in 1936 the flights were extended to Rio de Janeiro, having previously terminated at Recife. The Brazilian government had built a handsome terminal at Santa Cruz, near Rio, reacting no doubt to the popular belief at the time that airships, not airplanes, were to be the answer to the transocean air service problem.

## A Brief Claim to Fame

The Luftschiffbau Zeppelin's flagship could correctly claim to have started the world's first transocean passenger air service open to the general public. The *Graf Zeppelin's* 1932 inauguration preceded the **Pan American** transpacific *China Clipper* service by four years. The airship schedule was admittedly seasonal, operating during the summer months only, and it was less frequent. But its 90-mph average speed was not unacceptably slower than the **Martin M-130**'s 130 mph, it had range to spare, and it carried an average of about 15 passengers per flight, whereas the Martin was normally restricted to only three or four on the critical San Francisco–Honolulu segment.

Thus the airship case still seemed to be valid in 1936. But the dream was shattered when the *Hindenburg* holocaust at Lakehurst, New Jersey, put an abrupt end to all the hopes and aspirations. The *Graf Zeppelin* was actually en route

The *Graf Zeppelin* at Berlin, Staaken airfield.

back from South America on the fateful day in May 1937, although the captain did not inform the passengers of the tragedy until arrival. It was a sad end to a great enterprise.

### GERMAN SCHEDULED AIRSHIP SERVICES ACROSS THE ATLANTIC 1930–1936

| Year | South Atlantic | | North Atlantic | |
|---|---|---|---|---|
| | Airship | One-Way Flights | Airship | One-Way Flights |
| Luftschiffbau Zeppelin | | | | |
| 1930 | *Graf Zeppelin* | 2[1] | | |
| 1931 | " " | 6[1] | | |
| 1932 | " " | 18 | — | — |
| 1933 | " " | 18 | | |
| 1934 | " " | 24 | | |
| TOTAL | | 68 | | — |

### DEUTSCHE ZEPPELIN-REEDEREI

| | | | | |
|---|---|---|---|---|
| 1935 | *Graf Zeppelin* | 32 | — | — |
| 1936 | *Graf Zeppelin* | 22 | | |
| | *Hindenburg* | 12 | *Hindenburg* | 32 |
| 1937 | *Graf Zeppelin* | 2 | | |
| | *Hindenburg* | 2 | *Hindenburg* | 1[2] |
| TOTALS | | 70 | | 33 |

Grand Total: 163 scheduled flights

[1]Experimental and proving flights. [2]Destroyed by fire on arrival at Lakehurst, New Jersey, on 6 May 1937.

The dining room of the *Graf Zeppelin*.

The *Graf Zeppelin* in the shed at Lakehurst, New Jersey.

Lakehurst — Connections throughout U.S.A. by American Airlines

Connections throughout Europe by Deutsche Lufthansa

1936 (one westbound in 1937)

Frankfurt Friedrichshafen

*Hindenburg* 1936 (one round trip in 1937)

Seville — Barcelona

**GERMAN AIRSHIP ROUTES 1931-37**

Luftschiffbau Zeppelin GmbH until 22 March 1935
Deutsche Zeppelin Reederei 22 March 1935–April 1936

*Graf Zeppelin* 1931–37

AFRICA

Berlin–Rio in 4 days

1936

BRAZIL

Connections to the south and west by Syndicato Condor

Recife (Terminus until 1936)

0  500  1000  1500
Scale-Miles

Rio de Janeiro

REGD

# Zeppelin LZ 127 *Graf Zeppelin*

## 20 seats (in 2-berth cabins) • 72 mph

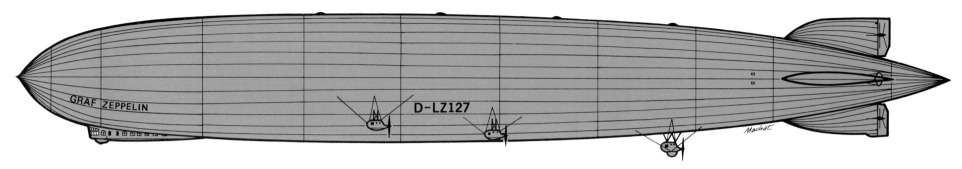

Maybach VL II (550 hp) × 5 • 150 tons max. gross lift • 7000 statute miles range

## The Case for the Airship

During the formative years of long-range air transport, the lighter-than-air dirigible airship was considered to be the logical solution by many specialists. Outweighing the serious disadvantages of enormous size, high operating costs (mainly because of the large air crew and the small army of ground crew required), and serious vulnerability to fire and weather, the dirigible's range of several thousand miles was far beyond the wildest dreams of any designer of heavier-than-air machines, either landplanes or seaplanes.

## The Thoroughbred

In 1920 Dr. Hugo Eckener had taken over from Alfred Colsman as head of the Zeppelin company. He received unintentional encouragement from the United States, which directed the construction by Luftschiffbau Zeppelin of the airship LZ 124 *Los Angeles,* delivered across the Atlantic in a nonstop flight in 1924. Eckener then seized his chance in May 1926 when the Paris Agreement lifted Allied restrictions on aircraft manufacture in Germany. He appealed to the German public to subscribe to the construction of a giant airship, and the government matched these funds. Work started early in 1927, and LZ 127 *Graf Zeppelin* made its maiden flight on 18 September 1928. Uniquely, the five 550-hp Maybach engines were fueled by *Blaugas* as well as by gasoline, and almost a million cubic feet of this gaseous concoction were carried in gas cells separated from the huge hydrogen cells above.

The great airship made its first Atlantic crossing in October 1928 and proceeded to attract newspaper headlines worldwide, as it made a series of demonstration, publicity, and revenue-earning flights within Europe, to the Middle East, and in 1929, most spectacularly, around the world with only three stops. It then went into service to South America (see opposite page).

Exact figures covering its ability to operate at a profit are not available, but shrewd calculations by P. W. Brooks, an impartial authority, suggest that the hidden subsidy assumed to be included in the balance sheet was not an unacceptable proportion of the revenue needed to cover costs. Of course, the tariffs were extremely high; the *Graf Zeppelin's* economics were as impractical as those of the Concorde today.

### Length 774 feet • Diameter 100 feet

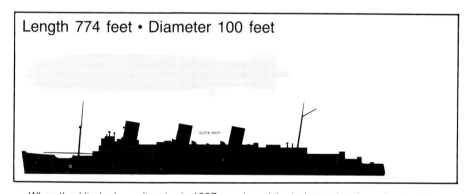

When the *Hindenburg* disaster in 1937 convinced the industry that the safer, but heavier, helium gas was essential, the *Graf Zeppelin* was retired immediately. But it would not have been able to operate with helium, even if it had been available. And so, in March 1940, it was broken up at Frankfurt, the duralumin no doubt being used for more urgent purposes.

**Dr. Hugo Eckener**, whose pioneering work and determination came so close to fulfillment.

# Aircraft Large and Small

## A Motley Crowd

"All things bright and beautiful, all creatures great and small," runs the popular hymn. **Deutsche Luft Hansa**'s fleet at the start of 1932 contained many creatures. One was great but most were small. Few could be described as bright and even fewer as beautiful, even by their creators. The two Junkers-G 38s (opposite page) were unrepresentative of the fleet as a whole, because of their size.

The Dornier Wal's elegant lines were remarkable for an aircraft that had first flown in 1922 (page 37), but most of the fleet looked a little outmoded, if not actually primitive. The Junkers-F 13s were perhaps exceptional. Together with their three-engined cousins, the Junkers-G 24s and the Rohrbach Rolands, they did most of the work. Many types were almost museum pieces, as can be discerned from the table opposite, spending almost all their time on the ground.

## Time for a Change

Aesthetics and age apart, the most important aspect of the fleet was that, of the 173 aircraft, 126—almost three-quarters of the total—were single-engined. Fortunately reinforcements were imminent, as the Junkers Flugzeugwerke was about to deliver an aircraft that was to become a legend, as described on pages 44–47.

The **Dornier Do X** was a huge 12-engined flying boat which was much publicized but never a commercial success.

This picture of the **Junkers-G 38** shows the large windows in the wing.

### THE D.L.H. MESSERSCHMITT FLEET

| Const. No. | Regist. No. Original | Regist. No. 1934 | Name | Year Deliv. | Remarks |
|---|---|---|---|---|---|
| **M 20**[1] | | | | | |
| 392 | D-1480 | D-UFON | Franken | 1928 | Lost while chartered to Luftwaffe 1941 |
| 421 | D-1676 | D-UDAL | Schwaben | 1929 | Destroyed during WWII, 1943 |
| 442 | D-1928 | — | Rhein-pfalz | 1930 | Destroyed by fire April 1931 |
| 540 | D-2005 | D-UNAH | Odenwald | 1931 | Totally damaged 1936 |
| 541 | D-2206 | — | Spessart | 1931 | Scrapped April 1932 |
| 542 | D-2025 | D-UKUM | Wester-wald | 1931 | Destroyed during WWII, 1942 |
| 543 | D-2026 | D-UREK | Schwarz-wald | 1931 | Destroyed during WWII, 1942 |
| 544 | D-2285 | D-UVOK | Sauerland | 1932 | Destroyed during WWII, 1942 |
| 545 | D-2290 | D-UXYN | Fläming | 1932 | Totally damaged 1937 |
| 546 | D-2341 | D-UKIP | Harz | 1932 | To VARIG (PP-VAK) 1937 |
| 547 | D-2349 | D-UMOK | Rhön | 1932 | Destroyed during WWII, 1942 |
| 548 | D-2352 | D-UJAR | Eifel | 1932 | Destroyed during WWII, 1943 |
| 549 | D-2359 | D-UHEN | Hunsrück | 1932 | Lost while chartered to Luftwaffe 1941 |
| **M 28** | | | | | |
| 527 | D-2059 | — | — | 1932 | Written off 1935 |

**Note** The first two M 20s were designated M 20a, the others M 20b.

The **Messerschmitt Me 20**, first delivered in 1928, was still serving **Deutsche Lufthansa** during world War II until 1943.

### THE FOCKE-WULF MÖWE SERIES

| Const. No. | Regist. No. Original | Regist. No. 1934 | Name | Year Deliv. | Remarks |
|---|---|---|---|---|---|
| **A 17 Möwe** | | | | | |
| 42 | D-1342 | — | Emden | 1928 | To D.V.S. Sept. 1933 |
| 43 | D-1358 | — | Aurich | 1928 | To D.V.S 1933 |
| 44 | D-1367 | — | Leer | 1928 | To D.V.S. Dec. 1933 |
| 45 | D-1380 | — | Olden-burg | 1928 | Destroyed Feb. 1933 |
| 46 | D-1388 | — | Stade | 1928 | Destroyed Dec. 1933 |
| 47 | D-1403 | — | Lüneburg | 1928 | To D.V.S. Sept. 1933 |
| 48 | D-1416 | — | Osna-brück | 1928 | To D.V.S. Sept. 1933 |
| 49 | D-1430 | D-UTOS | Hannover | 1928 | Written off 1936 |
| 50 | D-1444 | D-UNIK | Münster | 1928 | To D.V.S. Dec. 1933 |
| 51 | D-1484 | — | Bielefeld | 1928 | To D.V.S. Dec. 1933 |
| **A 29 Möwe** | | | | | |
| 61 | D-1757 | — | Friesland | 1929 | To D.V.S. Sept. 1929 |
| 62 | D-1775 | — | Jeverland | 1929 | Destroyed Aug. 1931 |
| 58 | D-1867 | D-ULIP | Westfalen | 1930 | To D.V.S. Sept. 1934 |
| 63 | D-1922 | — | Saarland | 1930 | Destroyed 1930 |
| **A 38 Möwe** | | | | | |
| 108 | D-2073 | — | Bück-eburg | 1931 | To D.V.S. June 1934 |
| 109 | D-2082 | D-UPIN | Hessen | 1931 | To D.V.S. Feb. 1934 |
| 110 | D-2107 | — | Lippe | 1931 | To D.V.S. March 1934 |
| 111 | D-2114 | D-UTAN | Thüringen | 1931 | To D.V.S. June 1934 |

**Abbrev.** D.V.S.: Deutsche Verkehrsfliegerschule

This **A 17** version of the **Focke-Wulf Möwe** series complemented the larger Junkers types during the 1920s and early 1930s.

# Junkers-G 38    34 seats • 112 mph

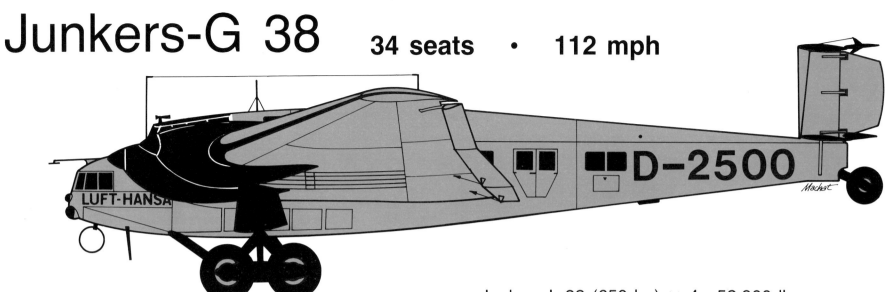

LUFT-HANSA    D-2500

Junkers-L 88 (650 hp) × 4 • 52,900 lb max. gross takeoff weight • 1200 statute miles range

## Size at any Cost

During the 1920s, German aircraft constructors seemed to be fascinated by large aircraft. In 1928, the *Graf Zeppelin* airship created the impression that size was synonymous with progress; and the heavier-than-air manufacturers followed the trend.

In 1923, Professor Hugo Junkers had designed an enormous 75-ton flying wing, the J 1000, but this project never got off the drawing board. Nevertheless Junkers persisted with his ideas for a big airplane, and on 6 November 1929, the four-engined **Junkers-G 38** made its first flight, four months after that of the mammoth flying boat, the Dornier Do X (page 42). Like the Do X, the G 38 was constructed by order of the German Ministry of Transport, to gain experience in building large aircraft.

Large it may have been. Handsome it was not. Publicists made much of construction features that permitted six passengers to sit inside the thick wing so that they had a forward view like the pilot's. The 26-ton weight was carried on only two wheels, the diameters of which were more than the height of a tall man.

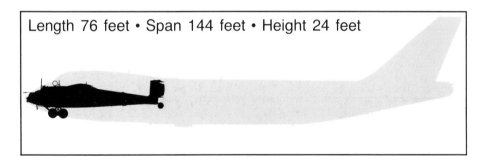

Length 76 feet • Span 144 feet • Height 24 feet

## Limited Service

The first G 38, registered D-2000, went into service with **Deutsche Luft Hansa** on 1 July 1931, from Berlin to London, via Hanover and Amsterdam. The second, D-2500, was added in June 1922 on a few selected routes. But in spite of their size—awe-inspiring for the period—the G-38s were not widely deployed. Even with 750-hp Junkers Jumo diesel engines, they cruised at only 127 mph, faster than some aircraft but not spectacularly so.

### THE D.L.H. JUNKERS-G 38s

| Const. No. | Regist. No. Original | Regist. No. 1934 | Name | Disposal |
|---|---|---|---|---|
| 3301 | D-2000 | D-AZUR | *Deutschland* | Crashed at Dessau 1936 |
| 3302 | D-2500 | D-APIS | *Generalfeldmarschall von Hindenburg* | Destroyed by Royal Air Force bombing at Athens during WW II |

**Note** Both aircraft underwent several modifications, including engine replacement, and each had several type designations.

### FLEET OF DEUTSCHE LUFT HANSA
1 January 1932
(before the first Junkers-Ju 52/3m)

| Type | First Year | No. | Type | First Year | No. | Type | First Year | No. |
|---|---|---|---|---|---|---|---|---|
| Albatros L 73 | 1926 | 3 | Focke-Wulf A 38 | 1931 | 4 | Junkers-G 31 | 1928 | 5 |
| Caspar C 32 | 1929 | 1 | Fokker-Grulich F II | 1920 | 12 | Junkers-W 33/34 | 1928 | 12 |
| Dornier Merkur | 1925 | 21 | Fokker-Grulich F III | 1921 | 7 | L.F.G. V 130 | 1927 | 1 |
| **Dornier Wal** | 1923 | 9 | Junkers-A 20 | 1924 | 5 | Messerschmitt M 20 | 1929 | 5 |
| **Dornier Super Wal** | 1927 | 2 | Junkers-F 13 | 1919 | 35 | Rohrbach Roland | 1926 | 15 |
| Focke-Wulf A 17a | 1928 | 10 | Junkers-F 24 | 1928 | 9 | Rohrbach Romar | 1929 | 3 |
| Focke-Wulf A 29 | 1929 | 2 | **Junkers-G 24** | 1925 | 10 | Sablatnig P III | 1921 | 2 |

**Note** 126 of the 173 aircraft were single-engined. Others are shown in bold type.

# The Standard Workhorse

## D.L.H.'s Silver Fleet

The late 1930s witnessed the domination of the Douglas DC-3 as the standard airliner in the United States. Every major U.S. airline had DC-3s, and Eastern Air Lines proudly promoted them with great flair as the Great Silver Fleet. Germany too had a silver fleet, twice as big as Eastern's. Throughout the 1930s, following the introduction of the first **Junkers-Ju 52/3m** in May 1932, **Deutsche Lufthansa** filled the skies of Germany and most of Europe with this reliable airliner.

By the outbreak of World War II, about 80 of D.L.H.'s official fleet inventory of about 145 aircraft were Junkers-Ju 52/3ms. Additional aircraft were operated on loan from the Reichsluftfahrtministerium (Aviation Ministry) and the airline probably operated more than 200 altogether. Those whose life spans can be ascertained with some confidence are listed in the table on this page, and there were many others, not precisely identifiable.

The Junkers 52/3ms of Deutsche Lufthansa composed the biggest single fleet of any one type of commercial transport aircraft ever assembled until the postwar period in the United States. The attrition during World War II, of course, was severe and finally devastating, as described on page 64. By 1945, however, as a fine representative of a thoroughbred line, *Tante Ju* had paid its dues.

### THE D.L.H. JUNKERS-JU 52/3m FLEET

| Years of Service First | Last[1] | Const. No. | Regist. No. Original | 1934 | Name |
|---|---|---|---|---|---|
| 1932 | 1933 | 4013 | D-2201 | D-ADOM | Boelcke |
|  | 1933 | 4015 | D-2202 | D-ADYL | Richthofen |
| 1933 | 1934 | 4019 | D-2468 | D-AFIR | Joachim von Schröder |
|  | 1941 | 4020 | D-2490 | D-AFYS | Gustav Doerr |
|  | 1937 | 4023 | D-2526 | D-AGAV | Zephyr/E. Schaefer |
|  | 1942 | 4022 | D-2527 | D-AGUK | M. von Richthofen/Kurt Wolff |
|  | 1941 | 4025 | D-2588 | D-AHIH | Rudolf Kleine |
|  | 1941 | 4021 | D-2600 | D-AHUT | H. J. Buddecke/Immelmann |
|  | 1941 | 4026 | D-2624 | D-AJAN | Rudolf Berthold |
|  | 1934 | 4027 | D-2640 | D-AZEV | Werner Voss |
|  | 1937 | 4028 | D-2649 | D-AJUX | H. Göring/U. Neckel |
|  | 1942 | 4029 | D-2650 | D-AKEP | Fritz Rumey |
|  | 1942 | 4030 | D-2725 | D-AKOK | Paul Bäumer |
| 1934 | 1941 | 4035 | D-3049 | D-ALAS | Heinrich Gontermann |
|  |  | 4036 | D-3050 | D-ALUN | Kurt Wintgens |
|  |  | 4037 | D-3051 | D-AMAM | Kurt Wüsthoff |
|  | 1941 | 4039 | D-3123 | D-ANAL | Gustav Leffers |
|  | 1938 | 4040 | D-3127 | D-APAR | Otto Parschau |
|  |  | 4041 | D-3131 | D-ARAM | Werner Voss |
|  | 1935SC | 4042 | D-3136 | D-ASEN | Paul Billik |
|  | 1934SC | 4043 | D-3356 | D-ABIS | Kurt Wolff |
|  | 1935 | 4044 | D-3382 | D-ABAN | Emil Thuy |
|  | 1935 | 4045 | — | D-AJYR | Emil Schäfer |
|  | D | 4046 | — | D-ADAL | Karl Allmenröder |

| Years of Service First | Last[1] | Const. No. | Regist. No. | Name |
|---|---|---|---|---|
| 1934 | 1942 | 4047 | D-AFER | Franz Büchner |
|  | 1941D | 4048 | D-AGIS | M. von Müller/W. Schmidt |
|  | D | 4049 | D-AHUS | Heinrich Kroll |
|  | 1936 | 4050 | D-AJIM | U. Neckel/H. Göring |
|  | 1941D | 4052 | D-AXES | Hans Berr |
|  | 1936 | 4053 | D-AXAN | H. J. Buddecke/Immelmann |
|  | 1942 | 4054 | D-ATON | Erwin Böhme |
|  | 1942 | 5010 | D-ALAN | Eduard Dostler |
|  | 1941 | 5014 | D-ANOL | Albert Dossenbach |
|  | 1937 | 5020 | D-AZIS | Von Bülow/Horst Wessel |
|  | 1935 | 5021 | D-AZAN | Joachim von Schröder |
|  | 1940lb | 5022 | D-AXUT | Lothar von Richthofen |
|  |  | 5023 | D-AXOS | Oswald Boelcke |
|  | 1942 | 5026 | D-ABES | Hermann Thomsen/Fritz Röth |
|  |  | 5034 | D-AHAL | Otto Bernert |
|  | 1938 | 5043 | D-ARYS | Hans Kirschstein |
|  | 1940SC | 5053 | D-AQUQ | Adolf von Tutschek |
|  | 1940P | 5060 | D-AMIT | O. von Beaulieu-Marconnay |
|  | 1942 | 5072 | D-ANEN | Fritz Puetter |
| 1935 | 1938 | 4068 | D-ABIZ | Erich Albrecht |
|  |  | 4070 | D-ADEF | Adolf Schirmer |
|  |  | 5278 | D-ADEK | Anton Schulz |
|  | 1938SC | 5120 | D-ADER | Hans Wende |
|  | 1940EC | 5074 | D-APOK | Max von Mulzer |
|  | 1937 | 5104 | D-AGES | Otto Kissenberth |
|  | 1940P | 5272 | D-AGIQ | Martin Zander |
|  | 1936N | 5429 | D-AKIY | William Langanke |
|  | 1939lb | 5098 | D-AKYS | Emil Thuy |
|  |  | 5180 | D-ALYL | Hans Loeb/Linke Crawford (XI Olympiade 1936 only) |
|  | 1937 | 5294 | D-AMAK | Volkmar von Arnim |
|  | 1938 | 4072 | D-AMIP | Fritz Erb |
|  | 1943 | 5128 | D-ANAZ | Willi Charlett |
|  | 1941 | 4071 | D-ANYF | Erich Pust |
|  | 1937 | 5329 | D-ANYK | Wilhelm Schmidt |
|  | 1938SC | 4075 | D-APEF | Karl Wessel |
|  | 1938SC | 4079 | D-APOR | Olaf Bielenstein |
|  | 1936 | 4055 | D-AQAR | Walter Höhndorf |
|  | 1936 | 5078 | D-ASIH | Rudolf Windisch |
|  | 1938 | 4074 | D-ASIS | Wilhelm Cuno |
|  | 1936 | 5169 | D-ATAK | Marschall von Bieberstein |
|  | 1939lb | 4073 | D-AVUL | Bruno Rodschinka |
|  |  | 5267 | D-AVUP | Kurt Steidel |
|  | 1936 | 4069 | D-ABIK | Manfred von Richthofen |
|  | 1936N | 4077 | D-ANOP | Fritz Simon |
| 1936 |  | 5555 | D-AGOO | Fritz Simon |
|  | 1937SC | 5478 | D-AJAO | Robert Weinhard |
|  | 1941 | 5484 | D-AKUO | Paul Billik |
|  | 1937 | 5502 | D-ALUE | Joachim von Schröder |
| 1937 | 1938 | 5777 | D-ABUR | Charles Haar |
|  | 1939 | 5800 | D-AFOP | Karl Hochmuth |
|  |  | 5685 | D-AGAK | Ulrich Neckel |
|  | 1943 | 5740 | D-ALAM | William Langanke |
|  | 1943 | 5734 | D-AMEI | Fritz von Roeth |
|  | 1938 | 5663 | D-ANOY | Rudolf von Thüna |
|  |  | 5682 | D-APUP | Marschall von Bieberstein |
|  |  | 5748 | D-ATAO | Alfred Bauer |
|  |  | 5797 | D-ATYZ | Hans Hackmack |
|  | 1939lb | 5851 | D-AUJA | Otto Fink |
|  | 1939lb | 5854 | D-AUKE | Wille Rabe |
|  | 1943 | 5693 | D-AXAT | Rudolf Windisch |

| Years of Service First | Last[1] | Const. No. | Regist. No. | Name |
|---|---|---|---|---|
| 1938 | 1942 | 5954 | D-ABVF | Franz Wagner |
|  | 1940 | 4059 | D-ACBO | V. Neubrand (ex-South Africa) |
|  |  | 6046 | D-ADED | Viktor Neubrand |
|  | 1941 | 5938 | D-AFCD | Erich Albrecht |
|  | 1939lb | 4060 | D-AGFD | Otto Parschau (ex-S. Africa) |
|  |  | 6030 | D-AGTC | Wilhelm Cuno |
|  | 1942 | 6047 | D-AHFN | H. Kricheldorf |
|  | 1941 | 6042 | D-AHMS | Martin Zander |
|  | 1939 | 5947 | D-ANJH | Hans Loeb |
|  | 1941 | 5979 | D-ANXG | Hans Kirschstein |
|  | 1942 | 5919 | D-ARDS | Robert Weichard |
|  | 1940 | 6014 | D-ASFD | Heinrich Mathy |
|  |  | 5940 | D-ATDB | Walter Bayer |
|  | 1939 | 5942 | D-AUJG | Hans Wende |
| 1939 | 1943 | 6432 | D-ABEW | Rudolf von Thüna |
|  | 1941 | 6385 | D-ABFA | Otto Parschau |
|  | 1942 | 6386 | D-ACEP | Adolf von Tutschek |
|  | 1941 | 6387 | D-ADBO | O. von Beaulieu-Marconnay |
|  |  | 6650 | D-ADBW | Emil Thuy |
|  | 1943 | 6066 | D-ADHF | W. Höhndorf |
|  |  | 6057 | D-AFFQ | Otto Falke |
|  | 1942 | 6659 | D-AGBI | Max von Mulzer |
|  |  | 4080 | D-AGDA | Wedige von Froreich |
|  | 1942 | 6452 | D-AGOB | H. J. Handke |
|  | 1942 | 5590 | D-AKEQ | Gustav Rubritius |
|  |  | 5933 | D-AMFR | Ludwig Hautzmayer |
|  |  | 6734 | D-APGU | Bruno Rodschinka |
|  | 1943 | 6149 | D-APXD | Robert Untucht |
|  |  | 6750 | D-APZX | Raoul Stoisavljevic |
|  |  | 6442 | D-AREB | Charles Haar |
|  | 1941 | 6180 | D-ARIW | Joachim Blankenburg |
|  |  | 6171 | D-ARAD | Volkmar von Arnim |
|  | 1942 | 6369 | D-ASLG | Alfred Viereck |
|  |  | 5727 | D-ATEA | Philipp von Blaschke |
|  | 1941 | 6370 | D-AVAJ | Olaf Bielenstein |
|  |  | 6561 | D-AWAS | Joachim Blankenburg |
|  | 1942 | 6372 | D-AXFH | H. E. Lochner |
|  | 1942 | 1301 | D-AZIR | Fritz Erb[2] |
|  |  | 6779 | D-ARCK | Van Vloten |
|  |  | 6790 | D-ARVU | Hans Wende |
| 1940 | 1943 | 6550 | D-ACBE | Emil Schäfer |
|  | 1941 | 6670 | D-AEAO | R. Fritsche |
|  |  | 6775 | D-AHGA | Paul Billik |
|  | 1940SC | 6800 | D-AHGB | Rudolf Kleine |
| 1941 | 1942 | 7029 | D-APAJ | Erich Pust |
|  | 1942 | 7077 | D-ASDI | Rudolf Kleine |
|  | 1942 | 7089 | D-ASHY | Gustav Doerr |
|  | 1942 | 7160 | D-ATAW | Lothar von Richthofen |
|  | 1942 | 7208 | D-AYGX | Johannes Höroldt |
|  | 1943A | 7256 | D-AVIU | Th. Schöpwinkel |
| 1942 | 1945 | 7390 | D-ACDA | Chartered from Aero O/Y (OH-LAP) |
|  | 1944 | 7493 | D-AEAC | Chartered from Aero O/Y (OH-LAO) |
| 1943 | 1945 | 4064 | D-AIAO | From Ala Littoria (I-BIBI) |
|  | 1945 | 6765 | D-AIAT | From Ala Littoria (I-BOAN) |

[1] The letters following the years in this column indicate disposal, as follows: A, to Aero O/Y, Finland; D, to Deruluft (1934–37); Ec, to SEDTA, Ecuador; Ib, to Iberia; N, to D.N.L., Norway; P, to D.L.H. Sucursal Peru; SC, to Syndicato Condor, Brazil. [2] *Fritz Erb* was built by A.T.G., Leipzig.

**Note** As noted in the text, many additional Ju 52/3ms were operated by Lufthansa during World War II, under various arrangements with the Reichsluftfahrtministerium.

# Junkers-Ju 52/3m   17 seats • 150 mph

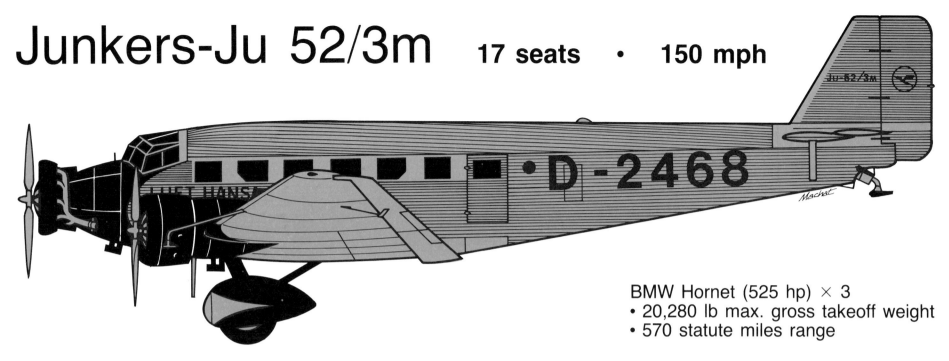

BMW Hornet (525 hp) × 3
• 20,280 lb max. gross takeoff weight
• 570 statute miles range

## The Junkers-Ju 52

After a decade of building transport aircraft based on the well-proven Junkers corrugated-metal-cladding formula, designer Ernst Zindel produced a further improvement. The **Junkers-Ju 52** made its first flight on 11 September 1930 and drew on the long experience of a famous pedigree that had begun with the F 13 in 1919, moving on to the trimotored G 24 and the larger G 31. Production of the heavyweight G 38 was abandoned. The Ju 52, a single-engined monoplane, was approximately the same size and about a ton lighter in loaded weight than the nine-ton G 31. Built as a freighter, it incorporated similar features such as several freight doors and a hatch in the roof. Its performance was impressive, one taking off in the winter of 1931 from Montreal, Canada, in 17½ seconds, carrying almost four tons of payload. But only seven Ju 52s were built, because the widespread deterioration of the world's economy handicapped Junkers's plans for air freight operations based on Kurt Weil's experience in Persia.

## A Better Mousetrap

In 1932, Deutsche Luft Hansa had to transfer two Rohrbach Rolands to Deruluft, to match the standard of the Soviet ANT-9, one of the early Tupolev designs. The German airline badly needed a replacement and Junkers obliged with the **Ju 52/3m**, which made its debut in April 1932. It was simply a Ju 52, but with three smaller engines in the 750-hp range. John Stroud describes it succinctly: "It was destined to become one of the best known European transport aircraft, and was almost certainly the type to be produced in the greatest numbers." Always a cautious commentator, Stroud understates the case, if the service record is any guide.

The Ju 52/3m carried up to 17 passengers or about three tons of freight. It cruised at about 150 mph and was able to use any contemporary airfield surface, even a football field. Its versatility was utilized by the Luftwaffe during World War II, as troop carrier, bomber, and ambulance, and, most spectacularly, in dropping parachutists. An armada of Ju 52/3ms parachuted troops into Allied-held Crete, and 170 of the fleet of 493 were shot down. Soviet sources claim that 676 alone were destroyed in the unsuccessful attempt to relieve Von Paulus's trapped army at Stalingrad.

Length 62 feet • Span 96 feet • Height 20 feet

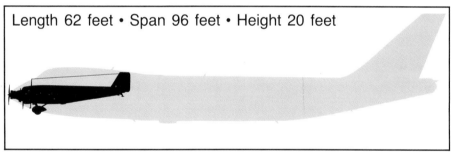

## An Amazing Record

The Ju 52/3m was used all over Europe. **Deutsche Lufthansa** bought them by the dozen. It was sold to many South American countries, to South Africa, and to China. Of the estimated 4,835 built, 2,804 were for the Luftwaffe during World War II. Additional numbers were produced in France as the **A.A.C.1** by the Ateliers Aéronautiques de Colombes, where construction continued after the war ended, as it did in Spain, where CASA maintained production of the **CASA 352/3m** until 1952.

Outmoded technically, the Junkers-Ju 52/3m was nevertheless like a well-worn old car that is kept in reserve because, in an emergency, it always starts and doesn't break down. It stayed on a few airline books until well into the jet age. Even the British used them, before and after the war; in the late 1940s, Air France operated no less than 85 of the A.A.C.1s, second only to the pre-war Lufthansa. The last one is believed to have been retired from service in New Guinea during the late 1960s. A few are still to be seen flying at air shows, and Lufthansa itself proudly maintains one in flying condition as a promotional tribute to a hall-of-fame heritage. Several are exhibited in museums around the world, and one, donated by Lufthansa, has found a home in the National Air and Space Museum in Washington, D.C.

# Consolidation in the 1930s

## The Passing of an Era

As described on page 42, the fleet of **Deutsche Luft Hansa** in 1932 appeared at first glance to be substantial, numbering 173 aircraft of 24 different types. But numbers were deceptive. The vast majority were old machines. Most were single-engined and well-worn. Some were almost decrepit. Twenty-seven aircraft of ten types had already been disposed of by 1930 (page 20). Now some further survivors of a bygone era were pensioned off.

One curious aspect of this cleaning of the hive was that many of the 1919-vintage Junkers-F 13s and the smaller A-20s, representative of the now-outmoded corrugated-cladding method of construction, resisted any dangerous thinking that they should all be banished to the scrapyard. They proved to be too useful.

The retirement of the Caspar C 32 is worthy of note, as it was a crop-spraying aircraft. D.L.H. also had a C 35, Caspar's eight-seat passenger aircraft. With the Albatros L 73, these were the only biplanes actually purchased by Luft Hansa after 1926.

## Cometh the Hour

One good reason for the cleanout was the debut of the **Junkers-Ju 52/3m**, a truly versatile and reliable aircraft, able to perform almost any duty demanded of it. By 1936, 59 of the now-reduced total fleet of 144 were Ju 52/3ms, and they were estimated to be carrying 85% of the total D.L.H. traffic.

They were to be found all over Europe, "taking care of the farm" while the airline planners were courageously branching out into foreign parts in faraway continents. While the overseas pioneers were catapulting themselves—literally—into the aviation history books, the Junkers 52/3m established itself as the flagship of the D.L.H. fleet. As the workhorse of the fleet, the 16-seat trimotor heralded the beginning of a new era of multiengined aircraft service with machines which could, without too much apology, be described as airliners.

This **L.F.G. V 130 Strela-Land** was used by **Deutsche Lufthansa** until 1936.

### DEUTSCHE LUFT HANSA
### AIRCRAFT RETIRED 1930–1936

| Last Year | Aircraft | Const. No. | Regist. No. | Name | Years of Service First | Years of Service Last | Remarks |
|---|---|---|---|---|---|---|---|
| 1930 | Caspar C 35 | 7015 | D-7015 | *Rostock* | 1928 | 1930 | Written off |
| 1933 | Caspar C 32 | 7008 | D-1143 | *Wismar* | 1929 | 1933 | Scrapped |
| 1932 | L.F.G. V 130 | 92 | D-455 | *Franzburg* | 1927 | 1930 | Sold |
| | | 93 | D-525 | *Greifswald* | 1927 | 1930 | Sold |
| | | 94 | D-547 | *Randow* | 1927 | 1932 | Sold |
| | | 95 | D-588 | *Kolberg* | 1927 | 1929 | Sold to Norway |
| | | 109 | D-759 | *Stralsund* | 1927 | 1928 | Written off |
| | | 110 | D-796 | *Stettin* | 1927 | 1930 | Sold |
| | | 112 | D-810 | *Stolp* | 1927 | 1930 | Sold |
| 1933 | Albatros L 73 | 10076 | D-960 | *Preussen* | 1926 | 1933 | Sold to D.V.L. |
| | | 10077 | D-961 | *Brandenburg* | 1926 | 1928 | Destroyed |
| | | 10118 } | | Never operational | 1930 | 1932 } | To Bulgarian Air Traffic Management |
| | | 10119 } | | | 1930 | 1932 } | |

**Abbrev.** D.V.L.: Deutsche Versuchsanstalt für Luftfahrt
**Note** Other aircraft retired during the 1930–1936 period are listed on other pages: Rohrbachs (22), Dornier Merkur (21), Fw A 29 and A 38 (42), Fokker F II (11), Junkers-G 31 (25), Messerschmitt M 28 (42).

**Erhard Milch**, whose airline career started with **Danziger Luftpost** in 1921, moved up the political ladder when the Nazis came to power in 1933 and controlled D.L.H.'s policies until the demise of the "old" Lufthansa in 1945.

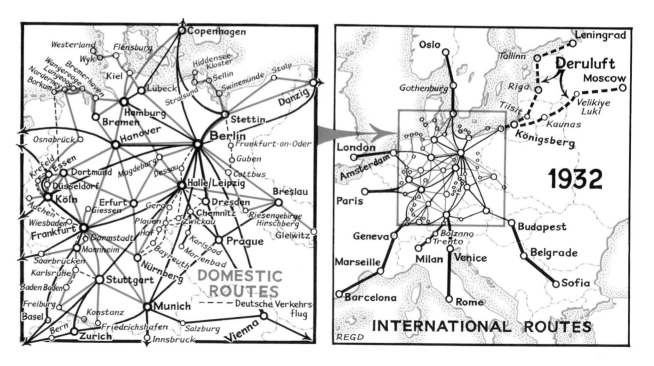

# Tante Ju and Gooney Bird

## Two of a Kind

Reviewing the critical stage of aircraft development during the interwar period of the 1920s and 1930s, one is tempted to make a comparison between the most successful (because they were built in the largest numbers) transport types from both sides of the Atlantic. The facts and figures showing the similarities between the **Douglas DC-3** and the **Junkers-Ju 52/3m** are shown in the table on this page.

Essentially the aircraft were about the same size. The Douglas was a better performer, having about a third more power, reflected in higher speed, higher all-up weight, and greater carrying capacity. Both were used in large numbers by the commercial airlines, and both served valiantly during World War II in their military colors and configurations.

More DC-3s were built than any other transport aircraft. The Junkers-Ju 52/3m ranked second on the list.

## From Different Worlds

The big difference was that the two aircraft were representative of two completely different eras of technology. The Ju-52/3m was built on the same principles as the 1919 Junkers-F 13 and was arguably just a bigger version, with more engines and a refined wing. The DC-3, in contrast, epitomized the introduction of the modern airliner, with multicellular stressed-skin wings superseding the simple spar-

The interior of the **Junkers-Ju 52/3m**.

and-rib construction of the Junkers; monocoque fuselage replacing a rectangular frame; retractable landing gear; and other refinements. All these had been incorporated in the DC-1 of 1933, usurping the Boeing 247 of the same period.

Technically, therefore, the corrugated skin of the Ju 52/3m represented the end of an era. The streamlined shape of the DC-3 was the flowering of a new. Yet they were both dominant for several years. Curiously the Junkers came on the scene four years earlier than the DC-3 but continued in production seven years longer, partly because in 1945 war-surplus DC-3s were a dime a dozen, whereas most of the Ju 52/3ms had been shot out of the skies, destroyed on the ground, or otherwise consigned to oblivion.

The two aircraft had one characteristic in common. Because of their reliability they were both known by their grateful uniformed clientele by an affectionate nickname. The American *Gooney Bird* had its counterpart in Germany, where the Junkers-Ju 52/3m will always be remembered as *Tante Ju*. It will also be remembered in Washington, D.C., where the Smithsonian Institution is pleased to report that Auntie has come to stay.

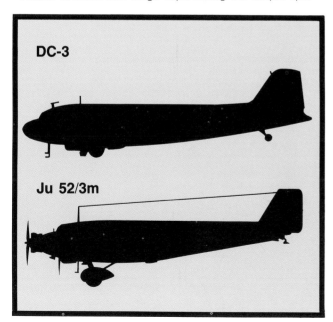

**DC-3**

**Ju 52/3m**

### THE JUNKERS-JU 52/3M AND THE DOUGLAS DC-3 COMPARED

| Type | Date of First Flight | Date of First Service | Dimensions | | | Normal Seating | Engines | | | Max. Gross TOW (lb) | Cruise Speed (mph) | Normal Field Length (ft) | Typical Practical Range (st. miles) | Total No. Built |
| | | | Length | Span | Height | | No. | Type | Hp (each) | | | | | |
|---|---|---|---|---|---|---|---|---|---|---|---|---|---|---|
| Junkers Ju 52/3m | April 1932 | 1932[1] | 62'0" | 96'0" | 14'10" | 15–17 | 3 | B.M.W. Hornet[2] | 600 | 20,280 | 150 | 2500 | 500 | 4835[3] |
| Douglas DC-3 | 17 Dec. 1935 | 25 June 1936 | 64'6" | 95'0" | 16'4" | 21–28 | 2 | P. & W. Twin Wasp[4] | 1200 | 25,200 | 180 | 3000 | 800 | 13,750[5] |

[1]The first Ju 52/3m (c/n 4013) was delivered to D.L.H. in May 1932. A.B.A. (Sweden) and Aero O/Y (Finland), followed by L.A.B. (Bolivia), were the next operators. [2]The license-built B.M.W. Hornets were the most commonly used. Others included Junkers Jumo diesels. [3]Includes about 4200 military versions, of which 2800 were built during World War II [4]All the earlier DC-3s, except those for United Air Lines, had Wright Cyclones. [5]All versions, including 2500 Lisunov Li-2s, license-built in the U.S.S.R., and 487 license-built in Japan. Only 423 were built originally as commercial DC-3s.

A **Junkers-Ju 52/3m** at Croydon Airport, London, during the 1930s.

The **Douglas DC-3**, the only transport aircraft built in greater numbers (in both civil and military versions) than the Ju 52/3m.

# Into a New Era

## A Symbolic Change

On 30 June 1933 the German national airline made a subtle change in its corporate structure, altering its name slightly from Deutsche Luft Hansa A.G. to **Deutsche Lufthansa A.G.** This coincided with a program of reequipment with modern aircraft types to replace the old, thereby changing the corporate image as well as the fleet composition.

Except for continued and expanded production of the ubiquitous Ju 52/3m, so adaptable as to be indispensable, Junkers turned away from the traditional corrugated metallic construction that had been its strength—in more ways than one—for almost two decades. The little single-engined **Junkers-Ju 60**, with a smooth-skinned monocoque fuselage (but retaining the corrugated wing), and its successor, the **Ju 160**, with smooth wing and fuselage, were introduced by Deutsche Lufthansa in 1934 and 1936 respectively. The vintage F 13s and W 34s were retired or scrapped and the last F 13 finally bowed out, still flyable, in 1939, to mark the end of an era.

## High Performance

Until the early 1930s, airlines on both sides of the Atlantic had been preoccupied with developing transport aircraft that were reliable, safe, and reasonably comfortable. Economical operation was not a powerful factor as yet, as the airlines were subsidized. Interline competition was almost nonexistent, so the airlines tended to compete with surface transport modes rather than with one another. Then, in 1931, Swissair acquired the **Lockheed Orion**, which cruised at 190 mph, 75% faster than anything on D.L.H.'s books. When the Swiss airline put the Orion on the Zurich-Munich-Vienna route, this seemed like an open challenge.

The German answer was the sleek single-engined **Heinkel He 70**, introduced in 1933, which could more than match the Orion in speed, to the extent that it set several world records for its class. Its fuselage was a duralumin monocoque and its landing gear was retractable, but its wings were wooden. It provided an express air service between Berlin and the other large cities of Germany and became familiarly known as the *Blitz* ("Lightning"). But the Heinkel He 70, weighing less than four tons, could seat only four passengers. Thus the unit costs were very high, and, with burgeoning traffic, Deutsche Lufthansa turned to bigger if not faster airliners than the He 70 and the Ju 160 to carry it through the decade.

The **Junkers-Ju 86**, built as both a commercial and a military aircraft.

The **Heinkel He 70** just before starting engines.

The **Junkers-Ju 160**, extensively used by **Deutsche Lufthansa** on feeder routes during the 1930s.

DEUTSCHE LUFTHANSA'S FIRST
MODERN SINGLE-ENGINED AIRCRAFT
Introduced 1933–1936

| Const. No. | Regist. No. | Name | Years of Service First | Years of Service Last |
|---|---|---|---|---|
| **Heinkel He 70** | | | | |
| 403 | D-UXUX[1] | Blitz | 1933 | 1934 |
| 437 | D-UBAF[2] | Sperber | 1934 | 1937 |
| 709 | D-UBIN | Falke | 1934 | 1937 |
| 710 | D-UDAS | Habicht | 1934 | 1935 |
| 711 | D-UGOR | Schwalbe | 1934 | 1937 |
| 909 | D-UJUZ | Bussard | 1935 | 1938 |
| 910 | D-UPYF | Adler | 1935 | 1937 |
| 911 | D-UBOX | Geier | 1935 | 1937 |
| 912 | D-UNEH | Condor | 1935 | 1938 |
| 913 | D-UQIP | Rabe | 1935 | 1938 |
| 914 | D-USAZ | Buntspecht | 1935 | 1938 |
| 915 | D-UVOR | Reiher | 1935 | 1935 |
| 916 | D-UXUV | Drossel | 1935 | 1937 |
| 917 | D-UMIM | Albatros | 1935 | 1938 |
| 918 | D-UKEK | Amsel | 1935 | 1937 |
| **Junkers-Ju 60** | | | | |
| 4201 | D-UPAL | Pfeil | 1934 | 1936 |
| **Junkers-Ju 160** | | | | |
| 4202 | D-UNOR | Luchs | 1935 | 1936 |
| 4206 | D-UMEX | Panther | 1935 | 1941 |
| 4207 | D-UPOZ | Wolf | 1935 | 1937 |
| 4208 | D-UFIR | Luchs | 1936 | 1941 |
| 4209 | D-UQOR | Löwe | 1936 | 1941 |
| 4210 | D-ULIK | Gepard | 1936 | 1941 |
| 4211 | D-UPYM | Puma | 1936 | 1936 |
| 4212 | D-UVOX | Rotfuchs | 1936 | 1941 |
| 4213 | D-UKAN | Marder | 1936 | 1941 |
| 4214 | D-UGAZ | Iltis | 1936 | 1941 |
| 4215 | D-UVUX | Wiesel | 1935 | 1941 |
| 4216 | D-UQOL | Tiger | 1936 | 1939 |
| 4219 | D-UFAL | Jaguar | 1936 | 1941 |
| 4220 | D-UGIZ | Hermelin | 1936 | 1941 |
| 4221 | D-UHIL | Kreuzfuchs | 1936 | 1941 |
| 4222 | D-UJIM | Blaufuchs | 1936 | 1941 |
| 4223 | D-URUQ | Weissfuchs | 1936 | 1941 |
| 4244 | D-UBIQ | Silberfuchs | 1936 | 1941 |
| 4245 | D-UJYM | Nerz | 1936 | 1941 |
| 4246 | D-ULUR | Schakal | 1936 | 1936 |
| 4247 | D-UQAS | Schakal | 1936 | 1941 |

[1]Formerly D-3, the D-2537. [2]Formerly D-3114.

# Junkers-Ju 86    10 seats  •  177 mph

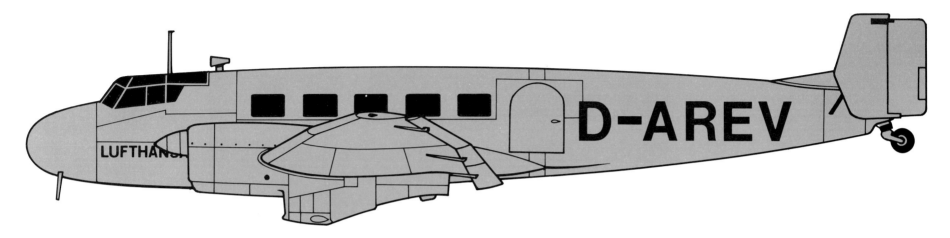

Junkers Jumo 205c (600 hp) × 2 • 16,975 lb max. gross takeoff weight • 680 statute miles range

## A Diesel-Powered Airliner

In contrast with many piston-engined aircraft of the 1930s era which were later fitted with diesel engines, the **Junkers-Ju 86** was designed with these from the start. It had two 600-hp Junkers Jumo 205Cs, and like many other aircraft built in Germany at the time, it was designed to be adaptable for both commercial and military users.

It made its first flight on 4 November 1934 and had some problems at first, although D-AXEQ made a 3600-mile nonstop flight from Dessau to Bathurst, West Africa, in 1936, and had ample fuel to spare on arrival. It settled down into service with **Deutsche Lufthansa**, which had about a dozen until 1940. Although the Luftwaffe took some, several remained operational with D.L.H. until May 1945.

## A German Export

The Ju 86 did not have the widespread application or popularity of its earlier cousin, the Ju 52/3m, but quite a few were exported. It was especially well received by South African Airways, which had 18, fitted with Rolls-Royce Kestrel or Pratt & Whitney Hornet engines—a rare reversal of the normal gasoline-to-diesel conversion procedure. The aircraft also saw commercial service with Swissair; A.B. Aerotransport, Sweden; L.A.B., Bolivia; LAN-Chile; and an airline in Australia; and five went to the South Manchurian Railway, operating air services in what was then a Japanese overseas territory.

The number of civil Junkers-Ju 86s sold exceeded 40, but the vast majority—as was true for many other transport aircraft of the time—were military versions, of which the total built may have approached 1000. One of these, delivered to the Swedish air force, is still preserved in its museum.

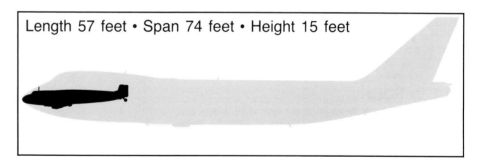

Length 57 feet • Span 74 feet • Height 15 feet

### DEUTSCHE LUFTHANSA'S JUNKERS-JU 86 FLEET

| Year of Introduction | Const. No. | Regist. No. | Name | Year of Introduction | Const. No. | Regist. No. | Name |
|---|---|---|---|---|---|---|---|
| 1935 | 4902 | D-ABUK | | 1937 | 016 | D-ANUV | *Wasserkuppe* |
| 1936 | 4904 | D-AREV | *Brocken*[1] | | 972 | D-AKOI | *Kaiserstuhl* |
| | 009 | D-AHYP | *Schneekoppe* | | 973 | D-AQEA | *Schauinsland* |
| | 010 | D-ALOZ | *Zugspitze* | | 974 | D-ASOE | *Hesselberg* |
| | 011 | D-AQER | *Inselberg* | | 975 | D-AVOE | *Obersalzberg* |
| | 012 | D-AZAH | *Feldberg* | | 976 | D-AMYO | *Melibokus*[2] |
| | 014 | D-AFAF | *Watzmann* | | 977 | D-AJUU | *Vogelsberg* |
| | | | | 1939 | 246 | D-AUME | *Annaberg* |
| | | | | 1940 | 502 | D-ADJO | *Hohentwiel*[3] |

[1]Crashed in 1937. [2]Reregistered in 1942 as D-AJEQ, because MYO was the three-letter radio code for "warning—enemy aircraft." [3]Originally ordered for the Japanese-controlled airline in Manchuria.

# Modern Airliners

## Eyes Across the Sea

The spectacular progress of transport aircraft development in the United States did not pass unnoticed by **Deutsche Luft Hansa**, which ordered three of the revolutionary twin-engined **Boeing 247**s in 1933. The world's first modern airliner, the 247 could carry ten passengers at 165 mph. It had a monocoque fuselage, stressed-skin wing surfaces, and a retractable landing gear. Its all-round performance was better than that of any of D.L.H.'s aircraft at the time.

Two B-247s were delivered to Lufthansa, but instead of the third, a **Douglas DC-2** was delivered to Berlin. Undoubtedly the U.S. construction methods and quality of workmanship of both types were well studied, although German aircraft engineers were no strangers to new techniques. The stressed-skin principle, key element in the structural revolution, had been heralded by Rohrbach's box spar in the 1920s (page 23).

## Single-Engined to Twin

And so the D.L.H. fleet composition underwent a radical change. The twin-engined **Heinkel He 111**, all-metal, with monocoque stressed-skin structure, retractable gear, variable-pitch propellers, and ten seats, came into service in 1936. Like the **Junkers 86** (page 49), the He 111 was designed as a bomber, so successfully that 6456 were built, as well as 236 by CASA in Spain. Field Marshal Milch had one for executive use.

## Twin to Four

The momentum of modernization was maintained and even accelerated during the latter 1930s. In 1938 the **Heinkel He 116**, a long-range four-engined development of the He 111, was intended for the South Atlantic and the Far East routes, the latter by the ingenious itinerary surveyed by von Gablenz (page 58). A special version, the He 116R, made a nonstop flight of 6200 miles in 1939, but a German air passenger service to the Orient was eventually opened by—who else?—*Tante Ju.*

More promising was the new airliner from Focke-Wulf, the **Fw 200 Condor**. This fine aircraft is fully described on pages 56 and 57.

## An Orderly Transition

In four momentous years, from 1935 to 1939, Deutsche Lufthansa had thus moved from operating a predominantly single-engined fleet to one which, in addition to the trusty armada of Junkers-Ju 52/3ms, could boast the fastest and most modern airliners in Europe. The transition is shown in the table on page 62.

### THE WORLD'S LARGEST PRE-WAR FOUR-ENGINED LANDPLANE FLEET

| Const. No. | Regist. No. | Name | Years of Service First | Years of Service Last | Aircraft Avail. 1939 |
|---|---|---|---|---|---|
| Focke-Wulf FW 200 Condor (see page 57) | | | 1938 | 1945 | 14[1] |
| Heinkel He 116 | | | | | |
| 545 | D-AJIE | Lübeck | 1938 | 1939 | 3 |
| 546 | D-ATIO | Hamburg | 1938 | | |
| | D-ARFD | Rostock | 1939 | | |
| Junkers-Ju 90 (see page 51) | | | 1939 | 1945 | 10 |
| TOTAL | | | 1938 | 1945 | 27 |

[1]Includes two with Syndicato Condor

The **Boeing 247**, one of two purchased by Deutsche Lufthansa.

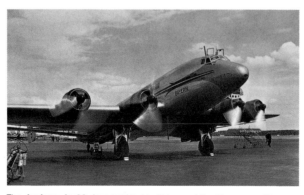

The **Junkers-Ju 90**, four-engined trailblazer of the European skies.

### DEUTSCHE LUFTHANSA'S MODERN TWINS

| Const. No. | Regist. No. | Name | Years of Service First | Years of Service Last |
|---|---|---|---|---|
| Boeing 247 | | | | |
| 1944 | D-AKIN | — | 1934 | 1937 |
| 1945 | D-AGAR (ex-NC-91Y) | Feldberg | 1934 | 1935 |

**Note** D-AGAR was destroyed at Nuremburg on 24 May 1935 when another aircraft taxied into it. D-AKIN crashed on a test flight at Hanover on 13 August 1937. Mainly experimental.

| Douglas DC-2 | | | | |
|---|---|---|---|---|
| 1318 | D-ABEQ | Taunus | 1935 | 1937 |

**Note** Acquired in lieu of the third Boeing 247. Delivered in February 1935 via Fokker, it was sold to LOT, Poland, in February 1937. Experimental only.

| Heinkel He 111 | | | | |
|---|---|---|---|---|
| 715 | D-ALIX | Rostock | 1935 | 1937 |
| 1828 | D-AMEY | Nürnberg | 1936 | 1940 |
| 1829 | D-AQYF | Leipzig | 1936 | 1940 |
| 1830 | D-AXAV | Köln | 1936 | 1937 |
| 1831 | D-ABYE | Königsberg | 1936 | 1940 |
| 1832 | D-AQUA | Breslau | 1936 | 1940 |
| 1833 | D-ATYL | Karlsruhe | 1936 | 1940 |
| 1968 | D-AHAO | Dresden | 1936 | 1936 |
| 2534 | D-AEQA | Halle | 1936 | 1940 |
| 2535 | D-AYKI | Magdeburg | 1937 | 1940 |
| 1884 | D-ACBS | Augsburg | 1938 | 1940 |
| 1885 | D-ADCF | Dresden | 1938 | 1940 |
| Junkers-Ju 86 (see page 49) | | | | |

### THE FOCKE-WULF FW 58 WEIHE FLEET
Replacement for the Junkers-F 13

| Const. No. | Regist. No. | Name | Years of Service First | Years of Service Last |
|---|---|---|---|---|
| 2697 | D-ONBR | — | 1938 | 1944 |
| 2698 | D-OAFD | — | 1938 | 1944 |
| 2699 | D-OORK | — | 1938 | 1943 |
| 2700 | D-OBJH | — | 1938 | 1944 |
| 3100 | D-OTRE | Rhein | 1939 | 1942 |
| 3101 | D-OHLM | Donau | 1939 | 1942 |
| 3102 | D-OUPG | Aquiri (PP-CBM) | To Syndicato Condor, 1939 | |
| 3103 | D-OKDN | Cacuri (PP-CBN) | | |
| 3104 | D-OVXF | Elbe | 1939 | 1942 |

**Note** First four (unnamed) aircraft used for aerial photography, before passing to Luftwaffe. Others used for commuter services.

# Junkers-Ju 90   40 seats  •  200 mph

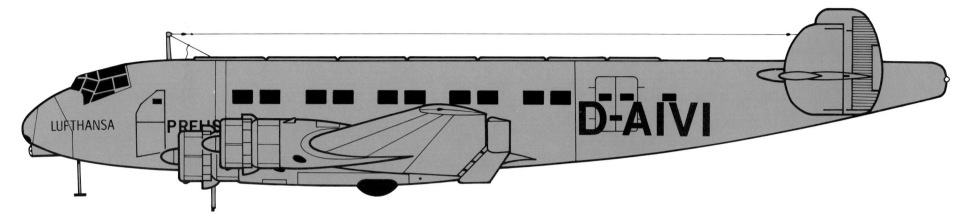

## BMW 132H (830 hp) × 4
- 50,700 lb max. gross takeoff weight
- 775 statute miles range

## The Big One from Dessau

The Junkers company had built a large airliner before, the ponderous G 38 of 1929 (page 43), but this had not been a success, in spite of its elephantine size, 25-ton weight, and windows in the leading edge of the thick wing so that privileged passengers could enjoy a forward view. Almost a decade later, in 1937, another 25-ton airliner, the **Ju 90**, developed from the Ju 89 bomber, emerged from the factory at Dessau. With smooth skin and flush riveting, it had clean modern lines, it was fast and powerful, and it looked good.

In some respects, it could be compared with the Boeing 307. Both had four engines, both had the same medium range of about 750 miles with full load, and total production, modest numbers in each case, was about the same. The 307 could carry 33 people in pressurized comfort and went into service with T.W.A. in 1940. The Ju 90 was not pressurized, but it was bigger, able to carry 40, and appeared on the European scene two years earlier, going into service with **Deutsche Lufthansa** in 1938.

The medium-range German contender, able to fly nonstop from Germany to the southern European capitals, nevertheless had a spotty career. The prototype, aptly named *Der Grosse Dessauer,* broke up in flight during the testing program on 6 February 1938. Because of barely a year of peacetime use immediately before the outbreak of World War II, it never became well known outside the German sphere of influence, although two were ordered by South African Airways. Military versions were built for the Luftwaffe, including the **Ju 290**, three of which were operated by D.L.H. in 1944–1945.

The Ju 90 represented a notable technical advance in commercial airliner construction. In partnership with the long-range Focke-Wulf Condor, it could have asserted German commercial aviation supremacy in Europe, had World War II not erupted in September 1939.

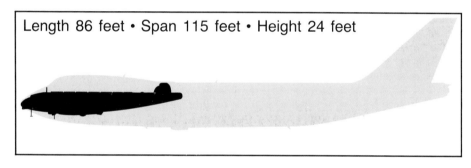

Length 86 feet • Span 115 feet • Height 24 feet

### DEUTSCHE LUFTHANSA'S JUNKERS-JU 90 FLEET

| Year of Introd. | Const. No. | Regist. No. | Name | Remarks |
|---|---|---|---|---|
| 1937 | 4913 | D-AALU | *Der Grosse Dessauer* | Prototype; first flight 7 June 1937; crashed 6 Feb. 1938; not D.L.H. |
| 1938 | 4914 | D-AIVI | *Preussen* | Crashed at Bathurst during tropical trials Nov. 1938. |
| | 4915 | D-AURE | *Bayern* | Bombed at Stuttgart Sept. 1944 |
| | 4916 | D-ADLH | *Sachsen* | Delivered as *Schwabenland;* to Junkers for tests and mods, 1939; DLH, 1940–42. |
| 1939 | 001 | D-ABDG | *Württemberg* | Operated by D.L.H. until 1942 |
| | 005 | D-AEDS | *Preussen* | |
| | 003 | D-ADFJ | *Baden* | |
| | 006 | D-ASND | *Mecklenburg* | |
| | 007 | D-AFHG | *Oldenburg* | |
| 1940 | 008 | D-ATDC | *Hessen* | |
| | 009 | D-AJHB | *Thüringen* | |
| | 010 | D-AVMF | *Brandenburg* | |

**Note** Const. nos. 002 and 004 would have been ZS-ANG and ZS-ANH of South African Airways, but were never delivered.

# North Atlantic Rehearsal

## Dornier 18 Flights

On 13 February 1936, a Dornier Wal flying boat made a preliminary survey flight from Hamburg to the Azores, via Las Palmas, Canary Islands. Meanwhile, the elegant **Dornier 18** was undergoing trials, in preparation for making four round trips across the North Atlantic between 5 September and 20 October, from Lisbon to New York, via the Azores and Bermuda. Then the depot ship *Schwabenland* (see pages 38–39) was transferred from its South Atlantic duties to take up position near Horta, in the Azores.

## The Blohm & Voss Ha 139 Flights

The following year this experimental series of flights was intensified. Handsome **Blohm & Voss Ha 139** four-engined floatplanes replaced the Dornier 18, while a brand-new depot ship of advanced design, the *Friesenland*, reinforced the *Schwabenland*. Between 13 August and 20 November 1937, with the depot ship catapults augmenting the takeoff performance, the Ha 139s *Nordwind* and *Nordmeer* made seven flights each way between Horta, the Azores flying-boat base, and New York, in times ranging from 14½ to 19 hours.

In 1938 the third series of flights had the *Schwabenland* based at Horta and the *Friesenland* at Port Washington, on Long Island, New York, where Pan American Airways had developed a flying-boat base in preparation for the launching of its Boeing 314 transatlantic scheduled service in the summer of 1939. With the positioning of the depot ships at each end of the route, an average saving of about two hours per flight was possible in both directions, and the Ha 139s made 26 crossings between 21 July and 20 October 1938.

A summary of all the catapult-launched flights, both from the ocean liners and from the depot ships, is shown in the accompanying table.

The **Ha 139** is hoisted aboard the *Schwabenland*.

### GERMAN CATAPULT EXPERIMENTAL PROGRAM ON THE NORTH ATLANTIC
#### Ocean Liners

| Year | Aircraft Type | Ship Used | One-Way Flights |
|------|---------------|-----------|-----------------|
| 1929 | Heinkel He 12 | *Bremen* | 7 |
| 1930 | Heinkel He 12 | *Bremen* | 18 |
|      | Heinkel He 58 | *Europa* | 4 |
| 1931 | Heinkel He 12 | *Bremen* | 13 |
|      | Heinkel He 58 | *Europa* | 17 |
| 1932 | Heinkel He 58 | *Bremen* | 17 |
|      | Junkers-Ju 46 | *Europa* | 18 |
| 1933 | Junkers-Ju 46 | (both ships) | 34 |
| 1934 | " " | " " | 36 |
| 1935 | " " | " " | 34 |
| TOTAL | | | 198 |

**Note** Aircraft were catapulted westbound to New York, and eastbound to Southampton, Amsterdam, Bremerhaven, and Cologne.

The **Blohm & Voss Ha 139** at Port Washington, New York.

#### Depot Ships

| Year | Aircraft Type | Route and Ships Used | One-Way Flights |
|------|---------------|----------------------|-----------------|
| 1936 | Dornier 18 | Azores (*Schwabenland*)–Bermuda–New York | 4 |
|      | " " | Azores (*Schwabenland*)–Sydney (N.S.)–New York | 4 |
| 1937 | Blohm & Voss Ha 139 | Azores (*Friesenland*)–New York (*Schwabenland*) | 14 |
| 1938 | Blohm & Voss Ha 139 | Azores (*Schwabenland*)–New York (*Friesenland*) | 26[1] |
| TOTAL | | | 48 |

[1] Total flights permitted by U.S. authorities was 28. But flights 8 and 9 were performed by the FW 200 Condor on its record-breaking flight (see page 56) as a substitution.

### AIRCRAFT USED FOR THE NORTH ATLANTIC CATAPULT SHIP PROGRAM

| Const. No. | Regist. No. | Name | Remarks |
|------------|-------------|------|---------|
| **Heinkel He 12** (owned by Norddeutscher Lloyd) | | | |
| 334 | D-1717 | *New York* | Assigned to liner *Bremen* 1929; crashed 6 Oct. 1931 |
| **Heinkel He 58** (owned by Norddeutscher Lloyd) | | | |
| 365 | D-1919 | *Atlantik* | Assigned to liner *Europa* 1930; renamed *Bremen* when reassigned 1932 |
| **Junkers-Ju 46** | | | |
| 2715 | D-2244 (D-OKUV) | *Europa* | Assigned to liner *Europa* 1932–33 |
| 2720 | D-2271 | *Hamburg* | Assigned to liner *Bremen* 1933; transferred to Syndicato Condor, as PP-CAU *Tocantins*, 17 Jan. 1934 |
| 2744 | D-2419 (D-UGUS) | *Mars* (*Jupiter*) | Landplane, *Mars*, not used on catapult flights; reregistered as D-OLMP; sold to Synd. Condor as PP-CBK 1939 *Tingua* |
| 2745 | D-2491 (D-UHYL) | *Sirius* | Assigned to liner *Bremen* 1934; reregistered as D-OBRA 1937; sold to Hansa 1939 |
| 2773 | D-3411 (D-UBUS) | *Europa* | Assigned to liner *Europa* 1934; sold to Hansa 1939 |
| **Dornier Do 18** (used only with depot ship *Schwabenland*) | | | |
| 661 | D-ABYM | *Aeolus* | |
| 663 | D-ARUN | *Zephir* | |
| **Blohm & Voss Ha 139** (used only with depot ships) | | | |
| 181 | D-AMIE | *Nordmeer* | |
| 182 | D-AJEY | *Nordwind* | |
| 217 | D-ASTA | *Nordstern* | Ha 139B (slightly larger and heavier) |

**Note** Other Do 18s were the prototype D-AHIS *Monsun*, D-AANE *Zyklon* (c/n 677), and D-AROZ *Pampero* (c/n 255). *Pampero* was lost in the S. Atlantic 1 Oct. 1938.

The **Dornier Do 18.**

# Blohm & Voss Ha 139 — 1000 lb. mail · 161 mph

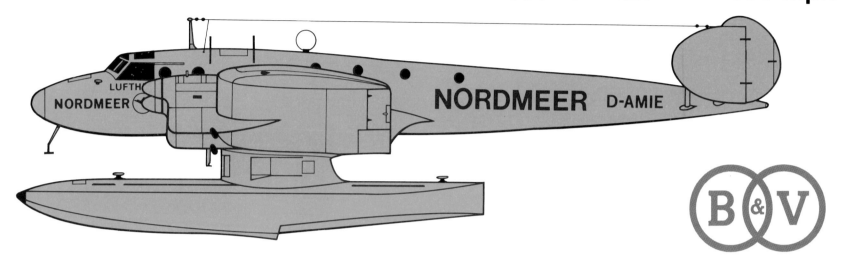

Junkers Jumo 205c (600 hp) × 4 • 38,580 lb max. gross takeoff weight • 3000 statute miles range

## Elegant Efficiency

The entry, in the mid-1930s, into a field already graced by famous names such as Junkers, Dornier, Heinkel, and Focke-Wulf by the Hamburg shipbuilders **Blohm & Voss** was somewhat surprising. In the event, the firm's associate, **Hamburger Flugzeugbau**, produced an aircraft that was unique not only for its elegant and instantly eye-catching design, but also for its remarkable strength and performance that met unusually stringent specifications.

The **Ha 139**, designed by Dr. Richard Vogt, was required to upgrade the German long-range transocean operations, for which the pioneering Dornier Wal was outdated and newer Dorniers such as the Do 26 were not yet available. It had to be capable of being launched from the powerful Heinkel pneumatic catapults installed on the latest depot ships and thus had to be stressed to withstand a form of mechanical torture. The center section of the spar was made of chrome-molybdenum sheet steel, formed into a flat hollow tube which also served as the main fuel tank. The four engines were 600-hp Junkers Jumo diesels, driving three-bladed Junkers-Hamilton variable-pitch propellers. The radiators were in the mountings for the large floats.

## An Impressive Performer

The first two Ha 139s were completed in 1936 and went into service with **Deutsche Lufthansa** in March 1937, performing excellently on a series of experimental flights between the depot ships based in the Azores and at Port Washington, New York (see table on opposite page). They were also used briefly in 1939 on the South Atlantic.

Because of its attractive lines, the Ha 139 was larger than it looked at first glance. Its normal loaded weight was 35,384 pounds, or, when catapulted, 38,690 pounds—almost exactly the loaded weight of a Sikorsky S-42 *Clipper* and only about 4000 pounds less than that of a Shorts S-23 Empire flying boat. It was almost certainly the largest floatplane ever built. The difference in takeoff weights, incidentally, is an indication of why the Germans persevered with the catapults. The extra 3300 pounds could be used for fuel, permitting a range of transatlantic proportions.

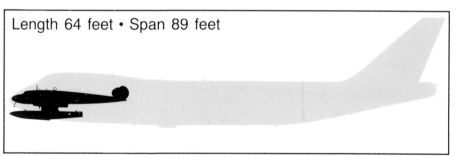

Length 64 feet • Span 89 feet

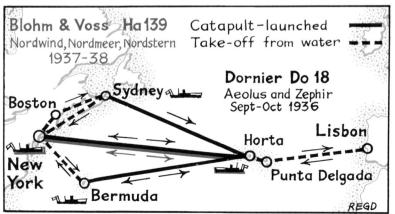

Blohm & Voss Ha 139
Nordwind, Nordmeer, Nordstern
1937-38

Catapult-launched
Take-off from water

Dornier Do 18
Aeolus and Zephir
Sept-Oct 1936

Boston · Sydney · New York · Bermuda · Horta · Lisbon · Punta Delgada

REGD

# End of the Airship Era

## North Atlantic Scheduled Air Service

While **Pan American Airways** can justly claim to have started the first *sustained* scheduled North Atlantic air services in 1939 with the **Boeing 314** flying boat, the **Deutsche Zeppelin Reederei** *Hindenburg*'s regular service from Frankfurt to New York throughout the summer of 1936 is often forgotten. It performed uneventfully, with an average journey time of 52 hours eastbound and 65 hours westbound against the prevailing winds. The one-way fare was $400, equivalent to ten times that amount today, or twice the price of a Concorde ticket; the service was probably profitable.

It was the star attraction of the aviation world in 1936. **American Airlines** advertised with pride a direct DC-3 connection to Lakehurst from Newark, then New York's air terminus. The *Hindenburg* took sports fans straight from Lakehurst to the Olympic Games in Berlin, and the airship carried the Olympic insignia to mark the occasion. (See page 40 for the service record.)

The control car of the *Hindenburg*.

The smoking room of the *Hindenburg*.

The passenger lounge of the *Hindenburg*.

## The Great Disaster

Pride came before more than simply a fall. Measured in human lives lost, the historic conflagration on 6 May 1937 at Lakehurst, New Jersey, as the *Hindenburg* was about to come to its moorings after its maiden voyage of the season, was far from being the worst disaster in aviation history. The miracle was that far more people (62) actually survived than lost their lives (36). However, the disaster was not only witnessed by hundreds but was filmed and shown to millions worldwide in a dramatic movie sequence so often repeated that millions more, of future generations not even born at the time, were later to have the image indelibly imprinted on their memories of events.

The controversy raged, and still resurfaces occasionally, as to whether the United States should have supplied helium for the *Hindenburg*. This is irrelevant. With full knowledge of the danger of hydrogen, with its high flashpoint risk, the company should never have operated with it. But perhaps it had no choice, considering the competitive and political environment of the times. One decision, however, was inescapable on 6 May 1937. Airships would never operate commercially again.

The LZ 129 *Hindenburg*.

# Zeppelin LZ 129 *Hindenburg*

## 50 seats (in 2-berth cabins) • 77 mph

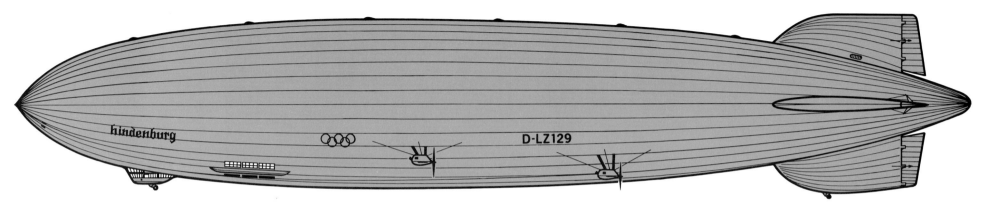

Daimler-Benz MB 502 (1000 hp) × 4 • 270 tons max. gross lift • 8400 statute miles range

## A Hesitant Beginning

Encouraged by the success of the *Graf Zeppelin* (see pages 40–41), the Zeppelin company embarked on a larger airship project that, if completed, would have been the **LZ 128**. Half as big again as the *Graf*, it would have carried half again as many passengers, even though it was designed to be about the same length. But after the British airship **R101** crashed at Beauvais, France, in October 1930, the designers concluded that the new airship must have nonflammable helium rather than hydrogen gas, and that the engines must be fueled by less volatile diesel oil rather than by gasoline or *Blaugas*.

## The Greatest Airship of Them All

And so, in 1931, work started on the new **LZ 129**, for which the German government cooperated with the State of Württemberg in building the massive construction shed, as well as paying for the airship itself. Unfortunately, the United States possessed a monopoly of the world's supply of helium, and refused to supply the precious gas to Germany. The United States was apprehensive about the possible future military use of airships, and the authorities in Washington were taking no chances.

The LZ 129 had to be redesigned, using hydrogen in the gas bags, and more powerful 1300-hp engines, Daimler Benz MB 502 (LOF 6) diesels; it needed only four, compared with the Graf's five. Named the *Hindenburg* for its first flight on 4 March 1936, it was twice as big as the *Graf Zeppelin* in volume. It could carry 50 passengers, and its total load-carrying capability was 32 tons, of which 11 tons were ballast. Its still-air range was a staggering 8700 miles. Its construction and entry into service represented a triumph of German engineering.

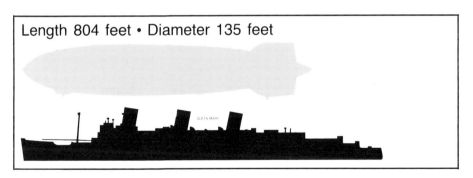

Length 804 feet • Diameter 135 feet

## Postscript

The *Hindenburg*'s passenger accommodation had been increased to 72 for the stillborn 1937 season. Interestingly, this was almost the same as the **Pan American Boeing 314**'s 70 seats, but the *Hindenburg* could carry them in far greater luxury and ten times as far. But the series production of airships was impossible, as was the prospect of coping with more than one at a time at the airports. The *Hindenburg* needed a ground crew of 240 men to receive it, and about half a square mile of space. In practical terms, airship services could only have been maintained for the privileged few, and further development of the breed was speculative, at best.

# Historic Landplane Sortie

## A Record-Breaking Flight

On 10 August 1938 a **Focke-Wulf Fw 200 Condor**, piloted by Capt. Henke of **Lufthansa**, flew nonstop from Berlin to New York. Registered D-ACON, the aircraft took off from the Staaken airfield in Berlin and landed at Floyd Bennett Field, because this was the only New York air terminal with adequate concrete runways. The nonstop distance of close to 4000 miles was covered in 24 hr 36 min, at an average speed of 160 mph.

The Lufthansa aircraft maintenance staff on board the *Friesenland*, the depot ship stationed at Port Washington for the Azores–New York experimental program, using catapult launching (see page 52), inspected D-ACON, gave it a clean bill of health, and three days later dispatched it back to Berlin, where it received an enthusiastic welcome.

## The Writing on the Wall

More than any other single flight, D-ACON's dramatic achievement established beyond doubt that landplanes could outperform flying boats, however elegant and spacious the latter were. Recognizing belatedly that heavy wing and wheel loadings could be compensated for by solid hard runways, aircraft designers the world over conceded that the era of the commercial flying boat was nearing its demise.

Other factors were to accelerate this trend. Chief among these was the enormous program of airfield construction undertaken by the United States—aided considerably by technical teams from **Pan American Airways**—during World War II. But the Fw 200, more than any other single airliner, even the pressurized **Boeing 307 Stratoliner**, heralded an irreversible change of course in the development of the commercial airliner.

The **Condor** welcomed at Berlin after its triumphal return flight in 1938.

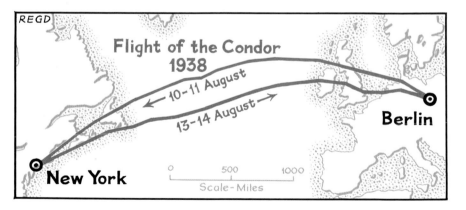

Flight of the Condor 1938
← 10–11 August
13–14 August →
New York
Berlin
Scale-Miles
500   1000
REGD

THE FOCKE-WULF FW 200 CONDORS

| Const. No. | Regist. No. | Name | Year Deliv. | Remarks |
|---|---|---|---|---|
| 2000 | D-ACON | *Brandenburg* | 1937 | Name only when flown as prototype, D-AERE. Record nonstop Berlin–New York, New York–Berlin, 10–13 Aug., 1938. Berlin–Tokyo, 28–30 Nov. 1938. Ditched and written off, Manila, 6 Jan. 1939. |
| 2484 | D-AETA | *Westfalen* • | 1937 | Operated until 1945 |
| 2893 | D-ADHR | *Saarland* • | 1938 | Written off in accident 1941 |
| 2895 | D-AMHC | *Nordmark* • | 1938 | Written off 1943 |
| 2994 | D-ARHW | *Friesland* • | 1938 | Crashed into sea 29 Nov. 1944 |
| 2995 | D-ASBK | *Holstein* | 1939 | Diverted to **Syndicato Condor** as PP-CBJ *Arumani* |
| 2996 | D-AXFO | *Pommern* | 1939 | Diverted to **Syndicato Condor** as PP-CBI *Abaitara* |
| 3098 | D-ACVH | *Grenzmark* | 1939 | To Reichsluftfahrtministerium. Used by von Ribbentrop to visit Moscow 1939 |
| 3099 | D-ARHU | *Ostmark* | 1939 | To Reichsluftfahrtministerium. Renamed Immelmann III and used as Adolf Hitler's personal aircraft. |
| 3324 | D-ABOD | *Kurmark* • | 1939 | Crashed 22 April 1940, during invasion of Norway |
| 0001 | D-ACWG | *Holstein* ° | 1940 | |
| 0009 | D-ASHH | *Hessen* ° | 1940 | Last service, Barcelona–Berlin, 14 April 1945; crashed at Piesenkofen, Bavaria, 21 April 1945 |
| 0020 | D-AMHL | *Pommern* ° | 1940 | Operated until 1945 |
| 0021 | D-ASVX | *Thüingen* ° | 1940 | Flew the last D.L.H. service on 5 May 1945, Aalborg–Flensburg |
| 2894 | OY-DAM | *Dania* | 1938 | Delivered to D.D.L., Denmark, by Kurt Tank, 14 July 1938. May have opened first Fw 200 scheduled service two weeks later. To England 8 April 1940 and seized. To BOAC as *Wolf*. Damaged beyond repair 12 July 1941 at White Waltham in Luftwaffe raid. |
| 2993 | OY-DEM | *Jutlandia* | 1938 | Delivered to D.D.L. Nov. 1938; flew on Copenhagen–Berlin–Vienna service until crash landing at Vienna, 17 Dec. 1941; repaired and served until 1945. Resumed service after World War II but badly damaged at Northolt in 1946 and scrapped. |

**Note** Those marked • delivered to Deutsche Lufthansa under contract. Those marked ° delivered to Deutsche Lufthansa but also used by Luftwaffe for logistics support during invasion of Norway, 1940.

# Focke-Wulf Fw 200 Condor

## 26 seats • 202 mph

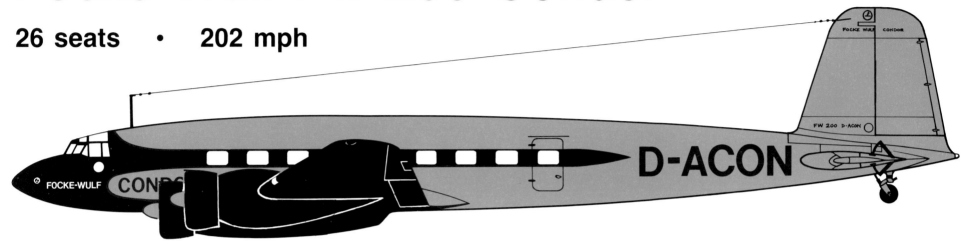

**D-ACON**

BMW 132G (720 hp) × 4 • 32,000 lb max. gross takeoff weight • 775 statute miles range

## An Inspired Project

In the summer of 1936, as the DC-3 entered service and the *Hindenburg* flew the Atlantic airways, the Bremen aircraft constructor Focke-Wulf began work on a revolutionary four-engined landplane. The **Fw 200 Condor** made its maiden flight just one year later. Its designer, Kurt Tank, had produced an aircraft that outperformed all others. It could carry 26 passengers at high speed, and could fly, with a smaller load, over long distances. Two notable demonstration flights are described on pages 56, opposite, and 59.

## Frustrated Potential

Deutsche Lufthansa took delivery of both the Fw 200 and the Junkers-Ju 90 in May 1938. The Condor went into service in June, from Berlin to Vienna, Frankfurt, and Munich. In November 1938 a Condor flew to Tokyo, a distance close to 9000 miles, in 46 hours. This outstanding airliner also went into service with the Danish **D.D.L.** in July 1938 and with **Syndicato Condor**, Brazil, in 1939 (page 32). It was ordered by airlines in Finland and Japan and by Lufthansa's Chinese partner, Eurasia; but it never entered service with them.

The outbreak of World War II put an end to ambitious plans for worldwide Condor marketing and sales. Besides the two prototypes and the ten aircraft of the first Fw 200 series, no less than 46 of the advanced Fw 200Bs were ordered by the summer of 1939. It was subsequently developed as a military long-range reconnaissance aircraft with the capability of bombarding shipping with a small bomb load. But it was never used as a heavy bomber. During the war it undertook long-range sorties between Bordeaux, France, and Stavanger, Norway, flying in a wide arc around the British Isles, often taking 16 hours in surveillance of Allied convoys. The two airfields were among the few in Europe at the time that could boast concrete runways.

Length 78 feet • Span 108 feet • Height 21 feet

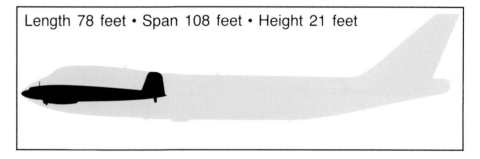

The **Focke-Wulf 200 Condor** at Floyd Bennett Field, New York, after its nonstop flight from Berlin in 1938.

# Eastward Bound

## Across Siberia

German airline aspirations in the Far East had focused on the establishment of a route through the Soviet Union. This was a geographically obvious solution, and the first tentative exploratory trips had been accomplished, not without incident, during the mid-1920s (see page 24). The objective was to fashion a direct route to Peiping, in cooperation with the Soviet airline, via Moscow and the larger cities along the whole length of the Trans-Siberian Railway.

Starting on 27 August 1928, in a cooperative venture by **Deutsche Luft Hansa** and the Soviet airline **Dobrolet**, a Junkers-W 33 D 1472 *Ural* flew from Berlin to Irkutsk, via Moscow and other intermediate stops. It made an immediate turnaround and was back in Berlin on 2 September, having flown the 7630 miles in 76 hr 15 min flying time. One week later the same aircraft repeated the exercise, this time tarrying awhile in Irkutsk to make some local surveys of possible onward extensions.

In August 1929 the famous airship *Graf Zeppelin* flew across northern Siberia on its round-the-world flight, taking 101 hr 49 min for the first nonstop segment of the journey, Berlin to Tokyo. It carried 20 passengers, who paid handsomely for the privilege—40,000 marks each.

## Change of Plan

Everything seemed to be going well. In 1930, **Deutsche Luft Hansa** established **Eurasia** (see page 26) as an associate airline in China, to secure a sound base at the far end of a prestigious transcontinental air route. At first the rail line was to be followed all the way to the Manchurian border; but this was not only circuitous, it was dangerous, as Eurasia discovered when one of its aircraft was forced down near Manchuli and its crew held captive by the local keepers of the law. A shortcut was sought across northern Sinkiang (then known as Chinese Turkestan), and a W 33 survey flight was made from Peiping to Urumchi in December 1931.

It was the end of the line in more ways than one. In 1933 the Soviet Union ceased to cooperate and the Germans had to seek a new route.

A heroes' welcome for **Von Gablenz** and his crew after their adventure in western China. Captain Von Schroeder is on the left.

## Over the Pamirs

Fortunately, **Deutsche Lufthansa** could fall back on another plan. Necessity being the mother of invention, Lufthansa began to consider a route which presented a much bigger challenge than the conquest of the oceans. For given the choice of the world's highest mountain massif or the world's stormiest oceans, most pilots would, in the 1930s, have chosen the latter for safety.

In June and July 1936, Capt. Drechsel made a survey flight in a **Junkers-Ju 52/3m** to Kabul. With this technically advanced aircraft, compared with the single-engined W 33s, he took the opportunity to survey the forbidding Hindu Kush and Pamir mountain ranges, his 7600-mile flight taking only 55 hr 43 min flying time. Possibly as important as the survey itself was the establishment of a meteorological station high up in the Pamirs.

The **Junkers-W 33** *Ural*, which made a pioneer flight to Irkutsk and back in 1928.

**Karl August Freiherr von Gablenz**, a great pilot and great operational and visionary innovator of blind flying and transocean flying techniques, pictured here both as a pilot and as an executive.

The **Junkers-Ju 52/3m** in China.

The strategy was to utilize the Wakhan region, a narrow strip of Afghan territory which acts as a buffer zone between India (now Pakistan) and the Soviet Union. By following the Pyandzh river valley and negotiating the 16,000-foot-high Wakhan Pass, it is possible to cross into China along this "Afghan Corridor" without overflying either the Soviet Union or India. Accordingly, to examine the feasibility of such an itinerary, the "Pamir Expedition" left Berlin in August 1937. Freiherr von Gablenz, flying with the **Junkers-Ju 52/3m** D-ANOY *Rudolf von Thüna*, piloted by Capt. Untucht, was partnered by Capt. Drechsel in another Ju 52, D-AMIP. They left Kabul on 24 and 26 August respectively, and D-ANOY, with a refueling stop at Ansi, arrived at Sian, Eurasia's main base at the time, on 27 August. D-AMIP landed about 20 miles short of Sian and was later transferred to Eurasia.

On the return flight, D-ANOY had engine trouble and had to make a forced landing near Chotan, in southern Sinkiang. The crew were promptly arrested and jailed by unfriendly troops from the local garrison. Held hostage for several weeks and badly treated, they eventually reached Kabul on 27 September having been "rescued" by a more sympathetic Chinese army contingent. They arrived back in Berlin on 10 October, to a heroes' welcome.

The "corridor" of Afghan territory, devised as a political buffer between Russian and British interests in the 19th century, served as a neutral passage for German survey flights to China.

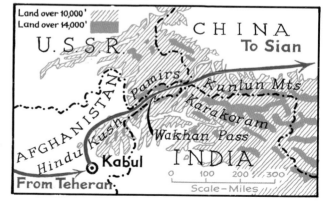

# A Far East Route at Last

## Into the Middle East

As early as November 1930, a **Junkers-W 33** had made an experimental mail and freight flight to Baghdad, as an extension of **Deutsche Luft Hansa**'s existing route to the east as far as Istanbul; but the little single-engined aircraft was not adequate for sustained service. On 29 October 1937, however, a scheduled mail and freight route opened to Baghdad, and this was extended to Teheran, Persia (Iran), with full passenger service, on 1 April 1938. The aircraft used was the versatile **Junkers-Ju 52/3m**, and two weeks later, on 15 April, it flew to Herat and Kabul, the Afghan capital, to open the longest route on the Lufthansa system at that time.

## *Auntie Ju* Spreads Her Wings

By the late 1930s, D.L.H. had many sleek and fast aircraft, but the challenging assignment to open a Far Eastern Service fell upon the trusty "old faithful," the Ju 52/3m trimotor, which had first gone into service in 1932. Its resilience and reliability had become legendary, and several had already been ferried out to **Eurasia**, the German airline affiliate in China, in 1934 and 1935.

After a survey flight all the way to Tokyo, flown on 22 April 1939 with Freiherr von Gablenz himself aboard, *Tante Ju* opened a twice-monthly scheduled service to Bangkok, on 25 July of that year. The journey took 4½ days by the southern route, via Baghdad, the Persian Gulf, and India; the 14-to-17-seat aircraft was fitted with only six special seats, to provide comfort for the long flight.

But this was little more than a token gesture. World War II erupted in Europe at the end of August. One aircraft, D-ANJH, had crashed at Rangoon on the return flight, and the third aircraft to arrive at Bangkok was confiscated. The crew managed to escape with their aircraft to Shanghai, whence they were able to reach their compatriots in Eurasia.

## On the Brink of a Breakthrough

In a dramatic flight matching its famous round-trip across the North Atlantic on 10 August 1938, the four-engined **Focke-Wulf Fw 200 Condor**, D-ACON, left Berlin on 28 November 1938 and reached Tokyo on the 30th. Making only three stops, it covered the 8870 miles in 48 hr 10 min, heralding a new era in airline operations to the Far East. Such a speed was far better than the British flying boats or any other landplane at the time could match. Alas, the Condor had to ditch in Manila Bay on its return journey, and the outbreak of war prevented any further flights.

Originally, D-ACON was to have made a round-the-world flight, but U.S. authorities refused landing rights in New York, Los Angeles, and Hawaii. In fact, the New York flight (page 52) was made by an astute manipulation of the flight program allocated to the Azores–New York depot ships and the Blohm & Voss Ha 139s.

Had a favorable political climate prevailed, there is little doubt that Deutsche Lufthansa could, by 1940 at the latest, have opened full Fw 200 services to Tokyo, as well as to New York and Buenos Aires. It would have been the world's first successful long-range landplane airliner.

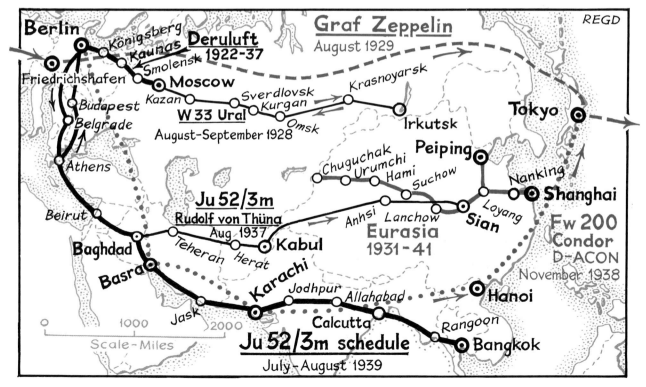

The **Focke-Wulf 200 Condor** made a dramatic flight to Tokyo in 1938 but never went into service on the Far East route.

The trusty old *Tante Ju* finally opened a Lufthansa scheduled route to the Far East in 1939.

# Outposts on the Pacific Rim

## SEDTA

Until 1937, German commercial aviation interests had been confined to Brazil, where Syndicato Condor (page 32) had a nationwide network. In Colombia, however, Juan Trippe, Pan American's wily leader, had usurped German control of SCADTA (page 28) as early as 1931, by an agreement under which Trippe had a free hand in Colombia, and Condor's presence in Brazil was not challenged. But D.L.H. was anxious to expand its routes more effectively to the Pacific Ocean.

On 24 July 1937 it established the **Sociedad Ecuatoriana de Transportes Aéreos** (**SEDTA**) in Quito, Ecuador. The driving force was none other than Fritz Hammer, the dynamic Condor Syndikat salesman-promoter. SEDTA had no support from the Ecuadorian government. It chartered its **Junkers-W 34**s and **Junkers-Ju 52/3m**s from Lufthansa in the spring of 1938, and was dependent on its own revenues and on D.L.H.'s help to cover costs.

A **Junkers-Ju 52/3m** of **D.L.H. Sucursal Perú**.

### THE FLEET OF SEDTA (ECUADOR) 1938–1941

| Regist. No. | Const. No. | Name | Remarks |
|---|---|---|---|
| **Junkers-W 34** | | | |
| D-OJIL | 489 | — | Crashed 4 March 1938, killing Fritz Hammer, one of the founders of Condor Syndikat |
| HC-SAA | 2608 | Pichincha | Ex-D-OGIF; crashed 11 Sept 1939, repaired, and transferred to Condor as PP-CBO 14 Jan. 1941 |
| **Junkers-Ju 52/3m** | | | |
| HC-SAB | 5915 | Ecuador | Ex-D.L.H. (D-APDF); crashed 10 Dec. 1938 |
| HC-SAC | 5053 | Guayas | Ex-D.L.H. (D-AQUQ); to Syndicato Condor as PP-CBR 13 Jan 1939 |
| HC-SAD | 5283 | Aconcagua | Ex-D.L.H. (D-AENF); chartered from Syndicato Condor 25 April 1941; requisitioned by air force, passed to USAAF as C-79 (42-52883) May 1942 |
| HC-SAE | 5109 | Azuay | From Syndicato Condor 20 Nov. 1939; requisitioned by air force |
| PP-CBG | 4075 | — | Chartered from Syndicato Condor 10 Feb. 1941 and returned |
| D-APDF | 5915 | | — |

## Death of a Master Salesman

The first few months of operation were soon marked by tragedy. Hammer was killed in the W 34 D-OGIF when it crashed on 4 March 1938. More than any single individual, he had carried the German commercial airline flags into foreign lands, using innovative marketing methods and displaying great tenacity and verve. In the art of founding new airlines he was decades ahead of his time.

SEDTA's proposal in May 1940 to open a service to the Galapagos Islands—not yet featured in the tourism brochures—sounded alarm bells in Washington. The U.S. airline PANAGRA was designated to operate its DC-2s precisely in parallel with SEDTA's Ju 52/3ms. Even *Tante Ju* was no match for the DC-2, especially since its fuel supplies were cut off. On 5 September 1941, the Ecuadorian government, under U.S. pressure, requisitioned the remaining Junkers trimotors. One of them was transferred to the U.S.A.A.F. as the sole C-79 and used in Costa Rica by the U.S. Roads Administration.

## Peruvian Branch Office

On 24, May 1938, **Deutsche Lufthansa Sucursal Perú** began service from Lima, Peru, to Arequipa and La Paz, Bolivia. This completed an ingenious multinational route across the middle of South America, entirely German-sponsored. It reached from Rio de Janeiro and São Paulo, Brazil, to Corumbá, on the Bolivian frontier, by **Syndicato Condor**; thence to La Paz by **L.A.B.**, the German-influenced airline in Bolivia; and finally to Lima and the Pacific Ocean by D.L.H. Sucursal. (See page 31.)

The Peruvian airline was not an associate or subsidiary. It was an overseas branch of D.L.H. and had no local shareholding. Its fleet consisted of two **Junkers 52/3m**'s, which were adequate for the limited task required. A connection with SEDTA in Ecuador was never made, although no doubt the idea was in the minds of the Lufthansa planning staff in Berlin.

### THE FLEET OF D.L.H. SUCURSAL PERU 1938–1941

| Regist. No. | Const. No. | Name | Remarks |
|---|---|---|---|
| **Junkers-Ju 52/3m** | | | |
| OA-HHA | 5060 | Huascarán | Ex-AMIT; to Peruvian govt. 31 March 1941 |
| OA-HHB | 5043 | Misti | Ex-D-ARYS; crashed 26 June 1938 |
| OA-HHC | 5272 | Huandoy | Ex-D-AMIQ; to Peruvian govt. 31 March 1941 |
| OA-HHD | 5283 | Aconcagua | Ex-D-AENF; chartered to SEDTA 29 Nov. 1940 |

**Note** All aircraft were delivered during 1938.

Pressure from the United States led to the Peruvian government's withdrawal of the operating permit, and flights were suspended on 31 March 1941. As in the case of Ecuador, PANAGRA was waiting in the wings to take over.

### LUFTHANSA BEZIRKSDIREKTION SÜDAMERIKA (SOUTH AMERICAN REGIONAL MANAGEMENT)

| Regist. No. | Const. No. | Name | Delivery Date | Remarks |
|---|---|---|---|---|
| **Junkers-Ju 52/3m** | | | | |
| D-ARUW | 4038 | Caiçara | 1938 | To Syndicato Condor 11 Sept 1939 (PP-CAV) |
| D-AGST | 5261 | Maipo | 31 March 38 | To Syndicato Condor 11 Sept 1939 (PP-CAZ) |
| D-AENF | 5283 | Aconcagua | 1 April 37 | To Syndicato Condor 11 Sept 1939 (PP-CBA) |
| D-APEF | 4075 | Pagé | 24 Sept 38 | To Syndicato Condor 11 Sept 1939 (PP-CBG) |
| D-AMYE | 5656 | Los Andes | 7 June 37 | To Syndicato Condor 11 Sept 1939 (PP-CBL) |

**Notes** D-AENF made the first D.L.H. Buenos Aires-Santiago flight on 13 Sept. 1937. D-ARUW made the first D.L.H. Rio de Janeiro-Natal flight on 1 Oct. 1938. D-APEF made the first D.L.H. Rio de Janeiro-Buenos Aires flight on 4 Nov. 1938.

# Dramatic Rescue

## The Hazards of War

Apart from the severe problems of terrain, climate, and maintenance, **Eurasia**'s and **China National Aviation Corporation**'s aircraft were targets for Japanese attack. Possibly the most spectacular incident—matching that of the famous "DC-2½" adventure when a C.N.A.C. DC-3, after being strafed by the Japanese, limped home with one DC-2 replacement wing—was an astonishing salvage operation performed in southern China on 13 April 1939. A Eurasia **Junkers-Ju 52/3m**, *Eu XIX*, was machine-gunned and bombed just north of the Indo-Chinese (now Vietnamese) frontier, and crash-landed on a mountain slope, tearing off its landing gear. An injured Capt. Rathje—the same who had narrowly missed death in the "Mongolian Incident" (see page 26)—was carried on a stretcher through the jungle for five days before reaching help in Indo-China on the railroad to Hanoi.

## Miracles Take a Little Time

Any transport aircraft was a priceless asset in wartorn China in 1939, and this one was considered much too precious to leave to rot on a mountainside. Accordingly, under the supervision of Ing. Schneider, a German master mechanic of Eurasia, 33 pack animals, loaded with spare parts and equipment, were sent to the crash site.

The series of pictures tells the story better than words. The aircraft was repaired and almost 1000 workers methodically dug out a runway on the steep slope. It was a masterpiece of ingenuity and improvisation. On 15 October, only six months after the crash, and with only 4 feet to spare on each side of the 900-foot mud-surfaced strip, Eu XIX flew to Kunming to resume its much-needed logistics support for the Chinese.

# A German Airline Empire

## Built-in Handicaps

Compared to the other European "empire" networks, serving dominions and colonies overseas, the German intercontinental map at the outbreak of World War II in 1939 was not too impressive. Germany had been deprived of all its overseas territories after World War I and its former adversaries controlled all the commercially significant airspace in the Eastern Hemisphere. Without sovereignty, Germany had no territorial bargaining cards to play; privileges to overfly, land, or carry traffic were granted reluctantly.

## Bricks Without Straw

German airlines were thus obliged to seek other avenues of geographical and political opportunity. **Junkers Luftverkehr** and then **Deutsche Luft Hansa** were at first active in the U.S.S.R., but political problems in 1933 ended this promising line of development towards the Far East, where D.L.H. had set up an airline in China, itself beginning to shake off the shackles of colonialism. Substantial progress was made, however, in South America, with cooperation from neutral Spain and Portugal, and with help from German expatriates and citizens in Brazil and other countries.

D.L.H. had been prepared to open services across the North Atlantic in 1939 with the **Focke-Wulf Fw 200 Condor** and the **Dornier Do 26** flying boat as the standard-bearers. But Martin Wronsky had been denied U.S. landing rights. Six Blohm & Voss BV 222 six-engined flying boats had also been ordered for luxury passenger service across the oceans; but these, together with seven more, were used for long-range reconnaissance during World War II.

Had the war not intervened, Deutsche Lufthansa could have developed a prestigious long-haul route network and would have been a force to be reckoned with in the world of international air transport. Instead, D.L.H. was obliged to contrive an amalgam of joint services, partnerships, and associated airlines. It was a masterpiece of improvisation.

Even in 1939 at the outbreak of World War II, two **Dornier Wal**s were still operating in the Baltic.

The long-range **Heinkel 116** was due for delivery in 1940 to supplement the Focke-Wulf Condor, but it never went into regular service.

When World War II broke out, Lufthansa had nine **Heinkel 111**s. Like the Heinkel 111s, the **Junkers-Ju 86**s were quickly requisitioned for the Luftwaffe.

### MODERNIZATION OF THE D.L.H. FLEET 1932–1939

| Aircraft Category and Type | Normal Seats | 1932 No. | 1932 Total Seats | 1936 No. | 1936 Total Seats | 1939 No. | 1939 Total Seats |
|---|---|---|---|---|---|---|---|
| **EARLY TYPES** | | | | | | | |
| **Single-engined** | | | | | | | |
| Junkers-F 13/A 20/W 33/34 | 4 | 49 | 196 | 9 | 36 | 2 | 8 |
| Fokker F II/F III | 4 | 18 | 72 | 1 | 4 | — | — |
| Dornier Merkur | 6 | 21 | 126 | — | — | — | — |
| Focke-Wulf Möwe | 8 | 16 | 128 | — | — | — | — |
| Junkers-F 24 | 9 | 9 | 81 | — | — | — | — |
| Others (Caspar 32, Ju 46) | — | 2 | — | 3 | — | — | — |
| Single-engined subtotal | | 115 | 603 | 13 | 40 | 2 | 8 |
| **Twin-engined** | | | | | | | |
| Dornier Wal | 10 | 9 | 90 | 5 | 50 | 2 | 20 |
| Other twins (Romar, Albatros) | 8 | 4 | 32 | — | — | — | — |
| **Trimotors** | | | | | | | |
| Ju-G 24/31 | 9 | 15 | 135 | 1 | 9 | — | — |
| Rohrbach Roland | 10 | 13 | 130 | — | — | — | — |
| Multi-engined subtotal | | 41 | 387 | 6 | 59 | 2 | 20 |
| **Total Early Types** | | 156 | 990 | 19 | 99 | 4 | 28 |
| **INTERIM TYPES** | | | | | | | |
| **Single-engined** | | | | | | | |
| Messerschmitt M 20 | 10 | 12 | 120 | 5 | 50 | 8 | 80 |
| **Trimotor** | | | | | | | |
| Junkers-Ju 52/3m | 16 | 2 | 32 | 59 | 944 | 78 | 1248 |
| **Four-engined** | | | | | | | |
| Junkers-G 38 | 34 | 2 | 68 | 1 | 34 | 1 | 34 |
| **Total Interim Types** | | 16 | 220 | 65 | 1028 | 87 | 1362 |
| **MODERN TYPES** | | | | | | | |
| **Single-engined** | | | | | | | |
| Junkers Ju 160 | 6 | — | — | 18 | 108 | 16 | 96 |
| Heinkel He 70 | 4 | — | — | 12 | 48 | — | — |
| Focke-Wulf Fw 58 | 6 | — | — | — | — | 8 | 48 |
| **Twin-engined** | | | | | | | |
| Heinkel He 111 | 10 | — | — | 7 | 70 | 9 | 90 |
| Junkers-Ju 86 | 10 | — | — | 6 | 60 | 13 | 130 |
| Dornier Do 18 | — | — | — | 2 | — | — | — |
| **Four-engined** | | | | | | | |
| Focke-Wulf Fw 200 | 26 | — | — | — | — | 4 | 104 |
| Junkers-Ju 90 | 40 | — | — | — | — | 4 | 160 |
| Dornier Do 26 | — | — | — | — | — | 2 | — |
| **Total Modern Types** | | — | — | 45 | 286 | 56 | 628 |
| **TOTAL FLEET** | | 170 | 1210 | 129 | 1413 | 147 | 2018 |

**Note** All figures as at 31 December. By the end of 1939 there were probably as many as ten Fw 200s and ten Ju 90s on D.L.H.'s register, but at least half of these were impressed into military service.

# Lufthansa in 1939

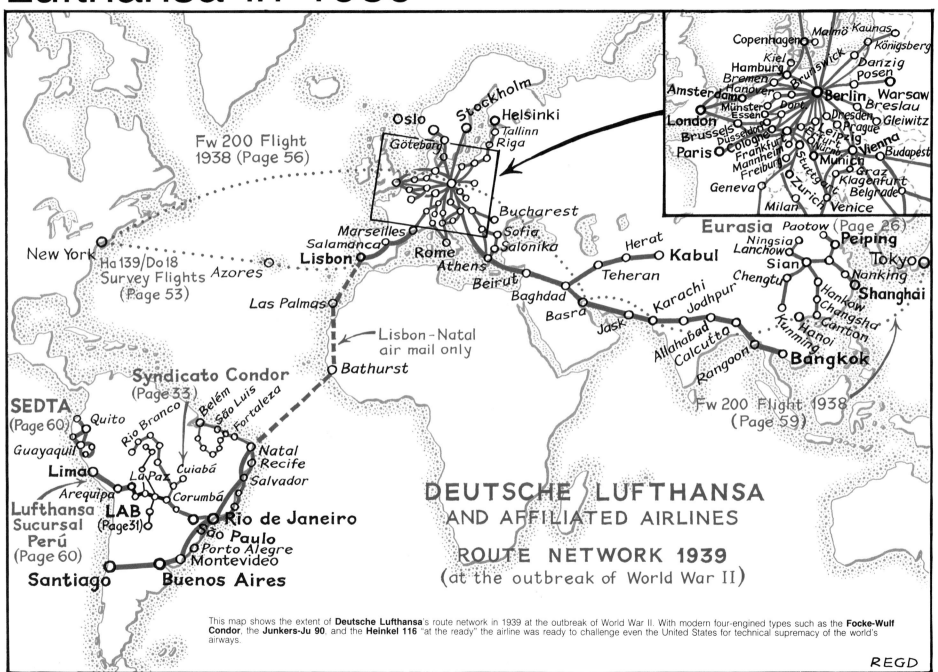

Fw 200 Flight 1938 (Page 56)

Ha 139/Do 18 Survey Flights (Page 53)

New York
Azores

Oslo
Göteborg
Stockholm
Helsinki
Tallinn
Riga

Marseilles
Salamanca
Lisbon
Rome
Athens
Bucharest
Sofia
Salonika
Beirut
Baghdad
Basra
Jask

Las Palmas

Lisbon–Natal air mail only

Bathurst

Herat
Teheran
Kabul
Karachi
Jodhpur
Allahabad
Calcutta
Rangoon

Chengtu
Kunming
Hanoi
Canton
Changsha
Hankow
Nanking
Shanghai
Sian
Lanchow
Ningsia
Paotow
Peiping
Tokyo

Eurasia (Page 26)

Fw 200 Flight 1938 (Page 59)

Syndicato Condor (Page 33)

SEDTA (Page 60)
Quito
Guayaquil
Lima
Arequipa
Lufthansa Sucursal Perú (Page 60)
Santiago

Rio Branco
La Paz
Cuiabá
Corumbá
LAB (Page 31)
Belém
São Luis
Fortaleza
Natal
Recife
Salvador
Rio de Janeiro
São Paulo
Porto Alegre
Montevideo
Buenos Aires

DEUTSCHE LUFTHANSA
AND AFFILIATED AIRLINES

ROUTE NETWORK 1939
(at the outbreak of World War II)

Copenhagen
Malmö
Kaunas
Königsberg
Kiel
Hamburg
Bremen
Hanover
Danzig
Posen
Warsaw
Amsterdam
Brunswick
Berlin
Münster
Dort
Breslau
London
Essen
Düsseldorf
Cologne
Dresden
Gleiwitz
Brussels
Frankfurt
Leipzig
Prague
Paris
Mannheim
Erfurt
Nürnb
Vienna
Freiburg
Stuttgart
Munich
Budapest
Geneva
Zurich
Graz
Klagenfurt
Belgrade
Milan
Venice

This map shows the extent of **Deutsche Lufthansa**'s route network in 1939 at the outbreak of World War II. With modern four-engined types such as the **Focke-Wulf Condor**, the **Junkers-Ju 90**, and the **Heinkel 116** "at the ready" the airline was ready to challenge even the United States for technical supremacy of the world's airways.

REGD

# Lufthansa and the War Effort

## The Bubble Bursts

Just when **Deutsche Lufthansa** had reached a high point in its development, all progress was brought to a halt by the outbreak of World War II on 3 September 1939. In line with nations on both sides of the war, German commercial airline services open to the public were discontinued.

The transition was swift and effective. Since 1933, Erhard Milch, a member of the airline's executive board since 1926, had also been Secretary of State of the Reichsluftfahrtministerium. The machinery for converting D.L.H. into an effective transport division of the armed forces was thus already in place and under control.

## A Fleet Transformed

Of the 145 aircraft on Lufthansa's books at the end of 1939, 22 **Heinkel 111**s and **Junkers-Ju 86**s were promptly requisitioned. Within three years, the fleet was reduced to 59, of which 47 were **Junkers-Ju 52/3m**s and the rest an odd mixture of obsolescent single-engined types and such representatives of the latest four-engined technology as the **Focke-Wulf Fw 200 Condor** and the **Junkers-Ju 90**.

Fleet reductions by Air Ministry requisition and by enemy action continued as the war ebbed and flowed around an alternately expanding and contracting Third Reich. Relief came from C.L.S., K.L.M., and SABENA (see table), from aircraft chartered from Iberia and Aero O/Y, seizure from Ala Littoria, and more charters from Air France in 1943. D.L.H.'s fleet in its last summer of 1944 included such unlikely types as the **Douglas DC-2** and **DC-3**, the **Bloch 220**, and the **Savoia Marchetti S.73**.

Two **Fokker F VIIb/3m**s, built in Czechoslovakia under license by Avia, and operated by C.L.S. (OK-ABP and OK-ABS), worked for Lufthansa during 1939 as D-AABP and D-AABS. In the occupied countries, the airlines cooperated with Lufthansa and a new airline, **Slovenská Letecká Akciová Spoleĉnost** (**S.L.S.**), operated in Slovakia from 1939 to 1944, with a fleet that included Junkers-Ju 86s.

The fleet count at the end of 1944 was officially 34:31 Junkers *Tante Ju*s and 3 **Focke-Wulf Fw 58**s. But all except three of the Junkers were chartered to the air force. Yet during the last few months into the spring of 1945 some incredible efforts were made to uphold the deeply entrenched traditions of a great airline. Three **Junkers-Ju 290**s, improved versions of the four-engined Ju 90s, and even commerical conversions of the **Ju 88** bomber were added for sporadic operations to support the FW 200 Condors and Ju 52/3ms.

## Business as Usual

Deutsche Lufthansa had a patriotic duty to link Germany with friendly and neutral countries, but there were voices of dissent within the airline. Some members disagreed with the policies of the Nazi regime, notably Klaus Bonhoeffer, head of the legal department, assisted by one of the company's lawyers, Otto John. Bonhoeffer was arrested after the attempted assassination of Hitler on 20 July 1944, and was subsequently executed. John was able to escape to a neutral country.

But as the Allied forces began to advance toward Germany from east, south, and west, the routes were curtailed. As described on the opposite page, like captains going down with their ships, a nucleus of Deutsche Lufthansa staff were still reporting for duty long after they could so easily have found excuses to be elsewhere.

### LUFTHANSA'S DOUGLAS FLEET IN THE WAR YEARS

| Const. No. | Regist. No. or Name Original | Luftwaffe | Lufthansa | Lufthansa Service From | To |
|---|---|---|---|---|---|
| **DC-2 (ex-C.L.S., Czechoslovakia)** | | | | | |
| 1582 | OK-AIB | — | D-AAIB | July 40 | 24 March 41[1] |
| 1565 | OK-AID | VG + FV | D-AAID | July 40 | Jan. 41[3] |
| 1562 | OK-AIC | — | D-AAIO | July 40 | 27 March 41[1] |
| **DC-2 (ex-K.L.M., Netherlands)** | | | | | |
| 1365 | PH-AKS | NA + LF | D-ABOW | 1 Aug. 40 | 11 Feb. 44[3] |
| 1355 | PH-AKI | NA + LD | D-ADBK | 25 July 40 | |
| 1363 | PH-AKQ | SG + KV | D-AEAN | July 40 | May 45[4] |
| 1364 | PH-AKR | PC + EB | D-AIAS | July 40 | [4] |
| 1366 | PH-AKT | NA + LA | D-AIAV | 23 July 40 | 9 Aug. 40[3] |
| 1356 | PH-AKJ | PC + EC | D-AJAW | July 40 | [4] |
| **DC-3 (ex-C.L.S., Czechoslovakia)** | | | | | |
| 2023 | OK-AIE | *Mährisch-Ostrau* | D-AAIE | 24 Aug. 39 | 9 Dec. 44[2] |
| 2024 | OK-AIF | *Brünn* | D-AAIF | 24 Aug. 39 | 43[2] |
| 2095 | OK-AIG | — | D-AAIG | 24 July 40 | 21 April 44[3] |
| 1973 | OK-AIH | *Prag* | D-AAIH | 24 Aug. 39 | 29 Oct. 40[3] |
| **DC-3 (ex-K.L.M., Netherlands)** | | | | | |
| 2110 | PH-ASR | VE + RR | D-ABBF | 16 Sept. 40 | 9 Dec. 42[3] |
| 1935 | PH-ALH | PC + EA | D-ABUG | Aug. 40 | |
| 2036 | PH-ASK | NA + LB | D-AOFS | 18 June 40 | April 45[4] |
| 1943 | PH-ALV | NA + LC | D-ARPF | 1 June 40 | May 45[4] |
| 2142 | PH-ASM | NA + LE | D-ATJG | 15 June 40 | |
| **DC-3 (ex-SABENA, Belgium)** | | | | | |
| 2093 | OO-AUH | — | D-ATZP | 6 Aug. 43 | 5 May 45[4] |

**Notes** [1]Transferred to Aero O/Y, Finland. [2]Destroyed by enemy action during World War II. [3]Crashed during World War II. [4]Still in service in 1944. The DC-2 D-AEAN and the DC-3 D-ATZP were in service on the last day of the war. DC-3 D-ARPF was scrapped in England in 1950.

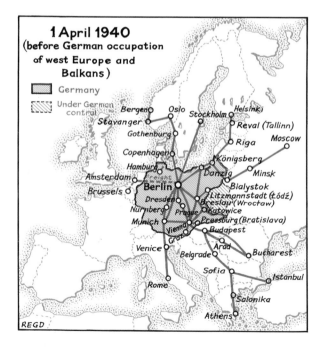

**1 April 1940** (before German occupation of west Europe and Balkans)

- Germany
- Under German control

Bergen, Oslo, Stockholm, Helsinki, Stavanger, Gothenburg, Reval (Tallinn), Riga, Moscow, Copenhagen, Königsberg, Hamburg, Danzig, Minsk, Amsterdam, Berlin, Bialystok, Brussels, Dresden, Breslau (Wrocław), Litzmannstadt (Łódź), Nürnberg, Katowice, Prague, Munich, Pressburg (Bratislava), Vienna, Budapest, Graz, Arad, Venice, Belgrade, Bucharest, Sofia, Rome, Istanbul, Salonika, Athens

REGD

**September 1941** (at the height of German control of Europe)

- Germany and Italy
- Under Axis control

Hammerfest, Kirkenes, Harstad, Tromsö, Narvik, Bodö, Trondheim, Oslo, Stockholm, Copenhagen, Königsberg, Danzig, Berlin, Breslau, Prague, Vienna, Munich, Lyons, Zurich, Graz, Budapest, Venice, Agram (Zagreb), Marseilles, Belgrade, Bucharest, re-opened 12 Aug. 1940, Sarajevo, Sofia, Istanbul, Lisbon, Madrid, Barcelona, Rome, Salonika, Athens

REGD

# Final Countdown

## Rise and Fall of the Third Reich

Throughout history, the complex frontiers of Europe have been in a constant state of flux, according to the demands of military conquest, the decisions of peace treaties, or even the fancies of royal families. But never did the map of Europe undergo such a convulsion as during the five short years of World War II, when the Nazi rulers of Germany enlarged the Reich to the scale of the old Holy Roman Empire, only to see it collapse like a house of cards.

During this frenzied era, **Deutsche Lufthansa**'s route network reflected the fortunes of this war, as the map series below illustrates. In 1940, during the period of preliminary sparring before the invasion of the Low Countries and the breach of the Maginot Line, services were maintained to neutral countries. (Map 1)

In little less than a year, after blitzkriegs to the west and to the Balkans, Deutsche Lufthansa expanded from the Arctic Circle to the Mediterranean and to the Balkan capitals. Particularly noteworthy were the routes to Lisbon and Stockholm, where German and British airline personnel eyed each other in a mood of mutual nonbelligerence. (Map 2)

This state of affairs did not last long. The tide of war turned and the Allies closed in inexorably. As the Axis forces retreated, D.L.H. adapted to each new emergency, first curtailing and then abandoning routes, often under artillery fire or when enemy troops were literally at the airfield perimeters. (Map 3)

## The Last Stand

During the last two weeks of the war, Deutsche Lufthansa was still in operation, but the end was near. There were forced landings, diversions, and encounters with enemy aircraft, including one occasion when the attacking Mosquito crashed but the D.L.H. Ju 290 survived. Vienna was evacuated on 5 April 1945; U.S. and Soviet troops met at Torgau, not far south of Berlin, on 25 April; Munich was occupied by American troops on 30 April. Some Lufthansa aircraft were stranded in a pocket of precariously held territory in Austria and Moravia and were abandoned or destroyed. (Map 4)

Deutsche Lufthansa moved out of Berlin on 22–23 April and took up temporary—very temporary—residence at Warnemünde, in one of the few small enclaves of territory on the Baltic coast not yet crushed within the giant Allied pincer movement. This refuge soon became too hot to hold, and all aircraft flew onward to Flensburg, in Schleswig. By this time, the fleet consisted of a **Focke-Wulf Fw 200 Condor**, a **Douglas DC-2** and a **DC-3**, a couple of **Junkers-Ju 52/3m**'s, and a **Junkers-Ju 88**.

## Finis

The last flights were made by the Fw 200 D-ASVX *Thüringen*, on a scheduled trip on 3 May to Oslo (only five minutes late) and arriving back in Flensburg after overnighting at Aalborg, on 5 May; and by the Ju 52/3m D-AFFF, which had been conducting an emergency courier service between Aalborg and Oslo and checked in on the same day. The dismembered route along the coast of Norway, operated by Ju 52/3m floatplanes, simply carried on until someone on the Allied side told everyone to stop. (Map 5)

Canadian troops entered Flensberg on 6 May 1945, and all German forces of the northern commands surrendered the following day. Disciplined to the end, the largest prewar airline in Europe was grounded. For the record, Deutsche Lufthansa A.G. was officially liquidated on 1 January 1951, and final settlements were made in 1965.

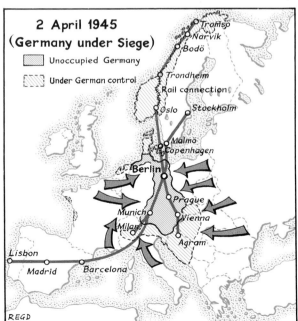

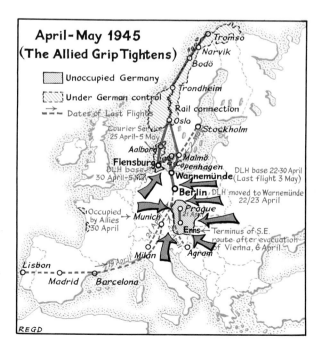

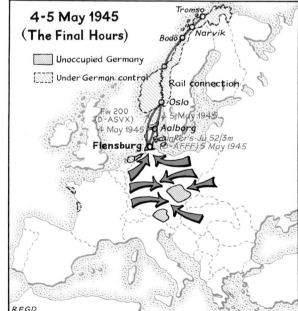

# A New Start

## Tragic Postscript

One of the great world promoters and pacesetters of air transport before World War II was Martin Wronsky, who had been the first to examine systematically the economics and operations of air transport while a director of Deutsche Luft-Reederei in 1919. He became a driving force in the commercial affairs of the old Lufthansa, particularly in the development of long-range international services in the early 1930s, and later represented the airline in important international negotiations. He was respected enough to be appointed U.S. custodian for D.L.H. after World War II.

In 1945 he tried to revive the fine traditions of the old company and planned to make the Hansa Werkstätten GmbH and the Hansa Reise und Verkehr GmbH the nuclei of a new airline. Alas, in submitting the paperwork to the American authorities, he was accused of falsifying a questionnaire on his background. He had not mentioned his association with the National Socialist Party, which he had been obliged to join in 1933. One of the airline industry's great pioneers, who had been almost ostracized by his colleagues during his latter career, Martin Wronsky took his own life on 12 December 1946.

## Büro Bongers

In 1950, Hans M. Bongers, former traffic director of the old Lufthansa, tried to establish an agency for airlines, to gain experience until Germany could once again operate air services. But the British occupation authorities would not grant the necessary permission. He thereupon set up his own consultancy business, the **Büro Bongers**, at Bitburg, where he lived. On 29 May 1951, Dr. Seebohm, the Minister of Transport, appointed him as adviser to the government of the Federal Republic, reporting to the **Vorbereitungsausschuss Luftverkehr (V.A.L.)**, or Aviation Preparatory Committee, which began work on 9 November 1951 and made its final report in October 1952.

## Luftag

By this time the government had, on 26 September 1952, already resolved to form an airline, and on 6 January 1953, a provisional stock company was founded, the **Aktiengesellschaft für Luftverkehrsbedarf (Luftag)**. It was backed by the federal government, the Deutsche Bundesbahn, and the state of Nordrhein-Westfalen. The first chairman was Dr. Weigelt, who had been a member of the board of directors of the old company when it was formed in 1926 and had been vice-chairman since 1936. His deputy was Kurt Knipfer, head of the air transport division of the Air Ministry; Bongers and Gerhard Höltje, another Lufthansa old-timer, were members of the executive committee. The capital was 6,000,000 marks.

On 26 June 1953, Luftag ordered four **Lockheed L-1049G Super Constellation**s for the long-haul routes, and on 28 September, four **Convair 340**s were acquired for the short-haul routes. In November of that year, Luftag increased its capital to 25,000,000 marks by the admission of private shareholders. On 2 December a contract was placed to develop the airport and to establish an engineering base at Hamburg.

## Rebirth

On 6 August 1954, Luftag changed its name to **Deutsche Lufthansa Aktiengesellschaft** and the capital was increased to 50,000,000 marks. Trading simply as **Lufthansa**, it began its first scheduled services, after some trials and proving flights, on 1 April 1955. The Convairliners D-ACOH and D-ACEF inaugurated the first German domestic routes, Munich-Frankfurt-Cologne-Hamburg and Hamburg-Düsseldorf-Frankfurt-Munich, on the same day. Until then, the internal services had been operated by other European airlines such as S.A.S. and SABENA.

The Federal Republic regained full air sovereignty, in ratification of the Paris Agreements, on 5 May. Three international routes, originating in Hamburg, were promptly started, to Madrid on 15 May, to London on 16 May, and to Paris on 17 May. The new Lufthansa was under way.

LUFTHANSA'S CONVAIRLINERS

| Const. No. | Regist. No. | Date of Deliv. | Disposal |
|---|---|---|---|
| Convair 340[1] | | | |
| 198 | D-ACAD | 20 Aug. 1954 | Sold to General Air 18 April 1969 |
| 210 | D-ACEF | 26 Oct. 1954 | Sold to General Air 18 April 1969 |
| 211 | D-ACIG | 18 Oct. 1954 | Sold to J.A.T. 17 March 1969 |
| 213 | D-ACOH | 28 Oct. 1954 | Sold to General Air 1 February 1971 |
| Convair 440 Metropolitan | | | |
| 408 | D-ACIB | 31 March 1957 | Sold to Air Algérie 21 June 1968 |
| 409 | D-ACUM | 31 March 1957 | Sold to Air Algérie 21 June 1968 |
| 448 | D-ACYL | 8 Aug. 1957 | Sold to Tellair 17 March 1969 |
| 451 | D-ACAP | 16 Aug. 1957 | Sold to Air Algérie 21 June 1968 |
| 460 | D-ACEX | 17 Sept. 1957 | Sold to Air Algérie 21 June 1968 |
| 464 | D-ACAT[2] | 1 Nov. 1961 | Crashed 28 Jan. 1968 |
| 470 | D-ACEK[2] | 1 Nov. 1961 | Sold to J.A.T. 21 Jan. 1968 |

[1]The Convair 340s were modified to Convair 440s during the winter of 1957–58.
[2]D-ACAT and D-ACEK were from *Condor Luftreederei*.

Hans M. Bongers *(top)*, who laid the groundwork for the rebirth of the new **Deutsche Lufthansa** in 1953.

Gerhard Höltje *(bottom)*, head of **Lufthansa**'s flight operations and engineering in the 1950s, steered the airline into the jet age.

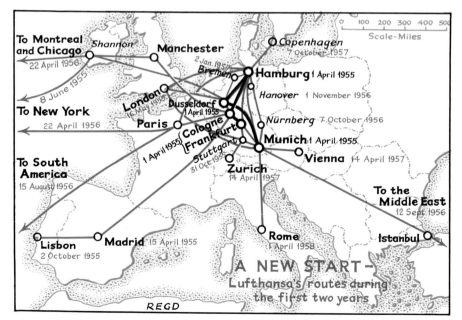

To Montreal and Chicago — Shannon — 22 April 1956
2 Jan. 1957
To New York — 8 June 1955
To New York — 22 April 1956
To South America — 15 August 1956
Manchester
Copenhagen 7 October 1957
Bremen
Hamburg 1 April 1955
Hanover 1 November 1956
London 16 May 1955
Düsseldorf 1 April 1955
Paris — 1 April 1955
Cologne
Frankfurt
Stuttgart
Nürnberg 7 October 1956
Munich 1 April 1955
Vienna 14 April 1957
Zurich 14 April 1957
To the Middle East 12 Sept. 1956
Lisbon 2 October 1955
Madrid 15 April 1955
Rome 1 April 1958
Istanbul
A NEW START – Lufthansa's routes during the first two years
REGD

# Convair 340

## 44 seats • 240 mph

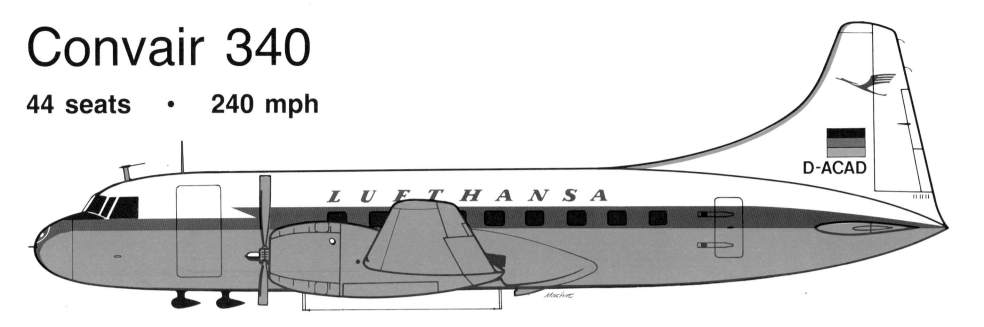

D-ACAD

Pratt & Whitney R2800-CB16 (2400 hp) × 2 • 45,000 lb max. gross takeoff weight • 700 statute miles range

## Development

After World War II the United States airlines, experiencing a boom in traffic, demanded supplies of new aircraft in all categories. In the competition for the short-haul airliner to upgrade the routes then served by the reliable but venerable Douglas DC-3, the **Martin** company seemed to have the edge at first. The **Model 2-0-2** went into service in November 1947, but it was unpressurized and had a structural deficiency. United Air Lines withdrew its support for the **Model 3-0-3**, but T.W.A. and Eastern started service with the improved and pressurized **Model 4-0-4** in October 1951.

By this time, however, most of the U.S. airlines, followed by those in Europe and elsewhere, had turned to Consolidated-Vultee, or Convair, as it became known, for its fine series of twin-engined short-haul airliners. American Airlines had sponsored the **Convair 240** with an unprecedented order for 100 in 1945, reduced later to 75 but still a welcome launching stimulus for the 40-seat replacement for the DC-3.

## Choice of Models

American Airlines put the Convair 240 into service on 1 June 1948, but the most popular model of the Convairliner series was the **Convair 340**, slightly larger than the 240 with an extra row of four-abreast seats. United Air Lines introduced it on 16 November 1952, just at the time when preparations were being made to form the postwar Luftag, which was to be the nucleus of the reborn Lufthansa.

At this time a technical battle was raging for technical leadership in the construction of commercial airliners. The British manufacturers were setting a challenging pace. The first jet airliner, the de Havilland Comet 1, went into service in 1952, and the first turboprop, the Vickers Viscount, on 18 April 1953. The operator of the latter was British European Airways (B.E.A.), which threatened to dominate the European airways with a large fleet.

**Lufthansa** had a difficult choice to make. The four-engined turboprop Viscount appeared to be technically, and possibly economically, superior. But the Convairliner came from an

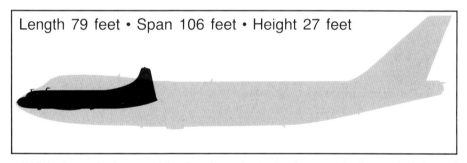

Length 79 feet • Span 106 feet • Height 27 feet

established manufacturer, and the American standards of support for the product, born of long experience of severe competition, were superior to those of the British, comparatively new to the business of commercial airliner marketing overseas.

Lufthansa took a conservative approach. It ordered the Convairliner and even reordered the more advanced **Convair 440 Metropolitan** for service in 1957, preferring to wait until the Viscount had proved itself in service and had been further developed.

### THE CONVAIRLINERS

| Series | Engines | | Dimensions (ft) | | |
| | Type | Hp (each) | Length | Span | Seats |
| --- | --- | --- | --- | --- | --- |
| 240 | P & W R2800-CA18 | 1000 | 75 | 92 | 40 |
| 340 | P & W R2800-CB16 | 1200 | 79 | 106 | 44 |
| 440 Metropolitan | P & W R2800-CB17 | 1400 | 79 | 106 | 52 |

Note   Other versions of the Convairliner had turboprop engines but were not used in Europe.

# Back to the Atlantic

## Claiming a Birthright

If ever an airline had a case for what the Civil Aeronautics Board in the U.S.A. termed "grandfather rights," then Lufthansa could stake a good claim for time-honored rights to fly commercial services across the Atlantic Ocean. As several previous pages in this book narrate, the German airline, together with its associated airship company and affiliates in South America, had pioneered the routes across both the North and South Atlantic. Surveys of the northern route had been made by von Gronau as early as 1930 (page 34); mail flights had been made from ocean liners (36) and from depot ships (38, 52); the *Graf Zeppelin* had operated a South Atlantic service during the mid-1930s (40); and the *Hindenburg* had operated for a year across the North Atlantic in 1936. The **Focke-Wulf Fw 200 Condor**, by flying nonstop from Berlin to New York and back in 1938 (56), had laid claim to the technical capability of starting a landplane service between Europe and North America.

## A Tradition Maintained

The new **Lufthansa** reestablished the traditions of the old in convincing fashion. Having been prevented from starting an airline earlier than in the mid-1950s, it had been able to bypass the problems of introducing early models of the postwar airliners and had not had to share the burden of solving all the technical and operational problems which only day-in, day-out airline service can reveal. Just as it had introduced the Convair 340, a developed version of the original Convairliner, it was able to skip the first generation of classic piston-engined airliners that laid the foundations of the postwar intercontinental route network after World War II.

On 8–9 June 1955 the crane emblem was proudly carried on a Lockheed **L-1049G Super Constellation** from Hamburg to New York, via Düsseldorf and Shannon. A few days earlier, on one of the proving flights, one of the guests on the "Super-G" was Commandant James Fitzmaurice, who had been one of the three-men crew who had made the first nonstop east-west crossing of the North Atlantic in 1928 (page 34). Lufthansa attained full IATA membership shortly thereafter, on 29 June 1955.

## Consolidation

On 22–23 April 1956, Lufthansa inaugurated a new North Atlantic service, the "Manchester Mid-Western." It provided, for the first time, a direct service from the north of England to North America, both to Montreal, Canada, and Chicago, as a second destination in the United States. The move was bold and innovative but carefully analyzed and planned, an approach that was to be the hallmark of Lufthansa's methods in the years to come. Originating from Hamburg, one of the two weekly flights called at Düsseldorf, the other at Frank-

furt—this latter city still only a staging point until it became the center of operations in 1960.

Four months later, on 15–16 August, the German flag was carried once more to South America, reviving memories of pioneering during the 1930s. The route was Hamburg–Düsseldorf (or Frankfurt)–Paris–Dakar–Rio de Janeiro. The second flight, on 18–19 August, continued on to São Paulo and Buenos Aires. Both were operated under a joint agreement with Air France, and this became a complete cost- and revenue-sharing pool agreement on 1 July 1957. By this time, Montevideo had been added to the South American route, on 10 April. A year earlier, on 12 September 1956, a Super-G had reestablished Lufthansa in the Middle East, with a route to Teheran, via Istanbul, Beirut, and Baghdad.

LUFTHANSA'S L-1049G SUPER CONSTELLATIONS

| Const. No. | Regist. No. | Date of Deliv. | Disposal |
|---|---|---|---|
| 4602 | D-ALAK | 29 March 1955 | Crashed Rio de Janeiro 11 Jan. 1959 |
| 4603 | D-ALEM | 19 April 1955 | Scrapped 1 April 1967 |
| 4604 | D-ALIN | 29 April 1955 | Presented to Hamburg Airport 7 Sept. 1967 |
| 4605 | D-ALOP | 28 May 1955 | Sold 2 Aug. 1967 |
| 4637 | D-ALAP | 20 Feb. 1956 | Scrapped Dec. 1966 |
| 4640 | D-ALEC | 28 March 1956 | Retired 6 Oct. 1967; sold 8 March 1968 |
| 4642 | D-ALOF | 25 July 1956 | Retired 6 Oct. 1967; sold 8 Dec. 1967 |
| 4647 | D-ALID | 7 Aug. 1956 | Retired 6 Oct. 1967; sold 23 Feb. 1968 |

The **Lockheed Model L 1049G**.

# Lockheed L-1049G Super Constellation

## 85 seats • 335 mph

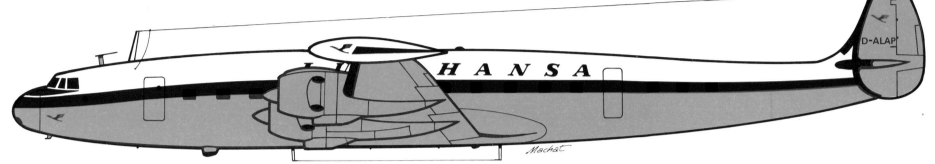

Wright 972 TC (3250 hp) × 4 • 137,500 lb max. gross takeoff weight • 4600 statute miles range

## A Thoroughbred Line

One of the best-known development stories of commercial airliner history is the way in which the **Lockheed Constellation** was produced, in almost complete secrecy, during World War II, in what was to become known as designer Kelly Johnson's "Skunk Works" at the Lockheed plant at Burbank, California. Inspired by Howard Hughes, owner of T.W.A., it made its first flight on 9 January 1943. It combined pressurized comfort with high speed; it was faster than any Douglas aircraft and took Washington by storm when Hughes and Jack Frye flew the prototype to Washington in less than seven hours on 19 April 1944.

**T.W.A.** put the "Connie" into service on the transcontinental route from New York to Los Angeles on 1 March 1946. Its comfort and speed combined with an elegance of design which quickly attracted the attention of the public and the airline industry alike. Although most of the big flag carriers and trunk airliners resumed postwar long-haul services with the trusty Douglas DC-4, they soon ordered the Constellation, which was 70 mph faster—almost half again as fast—and had 60 seats against the DC-4's 44 in normal layout.

## Fierce Competition

A battle royal began between Douglas, hitherto the dominant commercial aircraft constructor, and Lockheed, which had been a poor second in prewar competition for the airline market. **United Air Lines**, faithful to Douglas, opened a **DC-6** coast-to-coast schedule on 27 April 1947. Douglas had been spurred into action and had produced a faster and pressurized version of its four-engined transport. Both aircraft had severe problems. The Constellation was grounded during the late summer of 1946 and the DC-6 during the winter of 1947–1948.

United introduced a better DC-6, the **DC-6B**, on 11 April 1951, but T.W.A. trumped this ace with the Super Constellation **Model 1049** on 10 September 1952, this development having been baptized into service by **Eastern Air Lines** on 17 December 1951. Douglas then responded with the **DC-7** with **American Airlines** service on 29 November 1953, and T.W.A. came back with the **Model 1049G** on 1 April 1955. This was to prove the most popular of all the Lockheed Constellation series.

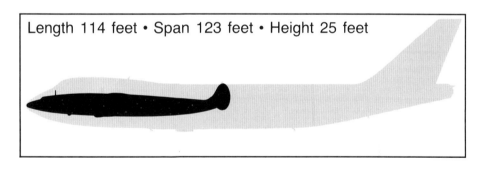

Length 114 feet • Span 123 feet • Height 25 feet

## Riding on the Wave

The Lockheed-Douglas rivalry was evident on the North Atlantic, where Pan American favored the Douglas stable and had the DC-6, DC-7B, and finally the DC-7C to take it through to the jet age. Some European airlines took the Douglas product, some the Lockheed, and many took both. Lufthansa would have preferred the DC-6B and had even signed a letter of intent for ten, but Douglas would not agree to the terms. And so Lufthansa went to Lockheed, and had the benefit of coming in at a late stage, like a star tennis player seeded until the final rounds of a tournament.

When, therefore, Lufthansa entered the fiercely competitive transatlantic market in 1955, it was able to face all challengers with an airliner second to none. Combined with a standard of service and reliability that was also second to none, the German flag carrier served notice that it would, in the future, be a force to be reckoned with.

# Turbine Power

## Struggle for Leadership in Europe

Even as, in 1953, **Luftag** decided to start European services with the route-proven Convairliners, **British European Airways (B.E.A.)** had started a new era in air transport by introducing the **Vickers Viscount** on its main-line services. In combination with the Airspeed Ambassador, B.E.A. gained undisputed domain over European airline skies during the 1950s. By 1956 the superiority of turbine power over the piston engine was firmly established and Vickers was already marketing a larger version of the original Viscount Series 700. B.E.A.'s first **Viscount 802** went into service on 13 February 1957, to strengthen the British airline's dominance even further.

The smooth-riding turbine-engined type simply had the edge in passenger appeal, giving B.E.A. high load factors, with consequent higher revenue-earning and profit-making potential to reinforce the parity with the Convairliner in operating costs. **Lufthansa** had to match the competition.

## The Viscount

On 15 June 1956, Lufthansa ordered nine of the larger Viscounts, Series 814, even though more Convairliners were soon to enter service, to Zurich and Vienna on 14 April and to Copenhagen on 6 October 1957. Brussels and Rome were added to the map on 1 April 1958.

The first Viscount service was from Munich to London, and the familiar crane symbol on the turboprop's tail was to be seen all over Europe within a matter of a few months. New services were started to Milan on 1 April 1959, to Stockholm on 20 April, to Athens on 10 May, and to Barcelona on 24 May.

## A Bold Initiative

On 8 November 1957, Hans Bongers, in a visionary memorandum to Air France—possibly with an eye to the north, where the three airlines of Scandinavia had amalgamated to form the S.A.S. consortium—proposed a cooperative union, to be called **Europair,** between Air France, Alitalia, Swissair, SABENA, and Lufthansa. Costs and revenues would be shared under an equitable formula which took into account various economic indices, traffic shares, and political and commercial considerations. Swissair declined, but K.L.M. agreed to attend the first meeting in Brussels on 29 December 1958. K.L.M. later withdrew. On 20 May 1959, traffic quotas were fixed at 34% for Air France, 30% for Lufthansa, 26% for Alitalia, and 10% for SABENA. The name of the joint airline was changed to **Air Union**, and full agreement was reached on tricky questions of cabotage and colonial traffic.

The proposed metamorphosis of the European air traffic system would have gone into effect on 1 April 1960, but Air Union never got under way or off the ground. Even with

political moves afoot to establish the European Common Market, the formula did not have enough safeguards or flexibility to allow for unforeseen circumstances. And so a promising experiment in international cooperation was still-born.

Later, in the 1970s, **K.S.S.U.** was to be a common-supplier maintenance, overhaul, and spares pool for **K**.L.M., **S**.A.S., **S**wissair, and **U**.T.A.; while **ATLAS** was a similar combination of Air France, Alitalia, Lufthansa, and SABENA. Hans Bongers's Air Union had been a prophetic harbinger of future developments in cooperation in the technical if not in the political arena.

While the **Viscount** began a new era, the piston-engined **Convairliner** still provided stiff competition as the last standard-bearer of a previous generation.

LUFTHANSA'S VISCOUNT 814-D FLEET

| Const. No. | Regist. No. | Date of Deliv. | Disposal |
|---|---|---|---|
| 338 | D-ANUN | 5 Oct. 1958 | To Condor 5 Feb. 1962–27 Aug. 1969; sold 7 June 1971 |
| 339 | D-ANOL | 19 Dec. 1958 | To Condor 12 March 1964–22 Jan. 1969; sold to Br. Midland (G-AWXI) 22 Jan. 1969 |
| 340 | D-ANAD | 10 Jan. 1959 | Retired 27 March 1970; sold 7 June 1971 |
| 341 | D-ANIP | 15 Feb. 1959 | To Condor 1 Nov. 1961–1 Nov. 1967; retired 31 March 1971; sold 7 June 1971 |
| 342 | D-ANUR | 8 March 1959 | To Condor 15 March 1963–27 Aug. 1969; retired 31 March 1971; sold 13 Jan. 1972 |
| 343 | D-ANEF | 26 March 1959 | Retired 31 March 1971; sold 13 Jan. 1972 |
| 344 | D-ANIZ | 4 April 1959 | Retired 8 Dec. 1969; sold 7 June 1971 |
| 368 | D-ANAM | 17 April 1959 | Retired 12 Feb. 1970 and used for training |
| 369 | D-ANAB | 29 April 1959 | Retired 28 Nov. 1969; sold 12 Nov. 1970 |
| 370 | D-ANAC | 30 July 1961 | Retired 1 July 1969; sold (G-AYOX) 19 Dec. 1970 |
| 447 | D-ANAF | 30 Nov. 1961 | Retired 30 Jan. 1969 and used for training from 12 April 1972 |

The **Vickers Viscount V-814-D**.

# Vickers Viscount 814-D

## 48 seats  •  312 mph

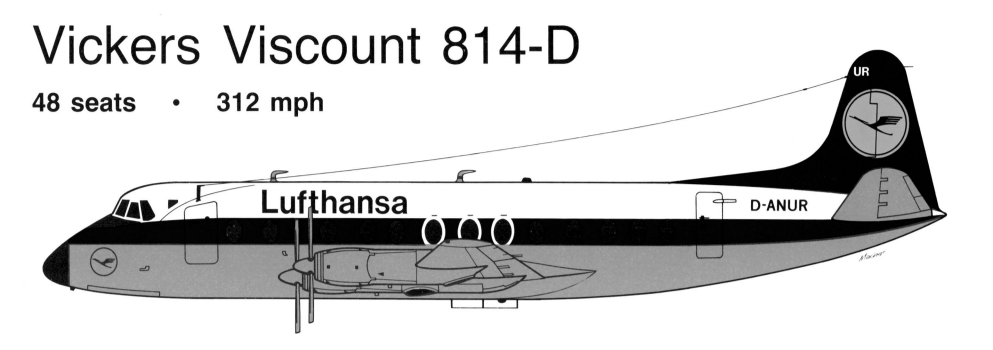

Rolls-Royce Dart (1650 ehp) × 4 • 64,500 lb max. gross takeoff weight • 2100 statute miles range

## Matching the Market

On 13 June 1945, at a meeting of the Second Brabazon Committee of the British Ministry of Aircraft Production, **Vickers-Armstrongs**, builders of the wartime Wellington bomber, proposed a new airliner, the **VC-2 Viceroy**, with four Armstrong-Siddeley Mamba turboprop engines. It had only 24 seats—fewer than a four-abreast DC-3—and this was clearly too small. By the time the **Series V.630**, as the VC-2 was redesignated, made its first flight on 16 July 1948, it was a 32-seater, powered by Rolls-Royce Darts.

Fortunately for Vickers and the entire British aircraft industry, **British European Airways (B.E.A.),** for which the aircraft was destined, insisted that even this was too small for the forecast traffic growth in Europe, a view that was confirmed by the public response to some experimental flights made between 29 July and 23 August 1950. By the time B.E.A. put the revolutionary turboprop into service on 18 April 1953, it had been enlarged to a comfortable 40-seater, designated the **Series V.700,** and renamed the **Viscount.**

B.E.A.'s launching order was for 20 **V.701s**, and Vickers was to sell more than 450 Viscounts of all series, the biggest success in the history of British commercial aircraft production. B.E.A.'s insistence on the V.700 specification was a creditable and visionary decision—in striking contrast with its subsequent appalling move to force de Havilland to shorten the fuselage of another potential world-beater, the medium-haul three-engined Trident.

## The Stretched Version

Almost without exception, the developed and invariably larger version of any commercial airliner has always been the most successful. Technical problems are ironed out, engine

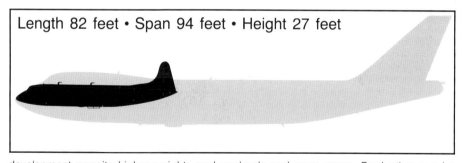

Length 82 feet • Span 94 feet • Height 27 feet

development permits higher weights and payloads and more range. Production can be made from the same jigs, with consequent economies in construction costs. And so it was with the Viscount.

B.E.A. ordered 12 of the larger Viscount 801 on 11 February 1953, and modified this on 14 April 1954 to the **Series 802**, with even better Dart engines. It entered service on 13 February 1957, and another version, the Series 806, was added on 27 January 1958. A further refinement, the Series 810, was the most successful of all.

Longer-range variants, first developed for the Australian transcontinental route, had the suffix -D. **Lufthansa's Viscount 814-D**s, therefore, were long-range aircraft, and the "4" indicated that it was the fourth customer after B.E.A.

# Goodbye to Propellers

## Keeping up the Pressure

During the last years of the four-engined propeller-driven airliners, the competition for intercontinental market shares raged unabated on the world's main air arteries, although there was an occasional case of mutually profitable pool agreements. When Lufthansa entered the North Atlantic market in 1955, traffic was increasing rapidly in the wake of the introduction of tourist fares, by unanimous agreement by IATA members, in 1952. By 1957, transatlantic passenger air traffic had reached the level of shipping volume, which thereafter began to decline.

As all the IATA members charged the same fares, competition was partly by the quality of service offered. Even this could be a problem as IATA tried to exert control over the standard of meals offered—there was a great debate over the definition of a sandwich—and of seating width and pitch.

## Equipment Competition

The only element in a competitive environment over which the airline retained control was thus the quality of the flying equipment, and thus the need for promoting the very best aircraft was never more intense. The **Douglas DC-7C**, the "Seven Seas" as it was neatly called, was used by some airlines, the **Super Constellation** by others—the choice was fairly equally balanced among the dozen or so flag carriers. Pan American and B.O.A.C. used the **Boeing 377 Stratocruiser**, mainly on first-class services on busy prestige routes such as New York–London; and B.O.A.C. and the Israeli airline El Al introduced the **Bristol Britannia**, the "Whispering Giant," in 1957.

## Nonstop Transatlantic

During the last years of the propeller era, genuine nonstop services began between European capitals and the eastern cities of North America, mainly New York. Such convenience, avoiding irritating stops en route, was one of the few competitive elements left to the airlines, and was, of course, equipment-related. El Al captured the mood well with its "No Goose, No Gander" slogan—a reference to former essential refueling stops in the eastern wilderness of Canada and Newfoundland—when it introduced nonstop Britannia service on 22 December 1957.

Into this arena came the **Lockheed L.1649A Starliner**, Kelly Johnson's last effort to extract the ultimate range out of the Constellation series. It was promoted vigorously by the part-creators of the pedigree line, T.W.A., still led by a shrewd and determined, if somewhat irrational, Howard Hughes. T.W.A. put the Starliner on the North Atlantic on 1 July 1957, but only Air France and Lufthansa, of the competing airlines, followed suit.

Lufthansa had ordered four L.1649A **Super Stars** on 24 May 1956. Service began on 15 December 1957, and on 13 February 1958, a Hamburg-originating flight opened nonstop Atlantic service from Frankfurt to New York.

## The Ultimate First Class

The IATA obsession with standardization had a loophole. Airlines were allowed to indulge their first-class passengers without protest from IATA, normally eager to stereotype everything. The two Stratocruiser operators had an advantage. The "Strat's" main attraction was the small downstairs bar where passengers could break the tedium of the 14-hour journey. Lufthansa's offering to its elite clientele was to fit the L.1649A (normally with 86 seats in economy class) with eight first-class and 18 deluxe-class seats, plus four beds, for a total of only 30. B.O.A.C.'s and Pan American's *Sovereign*- and *President*-class passengers may have had the bar; but none was pampered more than Lufthansa's *Senator Service* passengers.

The veteran **Douglas DC-3** was still pressed into service for special operations and feeder routes during the 1950s and early 1960s.

The **Lockheed Model L 1649A**, last of a great line.

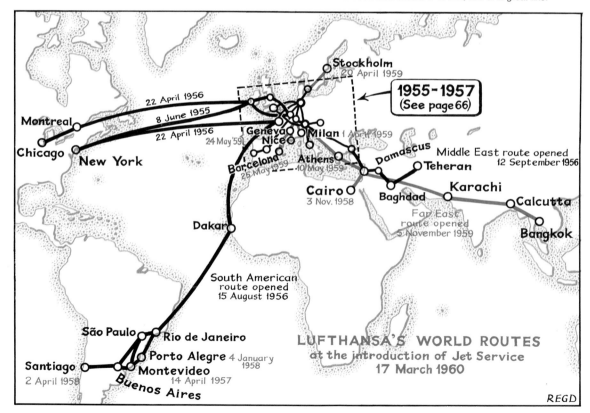

LUFTHANSA'S WORLD ROUTES at the introduction of Jet Service 17 March 1960

# Lockheed L.1649A Starliner

**85 seats  •  350 mph**

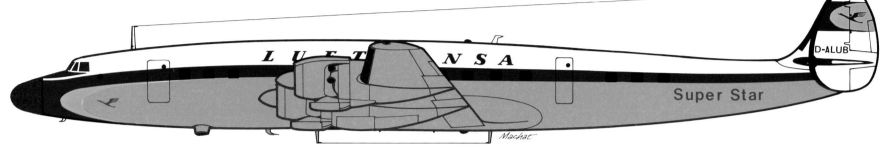

Wright 998TC (3400 hp) × 4 • 156,000 lb max. gross takeoff weight • 5280 statute miles range

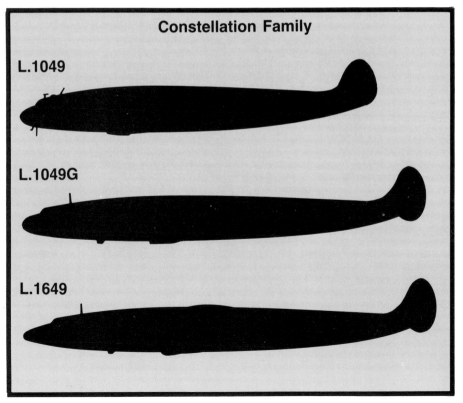

**Constellation Family**

L.1049

L.1049G

L.1649

Length 116 feet • Span 150 feet • Height 25 feet

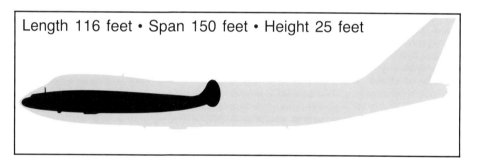

### LUFTHANSA'S L.1649A SUPER STARS

| Const. No. | Regist. No. | Date of Deliv. | Disposal |
|---|---|---|---|
| 1034 | D-ALUB | 27 Sept. 1957 | Converted to freighter and named *Isar*, 1 July 1960; sold 27 Jan. 1966 |
| 1040 | D-ALAN | 20 Dec. 1957 | Converted and named *Neckar*, 1 July 1960; chartered to World Airways 11 Oct. 1962–13 Feb. 1964; sold 17 Feb. 1966 |
| 1041 | D-ALER | 9 Jan. 1958 | To Deutsche Flugdienst 1 March 1960; sold to Trek Airways 13 Feb. 1964 |
| 1042 | D-ALOL | 17 Jan. 1958 | To Deutsche Flugdienst, 1 March 1960; sold to Trek Airways 1 March 1964 |

# Into the Jet Age

## Phenomenal Growth

By operating only the best aircraft of the propeller era and by offering superb service, in punctuality, reliability, and cabin standards, **Lufthansa** had regained with remarkable speed the leadership it had lost through the dormant period from the end of World War II until its resumption in 1955. Traffic was still growing during the 1960s at 30% or 40% per year. The jet age began in earnest toward the end of 1958, with B.O.A.C.'s Comet 4s and Pan American's Boeing 707s across the North Atlantic. Simultaneously, IATA-agreed economy fares stimulated traffic—to help fill the seats—by penetrating further down the discretionary income pyramid.

## The Boeing 707

By this time Lufthansa had rejoined the upper echelons of the world's leading airlines. It had ordered five **Boeing 707-430s**, with Rolls-Royce Conway engines, on 23 January 1957. These were placed on the nonstop Frankfurt–New York route on 17 March 1960, and frequency was increased to a daily flight on 1 April. On 20 May, service to the U.S. West Coast started, to San Francisco, and nonstop Frankfurt-Chicago flights began the next day.

## An Ambition Fulfilled

A few months before Lufthansa's jet age began, an old ambition, dating back to 1939, had been realized: a route to the Far East. A Super Constellation had started service to Bangkok, via Karachi and Calcutta, on 1 November 1959, in cooperation with Alitalia and the French airlines Air France and T.A.I. Now, on 23 January 1961, the Boeing 707 extended this route to Tokyo. Lufthansa veterans must have reminisced to the time when the Junkers-Ju 52/3m began its stillborn operation and when the Focke-Wulf 200 Condor flew to Tokyo in record time.

## The Boeing 720-B

One of the main problems faced by the leading jet airlines was that the available traffic to fill 150-seat Boeing 707s or Douglas DC-8s consistently and profitably was restricted to densely traveled routes. The jets were twice as big and three times as productive as the types they replaced. Not all routes were like Frankfurt–New York. Many generated less traffic, yet just as many airlines competed for it. The airlines needed a jet aircraft that was smaller but could fly just as far. Boeing came up with the answer: the 125-seat **Boeing 720-B,** shorter in the fuselage but with just as much range as its contemporary parent.

Lufthansa ordered four B-720-Bs on 30 January 1960 and four more later. It deployed them on its more lightly traveled routes to South America on 20 May 1961, and to the Middle East soon after on 1 July. Jet routes to Africa were added in 1962, to Lagos on 4 March, and to Johannesburg on 14 May.

## The Intercontinental Jet

In a process of constant refinement, Lufthansa reinforced its long-range jet fleet by ordering, on 31 October 1961, the first of its fleet of **Boeing 707-330 Intercontinental** jets. This was possibly the most successful single long-haul type of what were known as the Big Jets—although this claim would be challenged by the DC-8-63. Lufthansa inaugurated a polar route to the Orient, via Fairbanks, Alaska, on 28 May 1964, giving a new dimension to the Japanese market. (Anchorage was closed temporarily because of an earthquake.) The last continent, Australia, was added on 3–5 April 1965, with Boeing 707-330 service to Sydney.

By the mid-1960s, therefore, barring a few minor adjustments, Lufthansa's world map was complete. In company with its competitors, it was now ready to concentrate on its medium- and short-haul routes, and to upgrade them to modern jet standards.

The **Boeing 720B**.

This was the scene at Hamburg when Lufthansa's first jet aircraft, a **Boeing 707-430** (D-ABOB), was delivered on 2 March 1960.

## LUFTHANSA'S BOEING 707 AND 720 FLEET

| Const. No. | Regist. No | Name | Date of Deliv. |
|---|---|---|---|
| **707-430 (707A)** | | | |
| 17718 | D-ABOB | *Hamburg* | 24 Feb. 1960 |
| 17719 | D-ABOC | *Berlin* | 10 March 1960 |
| 17720 | D-ABOD | *Frankfurt* | 24 April 1960 |
| 17721 | D-ABOF | *München* | 1 Oct. 1960 |
| 18056 | D-ABOG | *Bonn* | 17 March 1961 |
| **707-330B (707B)** | | | |
| 18462 | D-ABOV | *Duisburg* | 28 Feb. 1963 |
| 18463 | D-ABOT | *Düsseldorf* | 5 March 1964 |
| 18819 | D-ABOX | *Köln* | 10 Jan. 1965 |
| 18923 | D-ABUB | *Stuttgart* | 4 Aug. 1965 |
| 18926 | D-ABUC | *Bremen* | 5 Oct. 1965 |
| 18927 | D-ABUD | *Nürnberg* | 24 Nov. 1965 |
| 18928 | D-ABUF | *Hannover* | 28 Dec. 1965 |
| 18929 | D-ABUG | *Essen* | 7 Jan. 1966 |
| 18930 | D-ABUH | *Dortmund* | 19 Jan. 1966 |
| 18931 | D-ABUK | *Bochum* | 27 March 1966 |
| 19315 | D-ABUL | *Duisburg* | 20 Jan. 1967 |
| 19316 | D-ABUM | *Bremen* | 30 Jan. 1967 |
| **707-330C (707C)** | | | |
| 18937 | D-ABUA | *Europa* | 10 Nov. 1965 |
| 18932 | D-ABUE | *America* | 11 March 1966 |
| 19317 | D-ABUI | *Asia* | 6 March 1967 |
| 20123 | D-ABUJ | *Africa* | 27 Feb. 1969 |
| 20124 | D-ABUO | *Australia* | 8 May 1969 |
| 20395 | D-ABUY | *Essen* | 16 Oct. 1970 |
| **720B** | | | |
| 18057 | D-ABOH | *Köln* | 8 March 1961 |
| 18058 | D-ABOK | *Düsseldorf* | 28 April 1961 |
| 18059 | D-ABOL | *Stuttgart* | 3 May 1961 |
| 18060 | D-ABOM | *Nürnberg* | 3 June 1961 |
| 18248 | D-ABON | *Hannover* | 5 Jan. 1962 |
| 18249 | D-ABOP | *Bremen* | 12 Jan. 1962 |
| 18250 | D-ABOQ | *Essen* | 23 March 1962 |
| 18251 | D-ABOR | *Dortmund* | 27 Feb. 1962 |

**Note** Of the total fleet of **Boeing 707s**, two crashed, D-ABOT at Delhi on 19 December 1973, and D-ABUY near Rio de Janeiro on 26 July 1979. All the others, except D-ABOD (retained for training and still in use), were sold over a protracted period from 1967 to 1985.

The last revenue service by a Lufthansa B-707 was by D-ABUL, from Rio to Hamburg, on 29 December 1984, by which time it had accumulated 70,718 flying hours. D-ABUF, retired from Lufthansa service on 28 June 1984, had flown 72,925 hours, the highest of any B-707-300 series.

Two of the **Boeing 720Bs** crashed, both on training flights, on 4 December 1961 and 15 July 1964, respectively. The others were sold between 1964 and 1966.

# Boeing 707-330B and 720B

## 135 seats • 600 mph

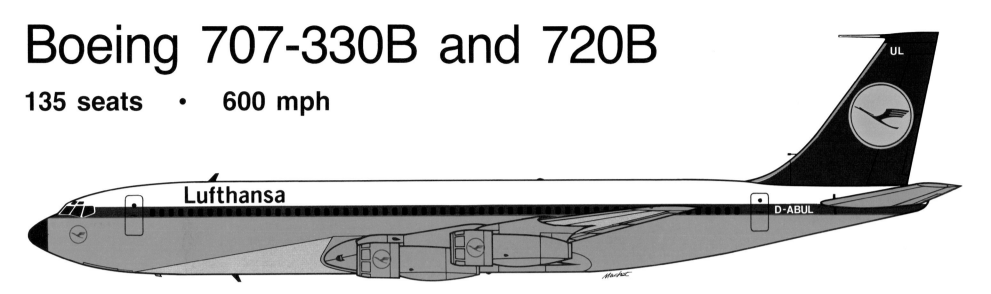

Pratt & Whitney JT3D (18,000 lb thrust) × 4 • 168 tons max. gross takeoff weight • 4000 statute miles range

## A Pedigree Line

Although the British **B.O.A.C.**, with the **de Havilland Comet 1**, could claim to have started the first commercial jet service on 2 May 1952, and the Soviet Union's **Aeroflot** began **Tupolev Tu-104** jet service on 15 September 1956, the jet age did not get into full swing until **Pan American** put the **Boeing 707-121** into service on the New York–London route on 26 October 1958. The Comet 1 service had lasted almost two years, but had ended in tragedy and the grounding of the aircraft. The Tu-104's deployment was confined to the U.S.S.R. and the overseas routes of the Czech airline, C.S.A. But within two years of Pan Am's service inauguration, Boeing 707s were flying all over the world, and the very name Boeing had become as familiar a term as Ford or Mercedes.

Although the 707's fuselage could not be lengthened to the same extent as the Douglas DC-8's, Boeing made the best use of its fine airliner, producing versions with better range and load-carrying capability. Some airlines specified the **Rolls-Royce Conway** as the power plant, especially those from the British Commonwealth; but other leading airlines chose the Conway too, including **Lufthansa**. (See *Pan Am: An Airline and Its Aircraft* for a fuller analysis and description of the Boeing types.)

## The Smaller Boeing

The **Boeing 720** was a smaller version of the 707, designed to fit the routes of lower passenger traffic potential. It was 16 feet shorter than the 707, but only a discerning eye could distinguish one from the other. Built to a specification by **United Air Lines**, which took the first delivery in 1960, it had some limited success.

Boeing soon produced a long-range version, with Pratt & Whitney JT3D-3 engines, designated the **Boeing 720B**. This had enough power and operating economy to fly 4000 miles with full payload, and for a short period it had the longest range of any commercial airliner. Lufthansa, which put 720Bs into service in 1961, was the first non-U.S. airline to buy this variant.

Length 153 feet • Span 146 feet • Height 42 feet

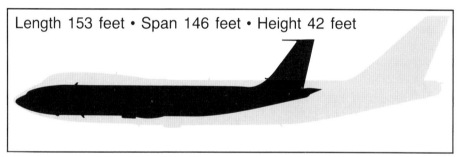

# The Europa Jet

## The Medium-Haul Boeing

**Lufthansa** had started North Atlantic services with the Boeing 707 on 17 March 1960. Satisfied that it had taken care of the problems of long-haul jet air services for a whole aircraft generation, it turned to the needs of short- and medium-haul traffic within Europe, and to the European hinterland in the Middle East and North Africa.

Easily rejecting the possible claims of the British Trident, when that pioneering design was compromised by an extraordinary decision to shrink it in size and power, Lufthansa ordered twelve **Boeing 727-100** medium-haul trijets on 28 February 1961. Designated the **B-727-30**, the first of these went into service on 12 April 1964 and were called **Europa Jets**.

Subsequently, as the accompanying table shows, Lufthansa recognized the versatility of this airliner, the biggest money-maker in history, by regularly ordering more, mostly the larger Boeing 727-200s. This steady supply not only kept pace with the ever-increasing traffic demands of a prospering and tourism-happy Europe, it updated the fleet periodically, replacing older aircraft with more efficient variants.

### LUFTHANSA'S FLEET OF BOEING 727s

| Const. No. | Regist. No. | Name |
|---|---|---|
| **727-30 (727A)** | | |
| 18360 | D-ABIB | Augsburg |
| 18361 | D-ABIC | Saarbrücken |
| 18362 | D-ABID | Braunschweig |
| 18363 | D-ABIF | Mannheim |
| 18364 | D-ABIG | Kiel |
| 18365 | D-ABIH | Wiesbaden |
| 18366 | D-ABIK | Heidelberg |
| 18367 | D-ABIL | Lübeck |
| 18368 | D-ABIM | (Condor) |
| 18369 | D-ABIN | Münster |
| 18370 | D-ABIP | Mainz |
| 18371 | D-ABIQ | Karlsruhe |
| 18933 | D-ABIR | Aachen |
| 18934 | D-ABIS | Freiburg |
| 18935 | D-ABIT | Heidelberg |
| 18936 | D-ABIV | Kassel |

**Note** The seven aircraft D-ABIK–D-ABIR were transferred to Condor Flugdienst in the later 1960s.

| Const. No. | Regist. No. | Name |
|---|---|---|
| **727-30QC (727C)** | | |
| 19008 | D-ABIW | Bielefeld |
| 19009 | D-ABIX | Würzburg |
| 19010 | D-ABIZ | Gelsenkirchen |
| 19011 | D-ABIA | Pforzheim |
| 19012 | D-ABIE | Oberhausen |
| 19310 | D-ABII | Wuppertal |
| 19311 | D-ABIO | Hagen |
| 19312 | D-ABIU | Ulm |
| 19313 | D-ABIY | Aachen |
| 19314 | D-ABIJ | Krefeld |
| 19793 | D-ABBI | Mainz |
| **727–230 (727B)** | | |
| 20430 | D-ABCI | Karlsruhe |
| 20431 | D-ABDI | Lübeck |
| 20525 | D-ABFI | Münster |
| 20526 | D-ABGI | Leverkusen |
| 20560 | D-ABHI | Münchengladbach |
| 20673 | D-ABKI | Bremerhaven |
| 20674 | D-ABLI | Ludwigshafen |
| 20757 | D-ABQI | Hildesheim |

| Const. No. | Regist. No. | Name |
|---|---|---|
| 20788 | D-ABRI | Esslingen |
| 20789 | D-ABSI | Hof |
| 20675 | D-ABMI | (Condor) |
| 20676 | D-ABNI | |
| 20677 | D-ABPI | |
| 20790 | D-ABTI | |
| 20791 | D-ABVI | |
| 20792 | D-ABWI | |
| 20899 | D-ABKA | Heidelberg |
| 20900 | D-ABKB | Augsburg |
| 20901 | D-ABKC | Braunschweig |
| 20902 | D-ABKD | Freiburg |
| 20903 | D-ABKE | Mannheim |
| 20904 | D-ABKF | Saarbrücken |
| 20905 | D-ABKG | Kassel |
| 20906 | D-ABKH | Kiel |
| 20918 | D-ABKJ | Wiesbaden |
| 21113 | D-ABKK | (Condor) |
| 21114 | D-ABKL | |
| 21442 | D-ABKM | Hagen |
| 21618 | D-ABKN | Ulm |
| 21619 | D-ABKP | Krefeld |
| 21620 | D-ABKQ | Mainz |
| 21621 | D-ABKR | Bielefeld |
| 21622 | D-ABKS | Oberhausen |
| 21623 | D-ABKT | Aachen |

**Note** The 727-30s were delivered from February 1964 to April 1966; the 727-30QCs from February 1967 to January 1968; and the 727-230s from January 1971 to January 1979.

All the 727-30s and 727-30QCs have been traded back to Boeing, or sold to various airlines and aircraft trading companies.

# BOEING
### The most popular family in the sky.

The **Boeing 727-30**, the original "short-bodied" version.

The **Boeing 727-230 Europa Jet** in flight.

The **Boeing 727-30QC**, the "quick-change" mixed passenger-cargo version.

The **Boeing 727-230**, the "stretched" version and the most successful of the series.

# Boeing 727-230

## 160 seats • 595 mph

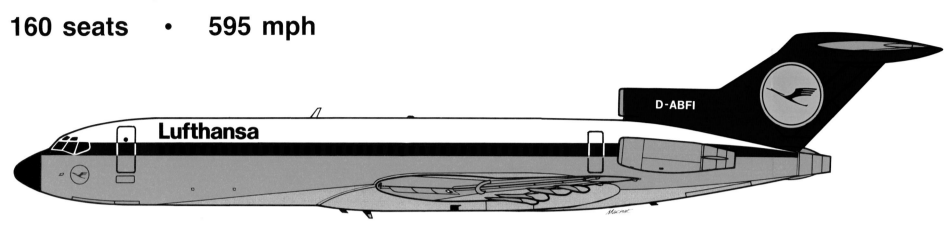

Pratt & Whitney JT8D-7 (14,000 lb thrust) × 3 • 86 tons max. gross takeoff weight • 2150 statute miles range

The table on this page outlines the main characteristics of the different versions of the **Boeing 727** and the **Boeing 737** series operated by **Lufthansa**. The early development of the 727, with Eastern Air Lines as the launching carrier in 1964, is reviewed on page 75 of the pilot book of this series, **Pan Am: An Airline and Its Aircraft**. Similarly, the later development of the Boeing 737 is described on page 77 of the same book, which notes that in this case, Lufthansa was the launching airline. As the tables on the opposite page show, the German company was an important customer for both types, contributing in no small measure toward Boeing's marketing success in Europe.

Length 152 feet • Span 108 feet • Height 34 feet

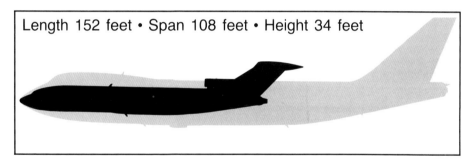

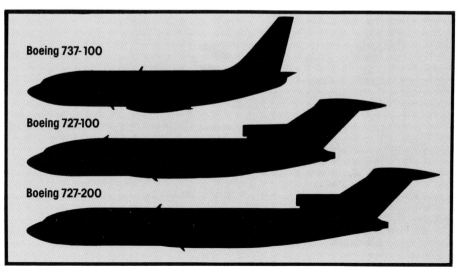

Boeing 737-100

Boeing 727-100

Boeing 727-200

### THE BOEING TWINS AND TRIJETS

| | | Dimensions | | | | Engines | | | | | | |
|---|---|---|---|---|---|---|---|---|---|---|---|---|
| Type | First Flight Date | Length | Span | Height | Pass. Seats | No. | Type | Thrust (each; lb) | Max. Gross TOW (lb) | Cruise Speed (mph) | Normal Range (st. miles) | No. Built |
| 727-100 | 9 Feb. 1963 | 133'2" | 108' | 34' | 119 | 3 | P&W JT8D | 14,000 | 160,000 | 605 | 2650 | }1824 |
| 727-200 | 27 July 1967 | 152'2" | 108' | 34' | 163 | 3 | P&W JT8D-7 | 14,000 | 172,000 | 595 | 2150 | |
| 737-100 | 9 April 1967 | 94' | 93' | 37'1" | 103 | 2 | P&W JT8D-7 | 14,000 | 100,500 | 570 | 1840 | }2000+ |
| 737-200 | 8 Aug. 1967 | 100' | 93' | 37'1" | 115 | 2 | P&W JT8D-9 | 14,500 | 114,500 | 570 | 2135 | |
| 737-300 | 24 Feb. 1984 | 109'9" | 94'9" | 36'6" | 141 | 2 | CFM 56-3 | 20,000 | 135,000 | 558 | 2660 | |

# The City Jet

## The Short-Haul Boeing

Warming to the advantages of an all-Boeing fleet, with commonality of spares holding and maintenance costs, Lufthansa made a procurement decision that astonished the airline world. Hitherto, U.S.-manufactured airliners had always been sponsored by U.S. airlines. Lufthansa now became the first non-U.S. airline to be the launching customer for a new U.S. type, which furthermore became the highest-selling single commercial airplane in history, with sales exceeding 2000.

The historic order, made in February 1965, was for 21 **Boeing 737-100s**. Based on the same fuselage cross section as the Boeing 727 and 707, but with two wing-mounted engines, it seemed to be going against the fashion of rear-mounted engines, initiated by the French Caravelle and successfully followed by the British B.A.C. One-Eleven and the Douglas DC-9. But the greater fuselage width was a powerful selling point and had passenger appeal.

Lufthansa put the Boeing 737 **City Jets** into service on 10 February 1968 and subsequently deployed the 727 and the 737 interchangeably, matching the size and range, from the 90-seat 737-100 to the 170-seat 727-200, according to traffic demand. By the mid-1970s, Lufthansa and its nonscheduled subsidiary, Condor Flugdienst, were operating more than 70 of both types, and only the arrival on the European scene of the wide-bodied twin-jet Airbus put a stop to the flow of Boeing deliveries from Seattle. Incidentally, all Lufthansa Boeing aircraft carry the number 30 as the last two digits, i.e. 737-130, as this is the Boeing customer designator.

The **Boeing 737-100**, the original version of the world's best-selling commercial jet, of which Lufthansa was the launching customer.

### LUFTHANSA'S FLEET OF BOEING 737-100s AND 200s

| Const. No. | Regist. No. | Name |
|---|---|---|
| **737-130 (737A)** | | |
| 19013 | D-ABEA | Coburg |
| 19014 | D-ABEB | Regensburg |
| 19015 | D-ABEC | Osnabrück |
| 19016 | D-ABED | Flensburg |
| 19017 | D-ABEF | Kempten |
| 19018 | D-ABEG | Offenbach |
| 19019 | D-ABEH | Solingen |
| 19020 | D-ABEI | Oldenburg |
| 19021 | D-ABEK | Konstanz |
| 19022 | D-ABEL | Mülheim a.d.R. |
| 19023 | D-ABEM | Wolfsburg |
| 19024 | D-ABEN | Tübingen |
| 19025 | D-ABEO | Göttingen |
| 19026 | D-ABEP | Wilhelmshaven |
| 19027 | D-ABEQ | Koblenz |
| 19028 | D-ABER | Goslar |
| 19029 | D-ABES | Friedrichshafen |
| 19030 | D-ABET | Baden-Baden |
| 19031 | D-ABEU | Heilbronn |
| 19032 | D-ABEV | Marburg |
| 19033 | D-ABEW | Bayreuth |
| 19794 | D-ABEY | Worms |
| **737-230 (737C)** | | |
| 20253 | D-ABBE | Remscheid |
| 20254 | D-ABCE | Landshut |
| 20255 | D-ABDE | Bamberg |
| 20256 | D-ABFE | Trier |
| 20257 | D-ABGE | Erlangen |
| 20258 | D-ABHE | Darmstadt |
| **737-230 (737B)** | | |
| 22114 | D-ABFA | Regensburg |
| 22113 | D-ABFB | Flensburg |
| 22115 | D-ABFC | Würzburg |
| 22116 | D-ABFD | Bamberg |
| 22117 | D-ABFF | Gelsenkirchen |
| 22118 | D-ABFH | Pforzheim |
| 22119 | D-ABFK | Wuppertal |
| 22120 | D-ABFL | Coburg |
| 22121 | D-ABFM | Osnabrück |

| Const. No. | Regist. No. | Name |
|---|---|---|
| 22122 | D-ABFN | Kempten |
| 22123 | D-ABFP | Offenbach |
| 22124 | D-ABFR | Solingen |
| 22125 | D-ABFS | Oldenburg |
| 22402 | D-ABFT | (Condor) |
| 22126 | D-ABFU | Mülheim a.d.R. |
| 22127 | D-ABFW | Wolfsburg |
| 22128 | D-ABFX | Tübingen |
| 22129 | D-ABFY | Göttingen |
| 22130 | D-ABFZ | Wilhelmshaven |
| 22131 | D-ABHA | Koblenz |
| 22132 | D-ABHB | Goslar |
| 22133 | D-ABHC | Friedrichshafen |
| 22635 | D-ABHD | (Condor) |
| 22134 | D-ABHF | Heilbronn |
| 22135 | D-ABHH | Marburg |
| 22136 | D-ABHK | Bayreuth |
| 22137 | D-ABHL | Worms |
| 22138 | D-ABHM | Landshut |
| 22139 | D-ABHN | Trier |
| 22140 | D-ABHP | Erlangen |
| 22141 | D-ABHR | Darmstadt |
| 22142 | D-ABHS | Remscheid |
| 22636 | D-ABHT | (Condor) |
| 22143 | D-ABHU | Konstanz |
| 22634 | D-ABHW | Baden-Baden |
| 22637 | D-ABHX | (Condor) |

**Note** The 737-130s were delivered from May 1968 to 6 February 1969, the 737-230s from December 1969 to February 1971, and the 737-230s from May 1971 to March 1982. Most of the 737-130s were sold to People Express.

A final batch of 737-230s was delivered between January and March 1985:

| Const. No. | Regist. No. | Name |
|---|---|---|
| 23153 | D-ABMA | Idar-Oberstein |
| 23154 | D-ABMB | Ingolstadt |
| 23155 | D-ABMC | Norderstedt |
| 23156 | D-ABMD | Paderborn |
| 23157 | D-ABME | Schweinfurt |
| 23158 | D-ABMF | Verden |

### LUFTHANSA'S BOEING 737-330 FLEET

| Const. No. | Regist. No. | Name |
|---|---|---|
| 23522 | D-ABXA | Giessen |
| 23523 | D-ABXB | Passau |
| 23524 | D-ABXC | Delmenhorst |
| 23525 | D-ABXD | Siegen |
| 23526 | D-ABXE | Hamm |
| 23527 | D-ABXF | Minden |
| 23528 | D-ABXH | Cuxhaven |
| 23529 | D-ABXI | Berchtesgaden |
| 23530 | D-ABXK | Ludwigsburg |
| 23531 | D-ABXL | Neuss |
| 23833 | D-ABWA | |
| 23834 | D-ABWB | |
| 23835 | D-ABWC | (Condor) |
| 23836 | D-ABWD | |
| 23837 | D-ABWE | |
| 23871 | D-ABXM | Herford |
| 23872 | D-ABXN | Böblingen |
| 23873 | D-ABXO | Schwäbisch-Gmünd |
| 23874 | D-ABXP | Fulda |
| 23875 | D-ABXR | Celle |

**Note** The 737-330s were delivered from August 1986 to February 1988. More are on order, including 39 of the advanced 737-500 version.

**Herbert Culmann**, chairman of the executive board from 1972 to 1982.

# Boeing 737-130

## 103 seats • 570 mph

Lufthansa

D-ABEF

Pratt & Whitney JT8D-7 (14,000 lb thrust) × 2 • 50 tons max. gross take-off weight • 1840 statute miles range

The **Boeing 737-200** (freighter version).

Length 94 feet • Span 93 feet • Height 37 feet

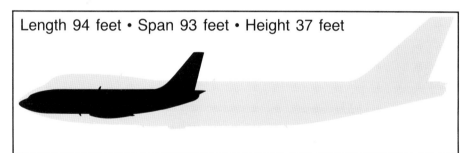

The **Boeing 737-300**. The engine intakes are flattened for ground clearance.

# Delivering the Goods

## An Old Tradition

Air freight is a very specialized category of air transport. It needs special ground equipment and handling and special aircraft with stronger and heavier floors and bulkheads, ingeniously designed larger doors, and on-board apparatus. Air freight travels only one way, whereas most passengers make round-trips. The traffic is often seasonal. The net result is that airlines find profitable air freight operation difficult to achieve, most companies giving it low priority and customarily carrying freight only as fill-up loads on passenger aircraft.

**Lufthansa** has traditionally taken a different view, believing that, properly organized and capitalized, the air freight business can be profitable. Demonstrating its faith, on 4 December 1957—within 2½ years of its first transatlantic passenger service—Lufthansa added an all-cargo flight on the same route, leasing an aircraft from Transocean Air Lines. It used a **Douglas C-54**, forefather of the DC-4, unpressurized and comparatively slow, but the air freight did not object.

The business was successful enough for nonstop **Super Constellation**s to be introduced in March 1959, and in 1961 Lufthansa chartered space on **Canadair CL-44**s operated by Seaboard World Airlines. This Canadian-built aircraft was a variant of the Bristol Britannia, and engineered so that the whole of the rear fuselage and tail was hinged into a "swing-tail" to permit maximum rear-end loading into the entire cross section of the fuselage.

## Jet Air Freight

Throughout the period of dynamic growth during the 1960s, when Lufthansa regained its leading airline role in Europe, the **Boeing 707** air freighters were given as high a status as the passenger aircraft. This respect was applied as much to the ground facilities as to the aircraft. Thus, on 2 October 1971, barely a year after delivery of Europe's first Boeing 747 wide-bodied jet, the world's largest freight-handling hall was opened at Frankfurt Airport, which by then had become the air freight hub for much of Europe. This event was promptly followed by the delivery to Lufthansa, on 10 March 1972, of the world's first all-cargo **Boeing 747**, and for several years it was the only one of its kind.

On 19 April Lufthansa introduced Boeing 747 all-freight service on the Frankfurt-New York route at a frequency of six days per week, and four years later Lufthansa ordered its first half-passenger, half-freight **Boeing 747-200B "Combi"** to meet the varying demands of a fluctuating market and routes of different freight traffic densities.

By the late 1980s, Lufthansa had become the largest scheduled air freight operator in the world.

## German Cargo Services (G.C.S.)

By this time the cargo division was operating as an autonomous unit, with its own allocated aircraft. On 10 March 1977, as an almost inevitable development, **German Cargo Services GmbH (G.C.S.)** was founded as a wholly owned subsidiary to operate air freight charters, mainly with Boeing 707s, to supplement the scheduled air freight services.

On 1 June 1983, it placed an order for four **McDonnell Douglas DC-8-73**s. These were former Douglas DC-8s, substantially modified and restructured by the **Cammacorp** company. Though their "narrow" bodies made them less attractive for normal passenger service, their General Electric/SNECMA CFM 56-2 turbofan engines gave them low operating costs, and they were ideal for freight. G.C.S. took delivery of the first aircraft on 12 July 1984 and put them into service almost immediately, replacing the Boeing 707s.

A **Douglas C-54** cargo aircraft, used by **Lufthansa** for its first all-cargo flights.

**Lufthansa** occasionally leased a **Curtiss C-46** for supplementary cargo operations.

THE DC-8-73s

| Const. No. | Regist. No. |
|---|---|
| 45991 | D-ADUI |
| 46003 | D-ADUA |
| 46044 | D-ADUE |
| 46047 | D-ADUO |
| 46106 | D-ADUC |

**Boeing 707**s were used for exclusive all-cargo services during the 1960s and later used by Lufthansa's affiliated **German Cargo Services**.

The **Cammacorp** conversion of the **Douglas DC-8**, the "Dash-Seventy" series.

Lufthansa's **Boeing 747F** is loaded through both the nose and fuselage cargo doors.

# Cammacorp-Douglas DC-8-73

## 269 seats • 530 mph

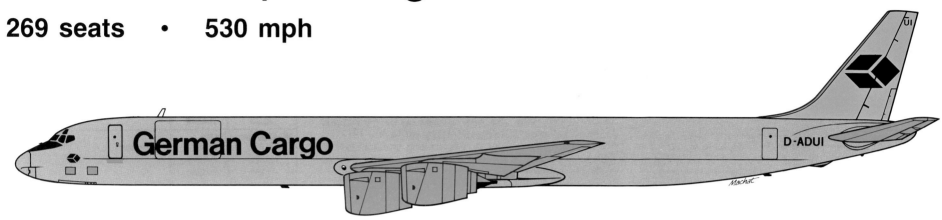

CFM International CFM56 (24,000 lb thrust) × 4 • 177 tons max. gross takeoff weight • 5200 statute miles range

## An Inspired Rescue Operation

During the mid-1970s, just as the wide-bodied Boeing 747s, DC-10s, and TriStars were threatening to sweep aside the last remnants of the once-proud fleets of 707s, DC-8s, and VC-10s, a remarkable operation was staged to rescue one of the earlier generation (now described as "narrow-bodied") from complete obliteration. In 1977, Jackson McGowan, who had been president of the Douglas Aircraft Company during the height of its marketing success in the 1960s, led a group of investors to form **Cammacorp**, headquartered at El Segundo, a Los Angeles satellite city near the airport, and once home of a Douglas wartime production line. The sole purpose of Cammacorp was to perpetuate the service life of the "stretched" **Douglas DC-8-60 Series**.

The idea was simple. The 19,000-pound-thrust Pratt & Whitney JT-3D engines would be replaced by 24,000-pound-thrust CFM56 engines, produced jointly by the General Electric and the French SNECMA engine manufacturers. These were not only more powerful but were far more economical, enhancing further the profit potential of an aircraft which some airlines had admitted to be "the nearest thing to printing your own money."

## New Lease on Life

McGowan sold the idea to a number of influential airlines, some of which already had DC-8-60s. Delta's DC-8-61s, for example, were converted at Delta's own base in Atlanta, from kits supplied by Cammacorp. For other customers, Cammacorp did the work, sometimes purchasing aircraft itself, and proceeded to inject them with new life at a modest production line at Tulsa. The cost was about $4,000,000–$5,000,000 per conversion, and both passenger and freight versions came off the line.

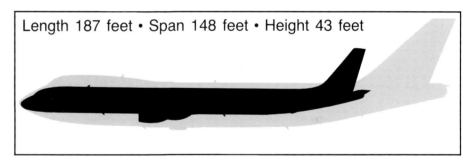

Length 187 feet • Span 148 feet • Height 43 feet

The first customers, in 1979 and 1980, were United Air Lines and Delta Air Lines, both for the **DC-8-71**. After the first flight on 15 August 1982, and F.A.A. certification, Delta took the first delivery in April 1982. Altogether 110 DC-8-61s, -62s, and -63s were converted to -71s, -72s, and -73s. **German Cargo Services (G.C.S.)** was one of the customers for the **DC-8-73**. Mission accomplished, Cammacorp shut its doors in December 1986.

## One Last Fling

The Douglas DC-8 had been dear to Jackson McGowan's heart, and he made sure that it would leave its imprint in the record books. On 29 March 1984, the pilot of a Cammacorp demonstrator DC-8-72 asked for clearance into the Los Angeles International Airport, stating that he had come from Cairo. A curious air traffic controller inquired, "Cairo, Illinois?" Not so. The aircraft had just flown 8230 statute miles nonstop in 15 hr 46 min from Egypt and still had 1½ hours of fuel left.

# The Jumbo Jet Takes Over

## Sharing the Leadership

When **Pan American** introduced the Boeing 707 in 1958 to introduce the first great jet age, it had a head start over most of its competition. Almost a year and a half was to pass before Lufthansa mounted its jet challenge, in March 1960. A decade later, the nature of the competition and the balance of power across the Atlantic had undergone a subtle change. European airlines such as Air France, British Airways, and Lufthansa were no longer overawed by threatened U.S. dominance of the transatlantic airways. When Pan American launched the new wide-bodied era with its **Boeing 747** service on 22 January 1970, **Lufthansa** was not far behind with its inaugural from Frankfurt to New York on 26 April, only three months later.

Following that epoch-making year, Lufthansa steadily built up its fleet of the giant airliner, for deployment on the most heavily traveled routes. Matching the flying equipment with its customarily sound ground support, it opened the world's largest maintenance hangar at Frankfurt in 1970, and the world's first all-cargo Boeing 747 service began in April 1972 (page 80).

## The Momentum Continues

Lufthansa did not favor the Boeing 747SP, which, to achieve Pan American's demand for nonstop New York–Tokyo capability, had had to trade off several seat rows of revenue-earning capacity. Instead the German carrier selected, and possibly insisted upon, the **Boeing 747SL**—Special Long-Range—version of the standard-sized 747 and put it into service on a two-stop route to Sydney, Australia, on 14 December 1976. This was followed up by the biggest single aircraft order in Lufthansa history, on 14 July 1977, for five of the 747SLs and six B-727s, totaling about $1 billion. Simultaneously arrangements were made to retire or dispose of the earlier Jumbos so as to reduce the average longevity of the fleet.

The last Boeing 707 was retired on 31 December 1984. Henceforward all Lufthansa's long-range routes were operated by wide-bodied aircraft, Boeing 747s or DC-10s. Perhaps one of the most unusual route assignments—and one only possible with a true Jumbo Jet—was that from Turin, Italy, to Detroit. In association with Alitalia and General Motors, an extraordinary cargo service began on 1 June 1987, with each Boeing 747 carrying 56 Pininfarina car bodies to the Cadillac Allanté assembly line.

| LUFTHANSA'S BOEING 747 FLEET | | | |
|---|---|---|---|
| Const. No. | Regist. No. | Name | Year Deliv. |
| **747-130 (747A)** | | | |
| 19746 | D-ABYA | Nordrhein-Westfalen | 1970 |
| 19747 | D-ABYB | Hessen | 1970 |
| 19748 | D-ABYC | Bayern | 1970 |
| **747-230 (747B)** | | | |
| 20372 | D-ABYD | Baden-Württemberg | 1971 |
| 20493 | D-ABYF | (Condor) | 1971 |
| 20527 | D-ABYG | Niedersachsen | 1972 |
| 20559 | D-ABYH | (Condor) | 1972 |
| **747-230F (747F)** | | | |
| 20373 | D-ABYE | | 1972 |
| **747-230B Combi (747D)** | | | |
| 21220 | D-ABYJ | Hessen | 1976 |
| 21221 | D-ABYK | Rheinland-Pfalz | 1976 |
| 21380 | D-ABYL | Saarland | 1978 |
| 21588 | D-ABYM | Schleswig-Holstein | 1978 |
| 21643 | D-ABYR | Nordrhein-Westfalen | 1979 |
| 21644 | D-ABYS | Bayern | 1979 |
| 22363 | D-ABYT | Hamburg | 1980 |
| 22669 | D-ABYW | Berlin | 1981 |
| 22670 | D-ABYX | Köln | 1982 |
| 22671 | D-ABYY | München | 1982 |
| 23286 | D-ABYZ | Frankfurt | 1985 |
| 23287 | D-ABZA | Düsseldorf | 1985 |
| 23393 | D-ABZC | Hannover | 1986 |
| 23509 | D-ABZE | Stuttgart | 1987 |
| **747-230B (747E)** | | | |
| 21589 | D-ABYN | Baden-Württemberg | 1978 |
| 21590 | D-ABYP | Niedersachsen | 1979 |
| 21591 | D-ABYQ | Bremen | 1978 |
| 23407 | D-ABZD | Kiel | 1986 |
| 23622 | D-ABZH | Bonn | 1987 |
| **747-230F Freighter (747C)** | | | |
| 21592 | D-ABYO | America | 1978 |
| 22668 | D-ABYU | Asia | 1981 |
| 23348 | D-ABZB | Europa | 1985 |
| 23621 | D-ABZF | Africa | 1986 |
| | D-ABZI | Australia | 1988 |

**Note** Ten 747-400s are now in the fleet.

Lufthansa's Boeing **747-230**.

A **Boeing 747 freighter**.

# Boeing 747-430

## 412 seats  •  590 mph

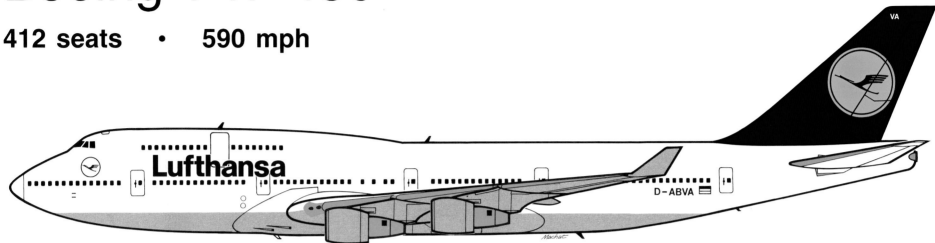

General Electric CF6-80 (58,000 lb thrust) × 4 • 435 tons max. gross takeoff weight • 8400 statute miles range

The aircraft illustrated above, the **Boeing 747-430**, is the latest development of the great airliner which, with its popular nickname, the Jumbo Jet, has become the symbol of mass air travel. **Lufthansa** ordered six of these aircraft on 23 June 1986, and from 1989 onward, with 11 orders and 12 options, will gradually replace its earlier versions of the 747.

The whole fleet is listed on the opposite page. It started with the earliest 747-100 Series, in 1970, the beginning of the career of the giant airliner, when it seemed far too big for all but the few most heavily traveled routes of the world. Starting cautiously with three, Lufthansa has already taken delivery of 32, not including the 747-430s to come. They fly to every corner of Lufthansa's world, which by 1990 embraced 183 destinations in 85 countries—more than reached by any other international airline.

The different types of wide-bodied aircraft, in their original versions, are listed in the table below. The Boeing 747 types up to the B-747-300 are tabulated on page 80 of *Pan Am: An Airline and Its Aircraft*, the first book in this series about the world's great airlines.

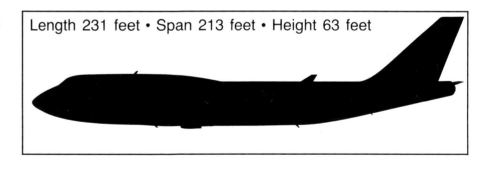

Length 231 feet • Span 213 feet • Height 63 feet

### WIDE-BODIED TYPES COMPARED
based on original series of each

| Type | First Flight Date | Dimensions | | | Mixed Class Seating | Engines | | | Max. Gross TOW (lb) | Cruise Speed (mph) | Normal Range (st. miles) | Approx. No. Built[1] | Launch Customer |
| | | Length | Span | Height | | No. | Type | Thrust (each, lb) | | | | | |
|---|---|---|---|---|---|---|---|---|---|---|---|---|---|
| B-747-100 | 2 Sept. 1969 | 231'0" | 195'8" | 63'5" | 350 | 4 | P&WJT9D | 43,500 | 710,000 | 595 | 5000 | 800+ | Pan Am |
| DC-10-10 | 29 Aug. 1970 | 181'5" | 195'4" | 58'1" | 270 | 3 | GE CF6 | 41,000 | 455,000 | 580 | 3000 | 382 | American |
| L-1011-1 | 16 Nov. 1970 | 177'8" | 155'4" | 55'4" | 260 | 3 | R/R RB211 | 42,000 | 430,000 | 580 | 3000 | 244 | Eastern |
| A 300-B2 | 28 Oct. 1972 | 175'11" | 147'1" | 54'3" | 230 | 2 | GE CF6-50 | 51,000 | 302,000 | 570 | 1600 | 600+ | Air France |

[1] All types, including developed versions, e.g. 747SP and DC-10-30, but not the narrower-fuselaged Airbus A 320.

# Nonscheduled Diversification

## Explosion of Mass Air Tourism

During the first 15 years after World War II there was a clear class distinction between the scheduled and non-scheduled airlines of Europe. The nations either owned or supported airlines which were recognized as official flag carriers. Small independent companies had to fight, mostly in vain, for traffic and operating rights. Well-established airlines such as S.A.S., K.L.M., and B.E.A. had inherited—and arguably had earned—such privileges as their birthright. The gulf between the two types of commercial operators was a form of aviation apartheid.

By the early 1960s, however, intensive travel demands by tourists who were prepared to exchange scheduled convenience for cheap fares enabled many small companies to find a niche in the regulation-protected scheduled airline armor. Nonscheduled flights, operated around the clock, with every seat filled, became as profitable as scheduled flights, operated during restricted hours and little more than half full. With guaranteed contracts comprising packages of air travel, hotel, and ground services, the Inclusive Air Tour was born. The expansion was phenomenal, the competition intense. Some airlines survived by the wit of individual entrepreneurs. Others were absorbed by flag carriers which, faced with the inexorable flood of mass air tourism, adopted a policy of "if you can't beat 'em, join 'em."

## Condor Flugdienst

One such marriage of convenience was the Lufthansa-Condor partnership. On 23 December 1955, **Deutsche Flugdienst GmbH** was formed in Frankfurt by Norddeutscher Lloyd, the Hamburg-Amerika Line, the Deutsche Bundesbahn, and Lufthansa. With three **Vickers Viking**s, it began service on 1 May 1956 to Palma de Mallorca, the first of many resorts throughout the Mediterranean. In 1960 Lufthansa purchased the entire company, and the next year it bought **Condor Luftreiderei**, which had two **Convair 240**s; it combined the two on 1 November 1961 to form **Condor Flugdienst GmbH**.

Lufthansa's position was consolidated further on 1 January 1968 by the acquisition of **Sudflug International**, another German charter airline. Lufthansa had allocated Viscounts to its junior partner in 1962, and Boeing 727 jets were added in 1965. On 1 May 1971, Condor became the first nonscheduled airline to operate its own **Boeing 747**, and in August the same year it gained the distinction of carrying the record number of passengers on any single airline flight, when 490 happy tourists from Frankfurt disembarked at Las Palmas, Canary Islands. On 14 May 1972, Condor 747s began charter service to New York, to establish tranoceanic credentials. Closer to home, on 6–7 September 1972, Condor broke a political barrier by becoming the first West German airline to carry visitors to the famous Leipzig Trade Fair in East Germany.

Condor has become one of the world's largest nonscheduled airlines. Its aircraft's distinctive yellow tails have become almost as familiar a sight at many of the world's busy airports as the emblem of its parent company. It has operated both Boeing 747s and **DC-10**s (pictured opposite), and its current fleet includes 737-300s and A310-300s. Its market is geared to long-range inclusive air tours. Condor's fleet of 17 jets in 1990 is operated by Südflug in the highly competitive business of mass air travel.

## Cargolux

Consistent with its policy of expanding its share of the air freight market as well as the air passenger market in the nonscheduled arena, Lufthansa increased its influence in December 1987 by purchasing a 24.5% share of **Cargolux**, the Luxembourg nonscheduled all-cargo carrier. It was founded on 4 March 1970 by a consortium from Iceland, represented by Loftleidir Icelandic Airlines; Sweden, represented by A.B. Salenia, a shipping company; and Luxair, representing the home country. As with Condor, Lufthansa has secured a firm foothold in the nonscheduled air charter market by taking an interest in one of the largest participants. Cargolux currently operates six Boeing 747 freighters.

## An Old Link Renewed

More than 60 years ago, in establishing a bridgehead for operations to South America, the old **Deutsche Luft Hansa** helped to set up one of Spain's first airlines, the first to be named **Iberia**, in 1927. After many vicissitudes, partly related to the Spanish government's wish to retain control over its own airline destinies, and later because of the conflicts of the Spanish Civil War, Lufthansa's interests waxed and waned according to political fortunes (see page 32).

The connection has, however, always been strong, and for several periods, Lufthansa supplied aircraft to the rejuvenated Iberia before the war; and possibly as a mark of traditional friendship, Madrid was the first destination to be served on the postwar Lufthansa's international network.

The cooperation between the airlines of Spain and Germany was recently strengthened with commercial considerations outweighing those of politics. To meet Spain's natural aspirations to obtain a larger slice of the enormous inclusive-tour market, a new airline was established at the very heart of the holiday traffic, Palma de Mallorca. On 24 February 1988, **Viva** was founded, with **Lufthansa** holding 48% of the shares. The acronym stands for **Vuelos Internacionales de Vacaciones, S.S.A.**, and the initial fleet of Boeing 737-300s began service in the spring of 1988. In 1990, Iberia decided it wanted fewer charters in Spain so Lufthansa turned over its shares in Viva.

This **Vickers Viking**, seen in **Lufthansa**'s markings, was first used by **Deutsche Flugdienst**, which later merged with **Condor Luftreiderei**.

This **Boeing 737-300** shows the striking markings of **Viva**, a Spanish charter airline in which Lufthansa held a substantial interest.

# McDonnell Douglas DC-10-30

## 270 seats • 564 mph

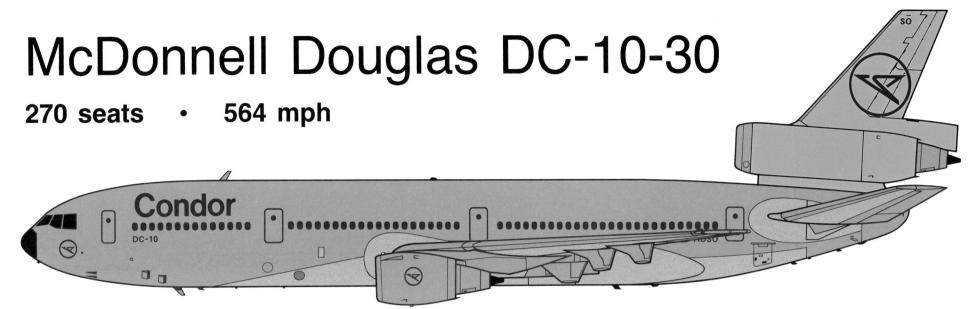

**General Electric CF6-50c (51,000 lb thrust) × 3 • 286 tons max. gross takeoff weight • 4600 statute miles range**

When **Lufthansa** put its first Boeing 747s into service on the North Atlantic route in April 1970, it realized that many years would pass before the traffic density on many of its other intercontinental routes would justify adequate frequencies of aircraft of the Jumbo Jet size. Accordingly, on 23 September 1970 it ordered four **McDonnell Douglas DC-10** trijet wide-bodied airliners, which had about three-quarters of the capacity of the Boeing. The first DC-10s entered service on the South American route in January 1974.

The aircraft continued to work those long-distance routes which could not support the Boeing 747 size yet demanded the sophisticated modernity of wide-bodied comfort. The latest example of such shrewd deployment was the inauguration, on 1 April 1987, of nonstop service from the West German hub at Frankfurt to Washington, D.C., where Dulles International Airport now serves a commercial community which has outgrown the confines of the federal capital.

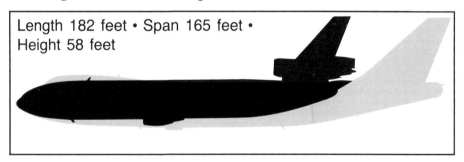

Length 182 feet • Span 165 feet • Height 58 feet

LUFTHANSA'S MCDONNELL DOUGLAS DC-10-30S

| Const. No. | Regist. No. | Name | Year Deliv. |
|---|---|---|---|
| 47921 | D-ADAO | *Düsseldorf* | 1973 |
| 47922 | D-ADBO | *Berlin/Bochum* | 1974 |
| 47923 | D-ADCO | *Frankfurt* | 1974 |
| 47924 | D-ADDO | *Hamburg/Duisburg* | 1974 |
| 47925 | D-ADFO | *München* | 1974 |
| 47926 | D-ADGO | *Bonn* | 1975 |
| 47927 | D-ADHO | *Hannover* | 1975 |
| 47928 | D-ADJO | *Essen* | 1975 |
| 47929 | D-ADKO | *Stuttgart* | 1975 |
| 46917 | D-ADLO | *Nürnberg* | 1975 |
| 46965 | D-ADMO | *Dortmund* | 1977 |
| 46595 | D-ADPO | (Condor) | 1979 |
| 46596 | D-ADQO | (Condor) | 1979 |
| 48252 | D-ADSO | (Condor) | 1981 |

One of the **Airbus A300B4**s that **Condor** used.

A **McDonnell-Douglas DC-10-30** of **Condor**.

# A European Mainliner

## The First Airbuses

Within two months of the first **Airbus A300B** flight, **Lufthansa** ordered three (plus four on option) on 20 December 1972. **Air France** had sponsored the whole project, but Lufthansa's support no less effective in setting the seal on the integrity of the Airbus idea. The order was modified on 7 May 1973 to the **A300B2** version of the basic design, and the first one entered Lufthansa service on 1 April 1976.

## Flexing the Airbus Muscles

Since then Lufthansa's enthusiasm for the breed has strengthened to the level of advocacy. The first of five larger **A300B4**s was delivered on 29 September 1977, and further orders followed. On 2 April 1979, Lufthansa and **Swissair** were the joint launching customers for the **Airbus A310**, a smaller version of the A300B. No token gesture, the order was for 50, of which 25 were firm, and worth $1.5 billion (U.S.). The first Lufthansa A310 entered service on a domestic route, Frankfurt-Stuttgart, on 10 April 1983. The first A310-300 long-range jet began transatlantic service in March 1990.

The order book for the Airbus family was further modified as the production line at Toulouse became more flexible to meet varying market demands. Seven larger **A300-600**s were ordered in July 1985, and the first of these entered service in April 1987. Eleven of the smaller, narrow-bodied **Airbus A320**s were in the fleet by May 1990; 20 more are on order. The airline also has ordered 20 **A321** models.

## Throwing Down the Gauntlet

Most dramatic of the series of important demonstrations of faith in a European airliner industry was Lufthansa's sponsorship of the **Airbus A340**. This is a four-engined version, designed primarily to challenge that segment of the long-haul market currently occupied by the McDonnell Douglas and Lockheed trijets. It may well be the most serious threat so far to the supremacy of a United States industry that has dominated the world air transport market since 1930, interrupted only slightly by the short-lived British and French challenges in the 1950s.

Lufthansa reached preliminary agreement for 15 A340s, with an option on 15 more, on 14 February 1987. The final deliveries, to start in 1992, will be split between the -200 version, with accent on very long range, and the -300, with more seats but still transoceanic range.

With Lufthansa's influential stamp of approval, Airbus Industrie has thrown down the gauntlet to McDonnell Douglas and— is it possible?—the omnipotent Seattle manufacturer itself.

**Heinz Ruhnau**, chairman of Lufthansa since 1982.

The flight deck of the **A320** is in striking contrast with that of the prewar **Junkers-Ju 52/3m** (above).

The flight deck of the **Airbus Industrie A320** *(left)*, the "narrow-bodied" Airbus, representing the latest state of the art. There are no central control columns, and no mechanical linkages with the controls—the so-called "fly-by-wire" system.

## LUFTHANSA'S AIRBUS FLEET (TO 1989)

| Const. No. | Regist. No. | Name | Year Deliv. |
|---|---|---|---|
| **A 300 B2** | | | |
| 21 | D-AIAA | Garmisch-Partenkirchen | 1976 |
| 22 | D-AIAB | Rüdesheim am Rhein | 1976 |
| 26 | D-AIAC | Lüneburg | 1976 |
| 48 | D-AIAD | Westerland-Sylt | 1977 |
| 52 | D-AIAE | Neustadt a.d. Weinstr. | 1978 |
| 132 | D-AIAF | | 1981 |
| **A 300 B4** | | | |
| 53 | D-AIBA | Rothenburg o.d. Tauber | 1977 |
| 57 | D-AIBB | Freudenstadt/Schwarzwald | 1978 |
| 75 | D-AIBC | Lindau/Bodensee | 1979 |
| 76 | D-AIBD | Erbach/Odenwald | 1979 |
| 77 | D-AIBF | Kronberg/Taunus | 1979 |
| **A 300-600** | | | |
| 380 | D-AIAH | Lindau | 1987 |
| 391 | D-AIAI | Erbach | 1987 |
| 401 | D-AIAK | Kronberg | 1987 |
| 405 | D-AIAL | Stade | 1987 |
| 408 | D-AIAM | Rosenheim | 1987 |
| 411 | D-AIAN | Nördlingen | 1987 |
| 414 | D-AIAP | Bingen | 1987 |
| **A 310A** | | | |
| 191 | D-AICA | Neustadt a.d. Weinstr. | 1984 |
| 201 | D-AICB | Garmisch-Partenkirchen | 1983 |
| 230 | D-AICC | Kaiserslautern | 1983 |
| 233 | D-AICD | Detmold | 1983 |
| 237 | D-AICF | Rüdesheim am Rhein | 1983 |
| 254 | D-AICH | Lüneburg | 1983 |
| 257 | D-AICK | Westerland-Sylt | 1983 |
| 273 | D-AICL | Rothenburg a.d. Tauber | 1984 |
| 356 | D-AICM | (Condor | 1985 |
| 359 | D-AICN | (Condor) | 1985 |
| 360 | D-AICP | (Condor) | 1985 |
| 397 | D-AICR | Freudenstadt (Condor 1988) | 1986 |
| 400 | D-AICS | Recklinghausen | 1986 |
| **A 310B** | | | |
| 434 | D-AIDA | (Condor) | 1987 |

# Airbus Industrie A300-600

## 267 seats • 553 mph

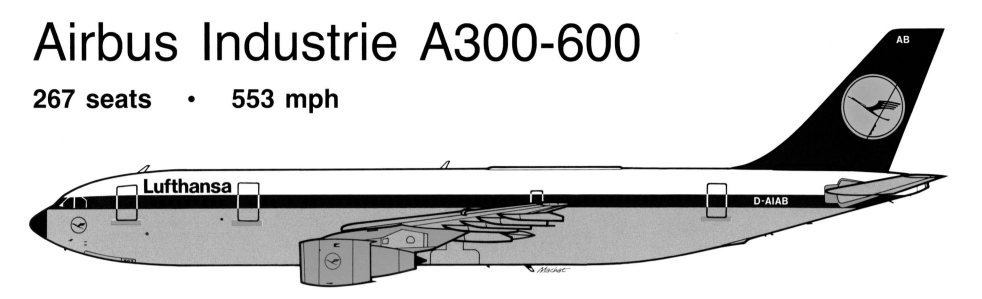

General Electric CF6-80c (59,000 lb thrust) × 2 • 182 tons max. gross takeoff weight • 3700 statute miles range

## A European Airliner

The early history of the **Airbus** consortium, builders of the **A300** family of airliners, is reviewed on page 87 of **Pan Am: An Airline and Its Aircraft**, the pilot book of this airline series. The Airbus was originally an Anglo-French project, but the U.K. withdrew and Germany eagerly took its place. Britain eventually returned as a full member, rather than as a subcontractor, in January 1979.

After the first A300 flight, on 28 October 1972, progress was slow. The impressive production capacity of the U.S. manufacturers had enabled them to put the Douglas DC-10 and the Lockheed TriStar into service in 1970, two years earlier than the A300. Even so, after a slow start, Airbus began to build a solid order book.

## The Right Answer

The Airbus Industrie design team at Toulouse demonstrated remarkable faith in the twin-engined concept as the most economical solution to short-haul air travel. As time went on, the permanency of the air traffic distribution curve, emphasizing the inescapable demographic elements of population and distance, dictated the emphasis on short-haul routes and the need for an airliner to match the demand. Airbus, meanwhile, reinforced by sustained engine developments, was able both to stretch and to compress the size and range of the A300. Simultaneously, the attitudes of the regulatory authorities became more flexible as engine efficiency and reliability reached truly impressive levels. In contrast with the early days, when overwater flights by twin-engined aircraft were regarded by the authorities as bordering on the suicidal, the latest variants of the Airbus family are flying across the Atlantic.

## A Complete Family

The most important development occurred in July 1978 when **Lufthansa** and **Swissair** jointly ordered the smaller **A310**, which first flew on 3 April 1982 and included a digital flight deck (with only two crew members) and the extensive structural use of lightweight composite materials. These improvements were later incorporated in a larger and longer-range **A300-600**, first ordered by the national airline of Saudi Arabia, Saudia.

Extending its grasp of the short-haul markets even further in March 1984, Airbus Industrie launched the smaller, narrow-bodied A320, in which the control stick is placed at the side of the cockpit, thus providing better vision and freedom of movement for the pilots. Fiber-optic technology replaces mechanical linkages between the flight deck and the controls, to introduce the revolutionary "fly-by-wire" technique.

Further down the road, the Airbus family will include a 295-seat long-range four-engined version, the **A340**, and an even larger twin, the 328-seat **A330**, which will have transatlantic range. For the first time since the 1950s, when the Comet, the Viscount, and the Caravelle pointed the way toward the jet age, Europe is once again taking the technical lead in the development of the commercial airliner and helping to shape the future course of air transport.

### THE AIRBUS FAMILY

| Type | First Flight Date | Dimensions | | | Pass. Seats | Engines | | Max. Gross TOW (lb) | Normal Range (st. miles) | No. Built |
| | | Length | Span | Height | | No. | Type | | | |
|---|---|---|---|---|---|---|---|---|---|---|
| A300 B2 | 28 Oct. 1972[1] | 175'11" | 147'1" | 54'3" | 281 | 2 | G.E. CF6-50C | 302,000 | 1615 | 300+ |
| A300 B4 | 26 Dec. 1974 | 175'11" | 147'1" | 54'3" | 269 | 2 | G.E. CF6-50C | 330,690 | 2994 | |
| A300-600 | 7 July 1983 | 177'5" | 147'1" | 56'6" | 267 | 2 | G.E. CF6-80C2 | 363,750 | 3710 | |
| A310 | 3 April 1982 | 153'1" | 144' | 51'10" | 234 | 2 | P & W JT9D-7R4[3] | 291,010 | 3224 | 150+ |
| A320[2] | 22 Feb. 1987 | 123'3" | 111'3" | 38'9" | 150 | 2 | CFM 56-5 | 145,500 | 2300 | 300+ |
| A340 | May 1992[4] | 208'10" | 192'5" | 54'11" | 295 | 4 | CFM 56-5 | 542,335 | 7800 | 89[5] |

[1]First flight date of original A300B. First flight of the A300 B2 was 28 June 1973. [2]All types are wide-bodied, except the A320. [3]Swissair. Lufthansa specified General Electric CF6 engines. [4]Estimated date. [5]Orders by April 1988.

# They Also Serve

## Regional Requirement

During the 1970s when the Economic Miracle reinstated West Germany as a world power, its people used their increasing incomes not only to buy new cars and houses but to do what Germans have always done: to travel, for business, for vacations, or just to visit friends. Such travel did not aspire necessarily only to jet to New York or Tokyo, or to seek sun and sand at Las Palmas or Dubrovnik. It included the wish to travel easily and quickly throughout the length and breadth of Germany.

A natural sequel to this aspiration was the creation of a number of small regional airlines, equipped mainly with small commuter aircraft to serve the smaller cities that could not support Lufthansa's Boeing 737s.

## Formation of D.L.T.

One of these was **Ostfriesische Lufttaxi GmbH (O.L.T.)** (East Friesian Air Taxi), founded at Emden, on the North Sea coast, on 11 December 1970. It took over Ostfriesischen Lufttaxi Dekker und Janssen O.H.G., founded in 1958, and changed its name on 29 December 1972 to **Ostfriesische Lufttransport GmbH**, finally changing again to **D.L.T.— Deutsche Luftverkehrsgesellschaft mbH** on 17 October 1974. It later disposed of its local routes to the Friesian resorts so as to concentrate on regional services.

These latter tended to be on the periphery of West Germany, not only in the North Sea area but also in the extreme south, with routes from Friedrichshafen, and in northeast Bavaria. The fleet consisted of four 18-seat **de Havilland (Canada) DHC-6 Twin Otter**s, augmented in 1977 by six 30-seat **Shorts 330**s. Then, on 29 June 1978, D.L.T. was restructured as a *Partner der Lufthansa* and the headquarters transferred to Frankfurt. Lufthansa's interest in D.L.T. was 40%, the remaining control being held by Aktiengesellschaft für Industrie und Verkehrswesen (A.G.I.V.).

## Modern Feeder Aircraft

Since then D.L.T. has become more than simply a local regional airline. In March 1981 it introduced the 44-seat **Hawker-Siddeley HS-748**, and the route network expanded considerably during the next few years to put hitherto deprived German cities on the airline map. Connections were made to most of Germany's neighboring countries, to provide service, for example, to provincial cities in Italy, Austria, the Netherlands, and the U.K.

On 3 February 1986 the 28-seat **Embraer Brasilia**, an excellent feeder airliner from Brazil, entered service; and during the summer of 1987 the **Fokker F-50**, latest of a fine line of turboprop twins from the Netherlands, rounded off the modernization of the D.L.T. fleet. Supplemented by aircraft such as the Jetstream and the Metroliner, chartered from other German regional carriers, D.L.T. now makes a substantial contribution (as the accompanying map shows) to Lufthansa's comprehensive airline system, which has brought air service within convenient reach of almost every citizen in the Federal Republic with the diminutive Brasilia as well as the Boeing 747. Lufthansa now holds 52% of D.L.T.

The **Hawker-Siddeley** (originally **Avro**, now **British Aerospace**) 748.

The **D.L.T.** network of today compares in extent with that of the prewar Lufthansa's European system in the early 1930s.

The **Embraer 120 Brasilia**, Brazil's contribution to the feeder airline fleets of the world.

# Dignity and Impudence

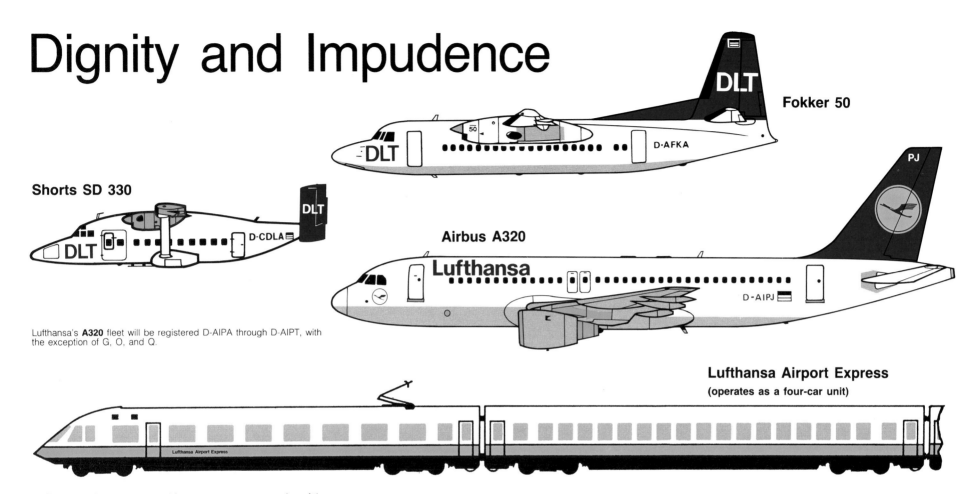

**Shorts SD 330**

**Fokker 50**

**Airbus A320**

Lufthansa's **A320** fleet will be registered D-AIPA through D-AIPT, with the exception of G, O, and Q.

**Lufthansa Airport Express**

(operates as a four-car unit)

The aircraft illustrated on this page are representative of the feeder types serving mainly the smaller cities of Germany and providing connections to provincial cities in neighboring countries. The **Airbus A320** could be regarded both as serving the lowest echelon of Lufthansa's main-line system—and the heir apparent to the versatile Boeing 737 Series—and the highest echelon of the feeder-route system, and is likely to be in service in such roles until the next century.

The **Lufthansa Airport Express** train is a novel solution to travel connections between a major traffic hub and neighboring cities which are too close to make air travel cost-effective for the operator or time-saving for the traveler. The Airport Express is operated by the **Deutsches Bundesbahn** exclusively for Lufthansa; airline tickets are required, and airline cabin service standards are provided by Lufthansa staff. It links Frankfurt Airport directly with Coblenz, Bonn, Cologne, and Düsseldorf, at the same time offering the passengers a delightful tour of the castles and vineyards of the scenic Rhineland Gorge. A second Airport Express train began operating between Frankfurt Airport and Stuttgart in May 1990.

## FEEDING THE MAIN-LINE ROUTES
### REPRESENTATIVE EQUIPMENT USED

| Type | First Flight Date | Dimensions | | | Pass. Seats | Engines | | | Max. Gross TOW (lb) | Cruise Speed (mph) | Normal Range (st. miles) | Operator |
| | | Length | Span | Height | | No. | Type | Hp (each) | | | | |
|---|---|---|---|---|---|---|---|---|---|---|---|---|
| Airbus A320 | 22 Feb. 1987 | 123'3" | 111'3" | 38'9" | 150 | 2 | CFM6-5 | 23,500 (lb thrust) | 145,505 | 560 | 2303 | Lufthansa[1] |
| Fokker F-50 | 28 Dec. 1985 | 82'8" | 95'2" | 28'2" | 50 | 2 | P & W 124 | 2160 | 43,500 | 320 | 1300 | D.L.T. |
| HS 748 | 24 June 1960 | 67' | 102'6" | 24'10" | 44 | 2 | R-R Dart | 2280 | 46,500 | 290 | 690 | D.L.T. |
| Shorts S-330 | 22 Aug. 1974 | 58' | 74'8" | 16'3" | 30 | 2 | P & W PT6A | 1173 | 22,900 | 220 | 450 | D.L.T. |
| Embraer 120 | 27 July 1983 | 65'7" | 64'11" | 20'10" | 30 | 2 | P & W PW118 | 1800 | 25,353 | 345 | 1,000 | D.L.T. |
| Lufthansa Express | 27 March 1982 | 358' | 9'7"[2] | 12'11"[3] | 164 | 16 | Electric Motors[4] | 240 Kw | 472,000 | 125 | — | Deutsche Bundesbahn |

[1]Included for purposes of comparison only. [2]Loading gauge width. [3]Loading gauge height. [4]Four power units in each of four cars. The units are manufactured by A.E.G., Brown-Boveri, and Siemens.

# INDEX

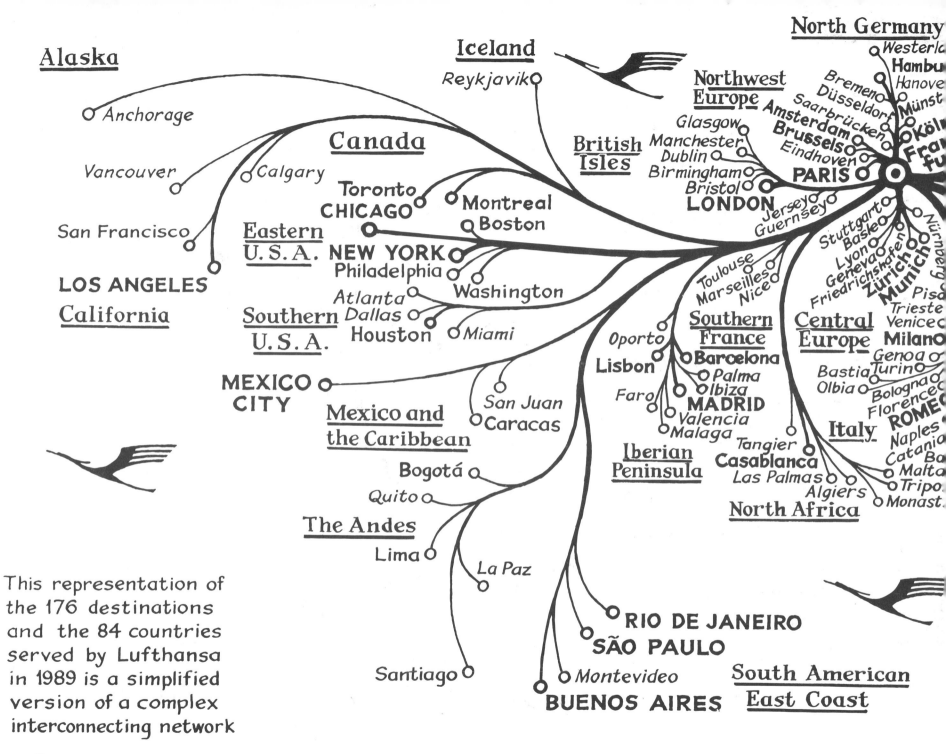

Alaska
Anchorage
Vancouver
San Francisco
LOS ANGELES
California

Canada
Calgary
Toronto
CHICAGO
Montreal
Boston
Eastern
U.S.A.
NEW YORK
Philadelphia
Washington
Atlanta
Dallas
Houston
Southern
U.S.A.
Miami

MEXICO
CITY
Mexico and
the Caribbean
San Juan
Caracas
Bogotá
Quito
The Andes
Lima
La Paz
Santiago

Iceland
Reykjavik

British
Isles
Glasgow
Manchester
Dublin
Birmingham
Bristol
LONDON
Jersey
Guernsey

Northwest
Europe
Amsterdam
Brussels
Eindhoven
PARIS

North Germany
Westerla
Hambu
Bremen
Hanove
Düsseldorf
Saarbrücken
Münst
Köl
Fra
fu

Stuttgart
Basle
Lyon
Geneva
Friedrichshafen
Zürich
Munich
Nürnburg
Pisa
Trieste
Venice

Toulouse
Marseilles
Nice

Oporto
Lisbon
Faro
Southern
France
Barcelona
Palma
Ibiza
MADRID
Valencia
Malaga
Iberian
Peninsula

Central
Europe
Milano
Bastia
Olbia
Genoa
Turin
Bologna
Florence
Italy
ROME
Naples
Catania
Ba
Malta
Tripo
Monast.

Tangier
Casablanca
Las Palmas
Algiers
North Africa

RIO DE JANEIRO
SÃO PAULO
Montevideo
BUENOS AIRES
South American
East Coast

This representation of
the 176 destinations
and the 84 countries
served by Lufthansa
in 1989 is a simplified
version of a complex
interconnecting network

© R.E.G.Davies

LUFTHANSA'S